SOCIAL MEDIA SPELLBOOK

SOCIAL MEDIA SPELLBOOK

366 WAYS
TO GET WITCHY ON THE WEB

Amy Blackthorn & Natalie Zaman

STERLING ETHOS
New York

STERLING ETHOS
New York

ISBN 978-1-4549-5384-5 / ISBN 978-1-4549-5385-2 (e-book)

Library of Congress Control Number: 2024933069

For information about custom editions, special sales, and premium purchases, please contact specialsales@unionsquareandco.com.

Printed in China

2 4 6 8 10 9 7 5 3 1

unionsquareandco.com

Cover and interior design by Stacy Wakefield Forte

Cover art from Shutterstock.com: Kuznetsova Darja; The Noun Project: Alex Burte (hashtag); Lele Saa (cat); riski nadia (laptop)

Interior icons from The Noun Project: Alice Design (photos); Ali Coskun (speaker); Creative Stall (fax); Eliricon (group); Iconographer (camera); NAPISAH (eye); Giulio Petrone (wand); Smashing Stocks (emoji)

To the bright star on my feed,
Judy of the West Tower. May
you find strength in the arms of
your ancestors. Rest in Peace.

—AMY

For Alex Davidson,
Rebecca and Josh DeVries, and
Jennifer Wood
#whatisrememberedlives

—NATALIE

HOW TO BE A CONFLUENCER

Magic spells "spell out" our intentions and the intangible steps we take to exert some control in our lives; coupling intention with action is the first (and often repeated!) step to manifestation. Bring spellwork online, and you take your ritual to a new level: you blend your energy into the collective energy of the web and everyone on it.

This book is designed to help you harness the collective energy of the internet—the real power behind social media. Tap into that energy and lend it to your workings, desires, and intentions for a push that can bring them that much closer to reality. You might pick up a follower or two by making internet magic, but there's more to this work than influence. Taking your intentions to the internet is about *confluence*, or merging your energy with that of others to make your dreams come true.

Spells, meditations, and rituals are presented in calendar format with something to try or adapt each day—but implement them in any format that makes sense for you. We've suggested how to share your spells through pictures, videos, and text, but if you encounter a day where we suggest posting a video, and you feel more comfortable or just want to share via a still image or text, that's valid. Tag us—we'll amplify!

THE RULES OF #MANIFESTATION

★ *Always* put safety and common sense first:

- NOTHING in this book should be used in place of medical, legal, or other professional advice.

- Be aware of handling herbs, oils, or any ingredients that may be irritants, especially if you have allergies, are pregnant, or planning to become pregnant.

- BEFORE you work with fire of any kind, make sure you have a means of putting it out at hand. Don't work with fire where it's not permitted, and NEVER leave a fire or a burning candle unattended; make sure it is completely out before you leave or discard it. And lastly, work with fires and scents (even those you can't smell!) in a well-ventilated area.

- Take note of where you can and cannot take pictures; don't put yourself or others at risk.

- Do not take or leave things where it is not permitted—respect of space is important for everyone!

★ By putting yourself "out there," you're vulnerable, so #bewarewhatyoushare.

★ The internet is an ever-evolving manifestation of our collective consciousness. Many of us feel and think on the same wavelengths. Copying is the magic at work—it's trying to multiply. ALWAYS give credit when using someone else's work!

★ A person's image, picture, or portrait is sacred and not to be used without their knowledge and permission. If you're doing a spell for someone else, respect their privacy. Don't name names unless they're okay with it.

★ The delete button doesn't erase, nor does editing. It is essential to say what you mean and mean what you say. Think about your post *before* posting it, keeping in mind that you may manifest EXACTLY what you state.

★ Sometimes, creating a private account may be best for you. Not all magic needs to be done under the public gaze.

★ It's not just about posting. Magic is about being aware of the mystical beauty and magical powers of everything around you.

★ As you go through the year, you may encounter different spells on the same topic. Consistency is vital to magical work; rarely does a single ritual address an issue, especially if deeply seated feelings and experiences need to be explored.

★ The spells and rituals in this book are based on our collective experiences, knowledge, and style. While there are certain things that are "fixed" (astrological dates, qualities of stones and herbs, etc.), there's no one right way to do anything. The more you personalize these spells and make them your own, the more powerful they'll be!

★ Intention first, aesthetics second. Don't be discouraged if a post doesn't come out exactly how you'd like. The important thing is your intention and focus.

★ Magic won't resolve all issues or fix everything. There are no guarantees, and magic should NEVER be used in place of professional help or advice. It can give a boost, help you ground and focus your energies, give you hope, and be a step in the process. In any situation, the mundane work still must be done. For example, if you're looking for a new job, do a spell—but if it ends there, you won't get very far. You must do the other work: research, craft a good resume, and put yourself out there.

★ Machines and technology CANNOT generate magic. If you ask Alexa or ChatGPT to pull a random tarot card for you, it'll give you a card, but it's not really a random draw. If you were to ask for cards, spells, or affirmations consistently from any AI or any computer-generated program with no human interaction, eventually a pattern would emerge. For all the patterns in nature, there is still a wild randomness that is the essence of magic, and machines are incapable of that. But we can use machine-powered apps to level up our random wonderfulness.

@AmyBlackthorn & @NatalieZaman

ICON GUIDE

use the spell with this icon at social media sites where you can...

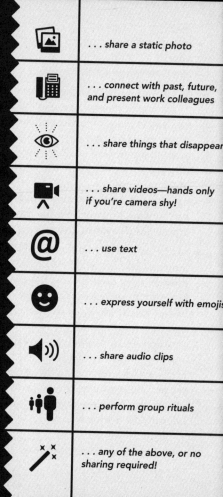

. . . share a static photo

. . . connect with past, future, and present work colleagues

. . . share things that disappear

. . . share videos—hands only if you're camera shy!

. . . use text

. . . express yourself with emojis

. . . share audio clips

. . . perform group rituals

. . . any of the above, or no sharing required!

THE
SPELLS

🎥 RISe AND SHINe!

It's the first day of the new year, the fresh start that everyone needs. This blank slate is a perfect time to dust off your altar and post your cleansing routine to keep you on the path to clear communication all year!

WHAT TO DO: Set up your camera to record in time-lapse. As you clean, visualize yourself "taking out the trash" to make room for the new energy you're hoping to manifest. If you're trying to be more organized, visualize choosing organizational items, donating gently used items, and getting rid of things that do not fit with your current goals. Grab some incense (mugwort is perfect for this) and charge it by singing to it or blowing on it, then get cleaning. Remove everything and put your treasures in a safe place while you clean. Give everything a gentle wipe down, being careful with soft stones and ones that can be damaged by water or salt. PRO TIP: Crystals with "-ite" in their name (selenite, hematite, celestite, etc.) can be damaged by salt, so don't use them in blessings or cleansings. Speak out loud to the stone to let it know how it can help.

Once everything is reset, give the space your blessing however seems appropriate. Upload the video to your platform and know that each time someone likes or views it, it reinforces your intention and adds their shine to your project.

CHARGING FOR MAGIC

Ritually cleansing and charging devices may have residual effects, like clearer responses to your emails or receiving sensitively constructed feedback on projects and proposals. Remember, it's all about EVERY STEP being intentional!

WHAT TO DO: You'll need salt, water, and incense (try sage, copal, or frankincense). Physically clean and clear the space where you'll be working. Gather all the devices and accessories you want to charge and lay them out in front of you. Walk around your workspace clockwise three times to establish sacred space. Take three deep breaths to ground and center. Add salt to the water, and light the incense. Dip your finger in the salted water and pick up your first device. Trace a symbol that holds meaning to you on its surface. As you trace, say: *This is a magical tool. I cleanse and charge it with the elements of water and earth. May it be an implement of clarity and stability. No harmful entities or energies shall pass through this portal.* Next, pass the item through the incense smoke and say: *This is a magical tool. I cleanse and charge it with the elements of air and fire. May it be an implement of mindfulness and creativity. All manner of harm will burn away and no evil thoughts or intentions shall pass through this portal.* Repeat for each device and accessory.

🎥 DIG IN, INTROSPECTION

The holiday lights are still up for another week or so. It's a great time to leverage those cheerful vibes into the work that needs to get done.

WHAT TO DO: When we think of the luxury of the senses, we often take for granted all the information that can accompany each sense. We only realize the depth of our loss when we notice its absence. When someone shares a photo of a large family dinner, we expect to be able to smell the air therein. So, inventory your space and see what scents bring up pleasant memories. Does the scent of pine make you think of pine boughs decorating a fireplace with cozy stockings? Because scent is so inextricably linked to our memories (remember, our scent must go through the "memory box" of our experiences before we can get to recognition!), a single scent can cause an entire avalanche of memories to erupt. Something as innocuous as a candy cane can remind us of a fight with a loved one rather than the holiday cheer many people might associate it with. Accessibility is key in magical work. Create a post on a video platform designed for storytelling to detail your feelings, sense memories, and experiences of each scent as they occur; really dig into those memories and recreate that magic for your followers.

⚡✦ YOUR ONLINE MAGICAL NAME

What's in a name? A lot. Names identify us. And we're constantly "gifted" with names—some unwelcome. You have the name given to you at birth, but you can also take on a magical name for magical work.

WHAT TO DO: Consider the name you'd like to use: What inspires you—people, objects, animals, crystals, plants, words? Visualize and meditate on a magical name. What thoughts come to you? Have you had any dreams that inspire you?

Take your time. (This does not have to be FINISHED today—but begin the work!) Write out all your ideas. Remember, your name embodies bits of your identity. Perhaps you have a name that is special to you already that you'd like to use, but consider playing with one of the many free name generators out there. Whether you share your magical name or not, it is a persona you can step into when you do magical work online.

Once you've decided on a name, you can start incorporating it into the platforms of your choice. Of course, you can always change it up, but be aware that magic likes consistency, so think long-term!

📹 PROSPERI-TEA

Let's blend up a prosperity tea to boost success!

PROSPERITY HERBS TO CHOOSE FROM: ORANGE BLOSSOM: attraction • BASIL: commanding, joy • MARIGOLD: commanding, praise • CHERRY: material gain • CINNAMON: good luck • NUTMEG: good luck • ORANGE PEEL: solar protection, transformation • PEPPERMINT: determination, good luck • STRAWBERRY: luxury goods • ALMOND: wisdom, manifestation • BERGAMOT: manifestation • GINGER: power • BLACK PEPPER: courage • BLACKTHORN/SLOE: destiny, justice

WHAT TO DO: We can boost our own personal prosperity in an ethical manner by looking at needed changes for our own lives, as well as ways to consistently draw that needed cash in a low-energy way. Perhaps today you have the energy to blend a prosperity tea to sip on throughout the morning, while working on real-world solutions to your conundrum. The flowers, fruit, and herbs above are just a handful of botanicals that are aligned with the energy of prosperity. Feel free to think outside the box, so to speak. If you're too busy to blend your own, you might grab a chai tea bag (try to identify the scents of cardamom for confidence, along with cinnamon and ginger), or hit your local independent coffee shop. Blending on camera (time-lapse) can include a lot of fun visual themes while staying within algorithm time constraints.

✎ ✕ DISCOVER YOUR ASTROLOGY

Astrology can be a handy tool for understanding yourself and others. Try casting your birth chart. It's easy, and there are loads of free resources to do this online.

WHAT TO DO: You'll need your exact date, time, and place of birth. Plug these into a natal chart generator, and you'll get a circular chart and key that shows the position of heavenly bodies (stars, planets, and even comets) as they appeared at the moment of your birth. There's much to interpret, but let's start with "the big three":

★ Your birth date determines your sun sign and identity.

★ Your ascendant or "rising sign" is the sign of the zodiac rising on the eastern horizon at the moment of your birth. Knowing your rising sign will help you understand how others see and perceive you.

★ Your moon sign is the sign of the zodiac the moon appeared in at the moment of your birth and can help you learn how you express your emotions.

If you follow your horoscope, read all three signs. Think of astrology as a weather forecast (changeable and open to interpretation). #bewarewhatyoushare: NEVER post your birth date, time, and place publicly; share with trusted friends only!

🖼 PROTECTIVE SEPIA FILTERS

We often neglect the magical aspect of a selfie. We're putting our best face forward, but are we also making ourselves vulnerable to magical attacks? By altering your image, you're changing the way that you appear online and therefore changing your appearance. Think of this as the technological version of turning your outer garment inside out and putting it back on, to elude harmful magic and the fae.

WHAT TO DO: Come up with a color scheme for your photo according to the correspondences of each hue, as detailed below.

BLACK: protection, grounding of harmful energies • BROWN: energy and stability • GREEN: healing energy from the earth, patching any energetic holes in our defenses • PURPLE: psychic protection • YELLOW: protection, solar fire burning away anything nasty before it gets to you

Once you've picked your color scheme, find the right background. Choose something that isn't personal because it could give away sensitive information to potential enemies. Apply a sepia filter: this way, the depth of the protection spell you've cast will be known only to you, but the sepia tones will shield you from outside influence. Use your new photo as an avatar for any photo-sharing applications where discretion is the better part of valor. Especially if you're "friends only."

✏️✷ ONLINE SACRED SPACES

Being on the internet is all about being connected—but not all connections are created equal.

WHAT TO DO: You'll need a pen, paper, a blue highlighter, and a black Sharpie. Meditate about where you want to live online:

★ Where are you most active?

★ What do you like to do?

★ Do you want to be private or public? You know what your security needs are.

Make a list of all the apps you're on, or considering being on, then read their terms of service. It's essential to understand *exactly* what you're giving up. What's the app asking you to share? How often are things changed up, and will you be notified? Remember, you're creating YOUR sacred (and safe) space.

Cross off all the apps that don't work for you with the black (protective) Sharpie. Highlight all the apps you intend to use or keep with the blue marker, visualizing clear communication of your intentions coming through the platform. (Blue is the color of the throat chakra and rules communication.) If you delete any apps or platforms, remember to request that they remove *all* your data. Protection work is both magical and mundane!

 # TOUCH OF THE SEASON

Amid the new year's hustle and bustle, it can be hard to hear our own voices, even inside our own minds. By taking time to allow yourself to forget your responsibilities for a moment, you can make room in that big, beautiful brain for a few other things such as self-care and clarity of purpose.

WHAT TO DO: If you're neurodivergent, it can be difficult to sit long enough to feel like you're doing it "right," but the truth is, if you're giving yourself some space in your own mind, you *are* doing it right.

Grab a large mixing bowl and sand, salt, or craft gravel. Pour a good amount until you have enough to bury one hand in the bowl. Practice picking up the sand or gravel in one hand, and allowing it to pour over the second hand, then repeat on the opposite side. While popular media has portrayed meditation as sitting on a yoga mat, entirely still, and thinking of nothing, there are plenty of ways to meditate that are as simple as finding something repetitive to distract the body and keep the mind free to find its own footing in your inner landscape (February 5). Make a post to memorialize this activity: it can be as simple as an artful capture of your sand and bowl, or as complicated as a video of you stirring the sand to loop in a post for others to center along with you.

Emojis may have evolved from the colon-and-parentheses smiley faces of yore, but we still use these tried and true "text pictures" to convey messages. And what are emojis, after all, but magical glyphs—combinations of letters, numbers, symbols, and images—that you can use to seal any text, email, or post with an extra bit of intention?

WHAT TO DO: How many texts, posts, or emails have you sent that include a smiley face? Smileys show that you're happy, that something another person said makes you happy, that you're sending happiness, or, if the convo was awkward or tough, that everything is okay. The smiley face is formed by typing a colon, which indicates a pause that usually comes before a list (read: all the reasons why), followed by closed parentheses that express completion ("You complete me!"). Keep that in mind the next time you use this figure. Visualize your feelings as you build the image and intend happiness when you press send!

@ MAGICAL HERB INVENTORY

Today, take a moment to organize your physical magical materials.

WHAT TO DO: Gather a notepad, index cards, labels, and anything else you need, like jars, bags, or boxes. Just for fun: if you have the time and energy, grab a book on magical herbs, too (*Blackthorn's Botanical Magic* is a great place to start). Take anything in a plastic baggie and transfer it to a jar. Remember, plastic is not an oxygen barrier, but glass is. If your plant material has lost all color and scent, it's time for the compost bin, because it doesn't have the volatile oils to "program" your magic any longer.

In one area, place your notepad and book, if you're using them. Grab your pile of herbs and make a label for it, including the common name, Latin binomial, and its spell correspondences, so that you can tell at a glance what it is intended to do, in case you need an on-the-fly magical substitution. Consider making a video in which you talk about your favorite success herbs in your magical practice. What success-spell ingredients can you find around you? Tell your friends about your favorite spells using easy-to-find success ingredients. *Suggested Success Herbs:* allspice, apple blossom, basil, cassia, chamomile, cinquefoil, frankincense, geranium, lemon balm, mustard seed, oak leaves, patchouli, vanilla, and yarrow.

✕ SLEEP MAGIC

Even technology needs a rest. Machinery just seems to work better when you shut it down for the night (not to mention that *you* may rest easier when technology is shut down for the night—the blue light of devices, even filtered, wreaks havoc on our circadian rhythms). This is a little ritual you can do daily to ensure that both you and your tech shut down occasionally.

WHAT TO DO: Make shutting down your tech not just a part of your daily routine but a ritual to refresh your machine and yourself. Research shows that between 10:00 p.m. and 11:00 p.m. is the "magic hour" for going to sleep—but of course, this does not work for everyone.

Shut down at least an hour before sleep. Sit in front of your device. Light up a scented candle or some incense (try lavender for restful sleep, pine for clearing the mind, or sandalwood for peace). Breathe deeply—take three deep breaths, then begin. Close each app or window (bookmarking as needed) one at a time. Before you close out, say "thank you" out loud. When you are ready to do the final shutdown, take three more breaths and say: *For the work we do, for info conveyed, / Sleep for now, until the new day.* Listen as your computer or device shuts down. Break the circle once all is silent.

🖼 SNOW MAGIC

Snow carries the magic of transformation, so it's a great spell ingredient for anything that involves changing up your game. Whether in its solid state as snowflakes, or as liquid, this medium carries the magic of transformation through all its phases.

WHAT TO DO: Grab a bowl. Clear glass allows you to check in and get some great photos. You'll also need snow and a piece of paper. Into the bottom of the bowl, place a piece of paper outlining the situation or, if safety is a concern, including a symbol instead. Next, fill the bowl with snow, the fresher the better. (Because of the environmental pollutants found in the air, we won't be consuming the snow.)

Grab a photo of the snow mounded in the bowl. Don't worry, you shouldn't be able to see the paper at the bottom of the bowl. Charge the bowl by telling it that you want to change your situation. As the snow melts, so does that situation. Come back in a while to take another photo when the snow is half melted. Post the photos and talk about the transformative nature of change. Never feel you have to share the exact nature of your posts with everyone—this is your time—but if you feel empowered to do so, share your thoughts on this subject.

If you live outside of a snowy area, feel free to substitute ice from the freezer for snow.

@  REWIND AND SHINE

We've all said and done things we wish we hadn't. Sadly, we cannot turn back time and get a do-over, but we can always begin again. Putting the baggage of guilt down is the first step in that process, and the first step to putting that baggage down is to own it.

WHAT TO DO: Create a video of yourself dropping or breaking something (that you won't be upset about losing!). Use the boomerang or rewind feature to show the motion in reverse. Thinking of your situation (you don't have to put that on display for the world), overlay the video with the below text or record it as a voice-over: *I take it back. / It's mine. / I forgive myself. / I put it down.*

Post the video publicly or privately and temporarily until you feel you have put the situation behind you. Once you feel free of it, delete the video from all platforms and devices.

🖼 HEALTHY HEART

While everyone has a different definition of health, only YOU know what makes you feel the healthiest version of yourself. Make a mood board to set some goals.

WHAT TO DO: Find a quiet place to sit with a notepad or journal. Divide the page into four squares. Label them "physical," "mental," "emotional," and "spiritual." Take some time to really examine what each of these words means to you. List things like colors, shapes, weather patterns, and more that come to mind when you think about each of these words. If negative feelings arise when meditating on one of these categories, lean in. This is your inner self trying to communicate a message to you. Look for visual cues that signal *health*. This isn't about competing or letting the pursuit of health get you down.

Once you've filled in all four squares, spend time translating those words into images that can be shared online. Whether you create a collage with magazines and glue or approach your board digitally with photo manipulations and graphics, you've got this. Upload your work as appropriate and use a bulletin board–style media page, a photo-editing application, or a bulk photo uploading site that can allow you to examine all the ways in which your feelings can be explored, categorized, and understood.

✳ ALERT! TIME FOR MAGIC!

We use alerts and reminders on calendars for birthdays, meetings, and appointments. We can also use them for timed mini rituals:

WHAT TO DO: Think of what you want to accomplish and write a one-liner or even one magical word to encompass your wish or goal: *Money!* or *The new job I want and need will present itself, indeed!* or even simply *Manifest!*

It is important to visualize your intention. Open your preferred platform for alarms and reminders and set up dates and times for your intention to be sent to you. By doing this, you're infusing the reminder with your will; it's not just some random phrase being repeated. Select times and dates that align with your wish—for example, set your message to go off in the morning for intentions for beginnings and at night for endings, or at noon for a boost of power. Make sure that you will be pinged and physically reminded (via email, text, or voice) at the appointed times. Every time you see or hear the reminder, the magic is re-energized.

🖼 CREATIVITY CASTLE

Home should be a place of comfort, security, and somewhere to put the cares of the day to rest. Let's make a home protection talisman—an object empowered to carry magical energy for a specific task. In this case, we'll create a box to keep your home's safety within.

WHAT TO DO: Find, build, reuse, or buy a box that you can close. It can be as large or small, elaborate or plain, as you'd like. Use color magic to prep the outside of the box: paint it black for protection, silver to invoke the moon's energy, or gold for the fiery protection of the sun. Allow it to dry thoroughly, then add small craft mirrors to all six exterior walls of the box to keep spells, curses, hexes, and jinxes from your door. You can decide if you'd like a contrasting color for the interior of the box or not. Once the inside of the box is prepared, the real creativity begins! Hit your favorite search engine to find images of home, whatever that means to you. You can print them, or you can make a photo post from your image search to share your ideal thoughts on what home means to you. Don't post actual photos of the outside of your home, including house numbers, as that can lead strangers to your door. Fill your box with images, photos, herbs, spices, or incenses that remind you of a strong, healthy home. Bless on a Sunday for protection.

✴ FOOLISH TECHNOLOGY

In the tarot, The Fool is a card of beginnings, blank slates, and potential. It's an excellent image for January, and for when you decide to try out a new app, platform, or device. Use the magic of The Fool to embrace and work with the newness of your experience.

WHAT TO DO: Whenever you get a new device or add a new platform or app to your device, "pair" it with The Fool. Access an image of The Fool card or have an actual physical card to look at as you load your new app or unpack your new tools. Before you load an app or platform or set up your device, speak this simple incantation with The Fool in sight: *I am The Fool with [name of item]. / I am wise to watch my steps.*

If The Fool teaches us anything, it is to proceed with caution. If there are terms of service to agree to before installing an app, read them! Be aware of what is being asked of you and ask yourself if you agree to it (e.g., do you really want to share all your contacts and personal information, or allow tracking even when you're not using the app?).

Remember The Fool each time you use the new app until you are seasoned and know its ways.

📷 FOUND FAMILY PHOTOS

Gratitude is an important part of our mental health, and wonderful for making those around us know that we care about them and what they contribute to our lives.

WHAT TO DO: Go through your albums, whether they're on your phone, in online storage, or in physical boxes. Feel free to post about your friends and family members one by one, or throughout multiple posts; the point of this exercise is to round up your memories and use them to express how much your loved ones mean to you. If you're worried about leaving anyone out, include that this will be an ongoing series when you post. Take photos or scan any physical photos you might have around and include them in your "pile" of loved ones. Then, once your collage is complete, write out all the warm contributions to your life your friends have made. In assembling your post(s), consider your end goal: to express gratitude for this person. If they're shy, come from an abusive household, or have other issues, they may ask you to remove them from such a post. If so, remember it isn't about you; it's about their own thoughts and feelings on the subject. If you're shy about expressing yourself, you can make the post friends-only or private—just know that privacy can limit the efficacy of the spell. You can still make magic with gratitude, even if no one ever sees it.

🎥 @ LIFTOFF!

Today we move from Capricorn, an earth sign, into Aquarius, an air sign; from the practicality of the sea goat, we are about to begin a journey into the fantastical and visionary ideals of the water bearer. This makes sense: fantastic ideas are a great deal easier to pull off when you have your feet on the ground. Use the potent energy of this time to ground yourself before soaring. It's time to break out a drone!

WHAT TO DO: Note that some places will require that you have a license to operate a drone (usually this depends on size). If you don't have a drone or access to one, you have options! Search "drone footage with a creative commons license"; this will allow you to use someone else's footage for noncommercial purposes. (Be sure to credit the creator!) You can also make a video of the drone's liftoff with your phone—the key is to have footage of liftoff. Ask yourself: what are your wildest ideas and dreams that you would love to see come to pass? Visualize these as you create or search for your footage. Keep them in mind as you layer the video with some magic words in text or as a voice-over: *Earth to sky, / Grounded am I! / Sky to earth, / I know my worth.* With your feet on the ground and your eyes on the stars, you have the perfect combination of sense and sensibility to make things happen!

🎥 AQUARIAN CANDLES

We have entered the sun sign of Aquarius, and now that you've "lifted off," it's time to be the motivator, the innovator, the philanthropist with some candles for your Aquarian spellwork.

WHAT TO DO: We're going to use the simplest of methods for this spell, but if candle-making is your jam, be as elaborate as you wish! You'll need candle wicking (braided wicks with a thick diameter are good if you plan to hang your candles after creating them; precoated wicks of a thinner diameter are for thinner candles and more delicate) and a candle base (there's soy wax, beeswax, paraffin wax, and solidified coconut oil). Because each base has a different melting point, make sure you choose the best base for your climate. Since Aquarius is an air sign, consider using blue candle dye. Carefully melt your base and add the dye once it comes up to temperature. Candle thermometers can come in handy, particularly if you plan to add perfumes. Dip the wick into the melted wax over and over again until you have the thickness you desire. Ask Saturn (the ruler of Aquarius) to bless your candles and allow them to firm up over twenty-four hours before using. While documenting this spell, remember that you are working with HOT liquids—SAFETY FIRST!

📷 🎥 CRYSTAL COLLECTION

As the magical meme goes (February 26), "one does not simply walk into a crystal shop." There's a world of crystals out there. Which ones do you really need?

WHAT TO DO: If you've not started already, think about building up your magical tool chest. Crystals are fabulous, portable magical tools, and all you have to do for an instant boost is look at or hold them (and they're pretty!). Here are some "working stones" that are always good to have on hand:

CRYSTAL	USE IT FOR . . .
Rose Quartz	Love, banishing negativity, healing emotional wounds
Jade	Healing, health, rest, dreamwork
Tiger's-eye	Success, grounding, practical matters
Lepidolite	Money, business, coping with change
Black Tourmaline	Protection, grounding, shielding

These are just a handful of the thousands of stones that can be used for magical work. Refer to your favorite crystal resources to find more. Share photos or video of your crystal inventory and ask friends and followers what they use to grow knowledge all around.

 # SATURN CLEANSING

It's an airy season in the astrological world, but that doesn't mean there is always enough "air" in the room. Let's refresh our space with the energy of Saturn (which rules over Aquarius) and banish anything that no longer benefits us.

WHAT TO DO: On a piece of paper, write down what needs banishing. Anoint a chime candle (October 1) with an oil that feels appropriate: for example, olive oil can help banish financial troubles, and jojoba can aid in any situation that feels insurmountable. Next, place the candle in a candleholder or fireproof dish, and lay the dish on top of your problem to overcome it. Light the candle. Grab your favorite incense—BONUS POINTS if it contains Saturnian herbs such as clary sage, cypress, eucalyptus, fir, juniper, myrrh, patchouli, or vetiver. Light the incense (now's the time to open a window if you can) and start in the northern part of your space, working counterclockwise (the direction of banishing), wafting the smoke into the corners as well as the main areas of the space, driving any negativity out the open window. Post ideas: a video of the incense burning as a meditative moment; or photos of candles in their box, lying on a table, or in the candleholder. This is especially effective if done on a Saturday!

🖼 MANIPULATION SHIELD

Build a shield that will work 24-7 to help block manipulators and give you extra strength and vision to recognize and stop them.

WHAT TO DO: You'll need a photo of your face, and black tourmaline (or another black stone such as obsidian), kyanite, lapis lazuli or amethyst, and rose quartz chips. Print the photo and do the following steps physically, or build the shield digitally with photos of stones.

★ Place the tourmaline (protective) on your nose (the center of your face) and say: *I protect myself.*

★ Take the kyanite and lapis lazuli or amethyst (these stones raise psychic ability) and create a ring of stones around the tourmaline, saying: *I see through you.*

★ Continue building the shield outward with another ring of tourmaline, saying, *I protect myself.*

★ Create another ring, this time using rose quartz, and say: *I love myself. I deserve love.*

★ Create a final ring of tourmaline around the rose quartz and say: *I protect myself.*

Cover the picture so that your face cannot be seen. When you are done, capture the image at any angle and use it as your cover or background image.

📠 BUSINESS RELATIONSHIPS

Social media enables us to keep in contact with business associates that aren't close enough to maintain through our personal profiles, coworkers, bosses, and even potential bosses who might check into your social media before hiring you. Whether or not you are out of the broom closet, you can share your magic in an under-the-radar way that helps keep your coworkers past and present feeling that they are in the loop and a part of your life. It's a way to show enough vulnerability to build trust with your friendships, without jeopardizing your career goals. Let's draw some like-minded friendships to your inner circle by putting out a beacon of light to all the fabulous "woo" people circulating in your extended network.

WHAT TO DO: The spell itself is as complicated as you'd like to make it. But for the sake of the post, keeping it as neutral as possible can prevent any awkward conversations later. Posting a picture of your candle before it is dressed, or only its flame, is a good idea. Take a light blue candle (wisdom) and carve the word "Connection" into the surface with a pen. Anoint your candle with olive oil for fruitfulness. Did you know the Vatican also blesses their candles with olive oil before Mass? If you have no time constraints, this spell is well suited to a Sunday for personal empowerment and success.

STAY GOLDEN

Want to insta-boost your success? Just add gold.

WHAT TO DO: Adding gold bling to a device can do more than make it sparkle. Gold is an earthy element ideal for stability and success. Cover your phone in a gold case, add a couple of gold stickers to your laptop or tablet, or consider gold if you're in the market for new charging cables.

When incorporating gold into your technology—as you place that sticker or pop your phone into its new case—VISUALIZE the help you expect to get from it. Picture your device holding its charge, working without glitches, and achieving successes large and small (for example, through the messages you send, the purchases you make, and the pictures you post with your device). Revisit the feelings these visualizations elicit every time you see gold on your device and elsewhere.

Remember: magical practices need to work alongside the mundane for the most significant effect; back up and charge your devices and be aware of how they work. (Technology usually gives us signs before it fails.) You'll always be golden when you're aware and alert. Share photos of your gorgeous new hardware.

🖼 JOYFUL JANUARY

The time has come to celebrate all you've accomplished, not just this year, but in life. So far, you've survived 100 percent of your worst days. Time to take a scroll through your timeline and find some things you're proudest of. This can include business and personal triumphs—nothing is too big or too small. It's all about how you feel looking back.

WHAT TO DO: Take a walk down memory lane with a variety of "look back" apps that catalog your timeline to see your posts from a specific date through the years or jump to your cloud-based uploads and search for specific photos or events like "birthday," "concert," or "wedding." Once you've found a few pieces to bring together, decide on the platform you'd like to use, whether it's a bulletin board–style application or a photo essay you'd like to condense into one image. Once you know where it will go, you can decide if you need a layout application to make multiple photos into an album, or create a board-style post in another medium. Looking through photos should give you ideas for the future as well. Consider doing this exercise with a notepad to jot down those golden threads before they are gone for good.

📷 HOUSEPLANT MAGIC

Houseplants (most, anyway) give so much and ask for so little in return: just a little water, sunlight, and the occasional shot of nutrients, and they're good to go. They brighten up our spaces, freshen the air, and can protect us in other ways. Try this spell to enhance your plants' inherent abilities.

WHAT TO DO: A houseplant can be your guardian and familiar (February 20) and can offer a layer of protection against illness, negative energy, psychic attacks, and the like. Choose a hearty plant: snake plants and pothos are great as they are hard to kill and can bounce back when they are under the weather or neglected.

Find a crystal or small token that represents you. Nestle it in the soil close to your plant without crowding it. As you place the object, say: *Watch over me, hide me when I need to hide. / Keep me healthy, safe, wealthy, and wise.*

Snap a photo and share it on your platform of choice to spread the plant power. Then take care of your plant as usual. If anything goes amiss—withered leaves, blight, or, sadly, if your plant dies—know that it has absorbed something for you.

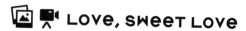 Love, sweet love

Honor the love you bring to the world with a Love Drawing Soda. For the base syrup, red plum creates a delightful, sexy flavor, but you can use any Venusian fruits, such as apples, peaches, cherries, strawberries, or raspberries.

WHAT TO DO: Gather your fruit, vinegar of choice, and sugar or another sweetener. Make sure your vinegar is 5 percent acidity or higher. This mixture is a 1:1:1 ratio, so you can scale it up or down depending on available supplies. Cut your ripe (or overripe) red plums, remove the seeds, then dice into ½-inch cubes. Measure the fruit, then use the same amount of vinegar and sweetener. Try apple cider vinegar and include the mother—the small wisps of probiotic material present in true apple cider vinegar—as the brown sugar it contains represents lust. Combine your ingredients in a bowl, cover with a tea towel, then allow to sit at room temperature for two days. Stir the mixture once a day to make sure all the sugar dissolves. Once two days have passed, strain the plum out and bottle. To make your soda, add 2 oz. of syrup to a glass, plus ice if desired. Then add 12 oz. of seltzer water to the syrup to make a fizzy soda. Charge the soda with your intent, and voilà! You just made a potion. Photograph or video the process, then post to your favorite platform.

🎥 @ HEALING FOR OTHERS

We all have loved ones who could use some healing. And even though healing is an inside job (you can't do it for them), you can send energy, support, and love their way, which will help them on their journey.

WHAT TO DO: Suffering, healing, and recovery are very personal. Depending on what they're dealing with, some folks don't want healing, empathy, or sympathy, especially in a public display. It is important to protect their privacy. There's no need to reveal who you are working for unless the other person wants recognition.

Find a visual symbol of the person you want to send healing to. It can be a photo, drawing, or video. Create your post with this image or video as a base, and layer it with these words (as text or audio of your own voice): *Who this is for I will not say, / Be well to fight another day! / If you see this and are in need, / Know that's why it's in your feed.* Keep the post up for however long the healing is needed.

📷 HAPPINESS HOLDER

In the dark of winter, it's easy to forget how far we have come. It's time to start a happiness jar. You'll need a jar with a lid, note cards (in bright colors if possible!), and a pen.

WHAT TO DO: Bless the jar with incense and give it a once-over with a citrus cleaning wipe if it's been sitting on a shelf for awhile—citrus carries the magic of happiness and joy. Consider adding color magic by painting or decorating the jar if desired and add crystals to your jar for added oomph. Stones for happiness include citrine, rose quartz (self-love), black tourmaline (releases negativity), celestite (divine joy), and carnelian (releases blocks to happiness). Place a pinch of orange peel (harmony), dill (happiness), or oregano (joy) into the jar to speak to your olfactory sense every time you open it. Once your jar is ready, think of one thing that happened in recent memory that made you happy. Write it on a notecard, fold it up, and place it into the jar. Now, when things happen to bring you laughter, joy, or happiness, write them down on the note cards and place them into the jar. Come back to the jar to pull out random cards on days when joy seems far away. Post your resulting jar on your favorite photo app along with something that brought you joy.

◼️📷 PEACEFUL PARTING

The month of February brings a lot of change into our lives. The mirth of the holidays has passed, and the low months of the year are nearly half gone. It is time to grant yourself some peace and let go of that which no longer serves you.

WHAT TO DO: Think of something whose time has come to an end. This could be a habit, a friendship, a job, a relationship, or even a hobby. The point isn't the what, so much as the how. Set up your camera to record a video or take photos of your process and/or the candle burning. Take a purple (divine guidance) or gray (neutralize harmful influences) candle and carve the word "Peace" onto its surface with a pen. Anoint the candle with jojoba oil for overcoming the odds. Place the candle into a candleholder or fireproof container and light. Say: *I wish you well, on this journey of yours. / I'm taking my peace, extending it hours.* Allow the candle to burn down. Remember, never leave a burning candle unattended!

🎥 👥 A CIRCLE OF LIGHT

While traditions vary from culture to culture, certain times of the year are pivotal points that mark shifts in the season and the stars. Today we celebrate the return of the light that comes with the spring.

WHAT TO DO: Create an online group ritual and spell to share light. All participants, including yourself, should wear white. Make a video of yourself (or just your hands if you're camera shy!) "lighting" a candle from the left side of your screen; the candle should be off-screen and lit when it is visible. Once the candle comes into view, say: *I light the night, I share the warmth, I share the light!*

Then move the candle off-screen to the right, as if you were lighting a candle for someone standing next to you. Have your participants create videos of themselves lighting a white candle from the left corner of the screen, after which they should speak an incantation: *I light the night, I share the warmth, I share the light!*

Pass the light to the right. Stitch the videos together, starting with your first video, then all participant videos, and ending with your second video. When the clips are put together, the light will be passed in a clockwise (invoking) circle.

Post this endless circle of light on a loop to celebrate the season and ensure good things in the coming year for everyone.

🖼 PROTECTION PHILTER

A philter is a potion, but also shares its cognate "filter," as in the photo filters used to change the appearance of a photograph in line with certain color values. Create a protection potion, and use a 16 oz. mug so you'll have room to pack in the flavor.

WHAT TO DO: Gather black tea, a tea infuser or reusable tea bag, cloves, cardamom, ginger, and cinnamon. Black tea carries the magic of manifestation; add two teaspoons of your favorite black tea to your infuser. Clove brings luck to the home and is a hex-breaker. Cardamom promotes confidence and strengthens unions. Ginger burns anything nasty headed your way. Cinnamon's magnetism deals in good luck, love, and protecting creativity.

For a single mug, work in ¼ or ½ teaspoon of each spice. Toast your herbs for two to three minutes over medium heat, stirring constantly to "open up" the spicy flavors. Don't forget to snap some photos or videos while you're working! Once the spices have been toasted, add your water, and bring to a gentle boil. Cut the heat before the boil starts to roll and toss in your infuser. Cover the pot to keep those precious oils from escaping and set the timer for five minutes, then strain out the materials, and add sweetener and milk for the perfect drink. Don't forget to empower the tea with protection magic, so that it's a true potion!

@ THE BEAUTY INSIDE

At first glance, labradorite can look like a plain, though beautiful, green stone. But turn it and its iridescent inclusions surprise and delight—butterfly wings are hidden in moss-green depths. Labradorite supports inner reflection, which is important for recognizing our own self-worth and building confidence.

WHAT TO DO: Get a piece of labradorite and make a video showing off the inward beauty of the stone. Where is the iridescence? Take your time capturing this, as this is where the labradorite's power is. Layer the video with text or your voice chanting: *I know my inner strength—know your inner strength! / I know my inner beauty—know your inner beauty! / Let's shine our inner light together!*

Post the video. Each time you view it, say the incantation along with the recording or text. View it when you need a reminder of your worth. Send it to friends who need this reminder also.

🖼 YOUR INNER LANDSCAPE

Our inner landscape is the resting place for our divine self. This is a powerful tool to create your own magic, as well as for discernment and divination.

WHAT TO DO: The information that we receive while in our own minds can be a very powerful tool that is less influenced by the outside world and brings things that need to be seen to the surface. *If it comes from my own head, how do I know I'm not making it up?* It's easier to tell than we think it might be—the hard part is believing it. The discernment I mentioned is key here, and that comes in the form of surprise. If you're getting information from within your inner landscape that surprises you, that's the feeling to hold on to. *How do I get an inner landscape?* You have to build it from scratch: Decide if your starting point is inside or outside.

Close your eyes and begin by relaxing every muscle group from toes to head. Try starting with a "home base" to begin from and to come back to at the end of each journey. You can build a house and fill the interior and then work out, or start with the 30,000-foot view and work your way inward. Whenever you have time to devote, close your eyes and get to designing. It's like interior decorating, but it's free and never ends. Share images of your home base on an app like Pinterest or use it as a mood board.

@ 🖼 A BIT OF CELTIC MAGIC

The word "Celtic" conjures up images of all things Irish—but Celtic culture runs through many countries and cultures, including Spain and Turkey. Ancient Celtic magic was religion, medicine, culture, family, tribe, and land all rolled into one. Knowing exactly what was done in the past is hard; there are many missing pieces. But we can honor the past in our magical practices by incorporating what we do know.

WHAT TO DO: Practice and share these Celtic mini spells:

★ Be like a bard and create a rhyming spell. Think of what you want to manifest, find some rhymes to express it, then share on your platform of choice. BONUS POINTS for sharing your spell with your voice; ancient Celtic traditions were passed on by word of mouth.

★ Many ancient Celtic stone formations aligned with the rising and setting of the sun at important points throughout the year. Find some pebbles, and try to balance them, one on top of the other. Snap a picture of your creation at sunrise or sunset with the caption: *By sun and stone, balance!*

★ Find and share an image of a triskele, a simple three-pointed knotwork that is probably one of the oldest human-made designs in the world. Post with the caption: *Mind, body, and spirit.*

📷 MARVELOUS MOON PHASES

A lunation, or moon's cycle, is twenty-eight days, which is why we can sometimes have a blue moon, or the second full moon in a month; or a black moon, the second new moon in a month.

WHAT TO DO: How do you know what the moon is doing? Give her a peek. Track lunar phases by making your own crystal lunar calendar.

You'll need fourteen stones and two bowls. Optional: black and white paint. If you choose to paint your bowls, one should be black and one white. The white bowl will be for the moon, and the black bowl for space. If you're starting on the new moon, all the stones will be in the space bowl. If you're starting on the full moon, each of the stones will be in the moon bowl.

Stones associated with lunar magic: moonstone (balancing), selenite (clarity of the mind), clear quartz (awareness of the body), aquamarine (courage). If you're starting at the new moon, take one stone each day and place it into the moon bowl. Take the time to center your energies and connect with your emotional self (ruled by the moon). As you pass through the different cycles you will begin to see the connections to your thoughts and patterns as the moon progresses through the month. Share photos of your lunar setup, the crystals you chose, or the designs of the bowls.

🎥 STITCH IT SHUT!

If you've ever been the topic of conversation, you probably know that as fun as spilling the tea can be, it has great potential to harm. That applies not just to the subject of the gossip, but to the spiller of the tea as well. When silence is needed, try this spell.

WHAT TO DO: Draw a picture of lips on a heavy piece of paper or on a piece of thin, recycled cardboard such as a cereal box. If you want to stop yourself from talking, make a lipstick print on the paper or cardboard. If it's someone else, subtly include the person's name in the lips when you color it in—no need to overtly name names or advertise. You know who it is, and that's what counts!

To assist with this work, light a clove-scented candle or incense. Cloves' nail-like shape mimics your needle and gives power and protection to your words. It also gets rid of negativity and heightens clairvoyance and empathy—essential for stopping gossip.

Set up your camera and start recording. Using black embroidery floss, carefully stitch three large Xs across the lips. As you work, say: *Speak no evil!* [as you stitch the first X] / *Spread no falsehood!* [as you stitch the second X] / *Stop. Gossiping.* [as you stitch the final X] Post and repost as needed.

✳ DISCOVER YOUR MOON SIGN

One of the easier ways to help people understand astrology is to relate it to their own lived experience. There are astrology social media apps, but stick to websites that aren't linked to social networks. Your birth chart contains sensitive information about you as a person and can be used as a targeting system for hexes, so only share those details with trusted friends.

WHAT TO DO: You'll need your date, time, and place of birth to generate the most accurate chart (January 6). If your birth certificate doesn't list your time of birth, it is common practice to choose noon, since it splits the difference as the middle of the day. To gain an understanding of your emotional center, look at the placement of the moon when you were born. Look for the moon symbol (☽) and decipher which glyph is next to your moon sign. Once you're armed with the information you seek, input the information into your favorite search engine and *boom!* You've got a world of information about how your emotions are processed, how to make yourself feel emotionally secure, and the best ways to nurture yourself. BONUS POINTS if you search for a test that lays out your attachment style and see how it plays a role in your vulnerability and security. Post about your moon sign and how knowing it impacts you, or use an app to organize your astrological information privately.

◀))) MAGICAL PLAYLISTS

The Universe has multiple ways of sending messages, whether it's tossing a coin with a special date in your path or randomly and unexpectedly hearing a song that plucks at your heartstrings. Music sets the mood which, in turn, boosts intention. What do you want to manifest today? Tap into the power of music to make it happen.

WHAT TO DO: Building a playlist seems simple, but this work requires more than creating a list of your favorite tunes. You are curating an auditory altar that will help you manifest your goals. Make unique playlists for each of your goals, dreams, or intentions, one at a time. Keep your desires in mind as you add songs. These are collections you build over time; you can always add more. Each piece of music or sound effect adds energy to your work. Hand-select your songs. Set your playlist on a loop as a part of any ritual or spellwork. And, of course, playlists can be shared! When others like and pick up your playlists, the magic you created blossoms further, along with the intentions for which you created them.

⚡ MINI ME, MIGHTY ME

Protection magic requires serious mental muscles, and we get them through practice and play.

WHAT TO DO: You don't need any materials for this spell. Find a comfortable place to sit or lie down where you won't be disturbed. This exercise helps hide your energetic self in times of stress, to make you a smaller target. Close your eyes and see yourself in the inner landscape that we've been building (February 5). Once you can work through your senses, see yourself from the outside as a three-dimensional avatar, like in a video game. See yourself shrinking to the size of a rabbit. Walk around your inner landscape at this size and feel how easy it would be to miss if someone were to throw a rock your way. Now see yourself grow to the height of a house, or even a skyscraper. Think of how ineffective that would be for the same rock to hit you. If someone were to try to hex tiny you, it would be easy to miss you. If someone tried to hex giant you, you wouldn't even feel it. Alternate shrinking and growing until you can do it on demand. This is a great skill in times of stress, such as when someone might be look-ing for you and you don't want to be found. Here's the social media post: "Where would you go, if you could be as large or as small as you wanted to be?"

✳ FINDING YOUR VENUS

In this month of hearts and flowers, it's a lovely time to find out where Venus lies in your birth chart. The planet named for the goddess of love reveals how we approach love, relationships, and pleasure. Knowing where Venus lives in your chart can reveal a lot about your personal tastes and what makes you happy when it comes to relationships.

WHAT TO DO: Just as with a birth chart (January 6), you'll need your birth date, time, and place to calculate your Venus sign. Many astrology sites that generate natal charts will most likely show your Venus sign (look for this symbol: ♀), but there are calculators dedicated to specific aspects. Search for "Venus Sign Calculator" for options.

The calculator will show you which astrological sign Venus occupies in your birth chart. Some offer brief interpretations. (A professional astrologer will be able to tell you more!) Share with friends and loved ones and have them discover their Venus as well. How can you help each other find and maintain fulfilling relationships?

 GOOD BOUNDARIES

Have you said yes to too many things and felt over-whelmed after? Are you too involved in other people's issues? Will you agree to just about anything to keep someone from being disappointed in you? Try this meditation to set good boundaries.

WHAT TO DO: It's easier to unfriend or block on social media platforms than in person, but it can be even more important to your health, safety, and mental well-being to do just that.

Emotional: You can choose how much of your personal history to share with your "public" friends.

Financial: Choosing to share or donate can come with emotional manipulation. By setting a boundary before people ask, you're staying true to yourself.

Intellectual: It's okay to keep some of yourself for you. You don't owe anyone a debate, no "devil's advocate"—none of it.

Physical: Your privacy, your body, and who you choose (or don't) to share it with is not only up to you, but you have the right to change your mind at any time, for any reason.

Sexual: Sexual comments about you, your photos, or anything else you choose to share are absolutely worth blocking if they make you in any way uncomfortable.

@ 😊 SEALED WITH <3

What better way to seal a Valentine's Day message than with a heart?

WHAT TO DO: When you place a heart on a message or a post today, fill it with intention. Visualize love and affection going into the post—and know the potential symbolism of the elements that go into making the text heart: the "less than" symbol (<) followed by the number 3.

To the ancient Greeks, the number 3 was considered a perfect number that embodied harmony, wisdom, and understanding: all traits that nurture love. Everything else apart from love is "less than," and 3, the perfect number, completes the heart. Interestingly, the keystrokes "alt" and "3" in succession create a solid heart—almost showing the "alternate text" of the number 3. In a broken heart </3, the three is cut off from completing the image, causing heartbreak.

BONUS POINTS for sealing your messages with XXX! Triple Xs mean lots of things, like three kisses. But XXX is also a sigil for asking for a wish to be granted. What do you desire on Valentine's Day?

 SPIRITUAL BATH SPELL

It's time to take cleansing to a whole new level with pine and sage. Cleansing magic is twofold: you have the physical act of bathing, which removes surface dirt and oils, but when you take the plants mentioned above, you get all the physical cleansing benefits of a bath along with the magical benefits of banishing evil, harmony, healing, purification, strength, hex-breaking, and peace.

WHAT TO DO: Gather a handful of fresh pine, or half that of dried pine needles, and a similar amount of fresh or dried sage. If you're not a gardener, many grocery stores have fresh sage in the herb section. Place your plant material in a muslin bag, tie it up in cheesecloth, or grab a cheap pair of nylons to be your reusable "bath tea bag." Video of you harvesting your plant material, going to find it in the grocery store, or assembling your bath bag are all appropriate. If you can't find pine, search out rosemary instead. You'll still have the consecration, harmony, and blessings, as well as the acne-fighting power as well. Start the tub water nice and warm, and when it's about half full, toss in your bath bag, saying: *Bath comes from near and far, / Water cleansing all my heart.*

@ HOW TO TAROT, BY PIXIE

Happy birthday, Pamela "Pixie" Coleman Smith! If you don't know who she is, you should. The images she created for the Rider Waite Smith Tarot deck are the most famous in the world. Many modern decks are based on her designs.

WHAT TO DO: Offer a one-card reading on your platforms using Pixie's method for reading. If you've never read tarot before, don't worry! Her method—revealed in an article she wrote in 1908, "Should the Art Student Think," and quoted in part on cartomancy (card reading) maven Mary K. Greer's Tarot Blog—works for everyone, and there are no wrong answers, because it's all about what you see and feel in the cards:

"Note the dress, the type of face; see if you can trace the character in the face; note the pose. . . .

First watch the simple forms of joy, of fear, of sorrow; look at the position taken by the whole body. . . .

After you have found how to tell a simple story, put in more details. . . .

Learn from everything, see everything, and above all feel everything! . . .

Find eyes within, look for the door into the unknown country."

Post a picture or write about what you've discovered.

@ HERBS OF POWER

Making friends with the spirits of magical herbs benefits us in so many ways as practitioners. By establishing
a connection to a plant, we no longer have to rely on
having a physical part of the plant for our magic. By
establishing a spiritual relationship, you can ask for the
commanding power, the fire, and the power of exorcism
of saffron without paying a hefty sum to own its threads.

WHAT TO DO: Research the plant you'd like to build a
connection with. Create a bulletin board post about
the magical, culinary, and medicinal uses of the plant to
refer to as your experience grows. Sit or lie comfortably
and slow your breathing. Connect to the inner landscape that we've been building all year, and within that
landscape, call to the spirit you'd like to work with (see
February 5). If you're ever concerned about meeting
a new spirit, feel free to call upon your spirit guide to
chaperone the first meetings for your comfort. Treat it
like a first date; get to know the spirit of the plant. Ask
questions based on your research of that plant. Get to
know them as a friend. In building this relationship you
not only have a new spirit ally, you have a new magical tool to call upon in times of need. Note: the more
popular the herb, often the more useful it is magically,
so start with plants that appeal to you personally for
initial contact.

✳ DAILY MAGIC

Just as each direction (May 28), and time (October 24) can boost your spells, so can the day on which you perform or start your spell.

WHAT TO DO: Remember to keep your own associations in mind: the day of the week on which you were born or married, or the day you started your current job or moved to your new home—these personal associations are powerful!

★ Sundays are great for celebrations, gratitude, and abundance spells.

★ Monday is the moon's day; because the moon is always changing, Mondays are wonderful for spells facilitating change.

★ Tuesday is great for courage and confidence spells.

★ Wednesday is ruled by the planet Mercury; perform communication and taking-charge spells on Wednesdays.

★ Thursday is Thor's day and is ruled by the planet Jupiter. Do luck spells on Thursdays.

★ Friday is ruled by Venus, so it's lovely for love spells.

★ Saturdays are great for protection and negativity-smashing spells.

CRYSTALS FOR CONFIDENCE

One of the best parts of being a witch is the ability to recognize your own self-worth and move forward as a confident person. That being said, we are not going to feel that we can take over the world every day. Here are some crystal allies that will be there to give you a boost if you need it.

WHAT TO DO: Investigate these allies for your journey:

★ **Amethyst:** it knows you're a witch of quality and helps you carry yourself that way.

★ **Aventurine:** a shield made for your heart, it lets you walk with your head up, knowing you're secure.

★ **Carnelian:** the bouncer for this energetic party, carnelian helps examine any potential issues before they occur so you can act with authority.

★ **Citrine:** not only does citrine refuse to collect negativity, it is also aligned with solar protection and prosperity (especially for Aries, Gemini, Libra, and Leo).

★ **Rhodochrosite:** balances emotions so that you're always putting your power foot forward.

★ **Topaz:** this stone of manifestation helps us to act in our best interest, for our highest good.

Look for and share images of these stones to grow your knowledge and share their power.

 # @ FIND A FAMILIAR

What is a familiar? Traditionally, familiars help witches extend their powers. Familiar familiars are cats, dogs, rats, mice, snakes, birds, and bunnies! But more than being a beloved pet, a familiar is an extension of yourself, as well as a connection to the natural world. You don't need to own your familiar; one that is drawn to you and with whom you feel a connection will be the best source of power and comfort.

WHAT TO DO: Find an image of the animal or plant that you would like as your familiar. If it's a wild animal or plant, take a photo of it or save one you find online. Layer the image with images of a rose quartz crystal for the love you will give and receive, a garnet for commitment to the relationship, and turquoise for the spirit connection. As you create this image, speak this incantation: *Creature of nature, your soul to mine, / Together we nurture a connection divine!*

Post the image on your platform of choice with the incantation as the caption. Repost or keep the image live until you connect with your familiar.

@ PROSPERITY CANDLES

Now's the time that we've been waiting for: time for the earth to awaken. Signs of seasonal change are likely to begin appearing now. Let's tap into the changing of the seasons for a prosperity spell to lend a bit of extra cash your way. Instead of a "get rich quick scheme," prosperity magic can be done as a long-term investment in your financial stability.

WHAT TO DO: First, we'll make a magical pen. Grab a 10 mL roller bottle and add one drop of juniper essential oil (avert hexes, prosperity) and then fill it the rest of the way with sunflower oil (solar prosperity). Place the roller ball and the cap and give it a gentle shake to incorporate the oils. (Don't forget to label it.) Take a brown (stability) candle (even more effective on a Thursday for abundance!) and carve "Prosperity" into it with a pen. Then anoint it with diluted juniper essential oil and place it into a candleholder. Set up your camera to record (or you can take a still photo of the candle once it's burning). Say: *Four score, coins and more, / Round them up, my heart will soar.* Allow the candle to burn completely. Then share your video or photo with the spell as a caption.

@  THRICE TWO

Numerology doesn't get much better than triple twos. Think about the energy of this number: duality (the presence of light and dark), balance, and, of course, multiplication.

WHAT TO DO: Tap into the power of the time, and today's date: Set an alarm to capture a screenshot TODAY at 2:22 a.m. (the true 2:22). If you're not an early riser, it's okay to perform this spell at 2:22 p.m. Post it with this intention: *Two for partnerships that benefit growth, / Two to double and stimulate both. / Two for the light and shadow to see, / Two is our friend, so mote it be!*

Note that all those twos add up to the perfect number:

$$2 + 2 + 2 + 2 + 2 + 2 = 12$$
$$1 + 2 = 3$$

The number 3 also represents the three faces of the Goddess—Maiden, Mother, and Crone—and the God—Youth, Hunter, and Wise Man—so divine power backs the magic of the day!

🖼 SOCIAL MEDIA JUSTICE

Here in the wilds of social media, you may find yourself looking to help the whole world. Wonderful—but also overwhelming. An effective approach to this feeling may include a practice called "simpling," which asks you to pick the top three issues that are most important to you and learn all you can about them.

WHAT TO DO: Start a bulletin board–style post about the three problems in the world that matter the most to you. (Don't worry, you can reevaluate your position later. Try examining your top-three list every year to help weed out unseen prejudices you didn't know you had.) Encourage your community to do the same. That way, you will create a network of experts with their own skill set. For example, this year your top three could be anti-racism, protecting trans youth, and the fight for clean water. If new laws are proposed that come upon one of your areas, your friend group knows they can ask you about the impact that could have. This makes for effective information-sharing and prevents burnout.

Remember: don't speak over marginalized voices. They know their lived experience better than you. Seek out voices to learn from, without the expectation of emotional labor. Examine your own prejudices daily. Support the voices from within that community, without centering yours.

Independence is awesome—but sometimes teamwork really *does* make the dream work. Create a video spell using the power of magnets to draw those you need to you.

WHAT TO DO: For this spell, you'll need your camera, some magnets (or better yet, a piece of hematite), and some small metal objects that will be attracted to your magnet or stone. Metal paper clips will work well for this spell (plus, they're literally "connectors"!).

Lay your paper clips in a circle, then place the magnet in the center. Set up your camera so that it captures the entire circle. Ground and center; then, using your finger, move the magnet clockwise (to invoke) in a spiral. With each turn, move the magnet or stone closer to the edges of the paper clips. As you do this, say: *Assistance is wanted; / My words, please heed; / Send me the people I need!*

Moving closer to the paper clips will attract them to the magnetic field and eventually cause them to stick to the magnet or hematite. Once all the clips have been captured, stop filming. Post the video with the incantation as a caption or voice-over, and keep it posted until you find your tribe.

◾ﭤ BYE, DRAMA LLAMA!

The dreaded Drama Llamas: those who seek to cause chaos and disaster while masquerading as Concerned Citizens. How can we maintain healthy boundaries in our online spaces, while keeping up to date on the goings-on in our communities?

WHAT TO DO: Setting a time limit or schedule for times you'll be available online and via social media is a great first step. Filtering your friends lists is also of the utmost importance, because not all eyes are friendly—some of them are surveillance cameras. This spell will banish the haters so you can get back to conquering your little corner of the globe. Set your camera to time-lapse video. Set up a mirror to make sure lurkers don't get any information they can use from outside means; think of it as a two-way mirror: they can't see you, but you can see them. Anoint the mirror glass with diluted frankincense essential oil for protection. Take a gray candle (confusing your enemies) and carve "Be gone" onto it with a pen. Anoint with diluted frankincense (banishing/cleansing) essential oil and place into a candleholder in front of the mirror. Say: *Foe not friend, your time's at an end; / Here you're not welcome, to someone else sell some.*

Best if done on a Saturday. Your target will get bored and go bother someone else, because that's the only way they can feel good about themselves.

@  MAGICAL MEMES

Humor is magic! Laughter generates energy and helps those who engage in it to let go and be open—an important aspect of magical work.

WHAT TO DO: The meme of Boromir from *The Fellowship of the Rings* saying, "One does not simply walk into a crystal shop" has been in circulation since the film came out. When creating magical memes, combine photos and text in cheeky, unexpected ways—with intention. Of course, you can be funny, but work *first* from your intention:

★ Think of your intention, wish, or desire. Write it down in one to two sentences.

★ The next part will take some time: Look for images and artwork that express your wish, possibly in a humorous way. Look for facial expressions, actions, and objects to juxtapose with your desire. A good place to start is classical paintings. Most are in the public domain and there are many from which to choose.

Post your meme as a spell—watch the laughter and blessings roll in!

🎥 WILD WELLNESS

If you're not feeling your best, it's hard to give it in your day-to-day life. Time to take some moments to rest, recuperate, and refocus on your own wellness. Note we didn't say "health," as everyone has a different level of wellness they are capable of. No one is going to be in perfect health every day, but some don't have the ability to feel healthy at all. You're looking to feel as best as you are capable of—don't compare yourself to friends, family, or social media acquaintances, as social media can be used as an escape, and few things are as rosy as they look in the right filter.

WHAT TO DO: Gather your favorite adult coloring book, color tools like gel pens or crayons, and don't forget a fun drink like a fruity seltzer or milk. The point is to recuperate some of the lost joy by allowing yourself to reconnect with the version of yourself that has gone to the wayside. Set up your camera to record and start coloring. For a few minutes you have no responsibilities other than listening to your muse and your inner child. Enjoy yourself. Watching a time-lapse video of you coloring geometric patterns, flowers, magical herbs, or something similar will also provide your followers with a few moments of emotional clarity, solace, and respite.

@ CABINET OF CURIOSITIES

02
28

Think of the purpose of a collection: the more pieces you have, the more variety you have and the stronger your theme. Create a collection of images and texts to build a virtual cabinet of your desires. Whatever your intention, this cabinet of curiosities will keep your secrets and add strength to your intention.

WHAT TO DO: Begin with your intention; how can it be expressed in words, images, or sound? On your platform of choice, open a new file, board, or folder and call it "Cabinet of [fill in the blank with one to two words to express your wish]."

Add images, text . . . whatever you come across. Think outside the box. For example, if your desire is to get a job as an accountant, use more than numbers; include images of wealth, Fibonacci sequences (representing balance and perfection), and what you would like to get out of this position. As you build, say or think this incantation: *With this curiosity / What I desire shall come to me!*

This is not something that will be completed in one day, but over time, as you never know what you will encounter while online. Group your objects together. The arrangement is important—juxtaposition tells a story. Continue curating until (and after) your wish comes to pass. Grow your collection and grow your wish—likes and views will boost this magic!

🎥 HAPPY LEAP DAY!

This day comes once every four years, and it is known for granting wishes! In times like these, we pay attention to the spaces between. In a non-leap year, the hush between December 31 and January 1 is a pivotal moment—why shouldn't February 29 get the same treatment?

WHAT TO DO: Set your camera on a tripod and start recording a time-lapse video. Gather a candle (in a color to match your specific wish, or in light blue for general wish fulfillment) and a candleholder, and crystals that align with your wish for prosperity, peace, protection, purification, or any other aim. Place your candleholder in the center of the clean space that you'll be working on. Start in the center and create a pattern dictated by your eye and the desire you're working toward. Arrange the stones, flowers, or other magical decorations radiating out in a circle. Make sure to leave enough space for fire safety, then light your candle. Once your candle is lit, the pattern surrounding it will send energy through your grid in all directions, which allows you to flavor and filter your magic for the best and most specific outcomes. Allow it to burn down until complete. As your candle burns in the time-lapse, your friends' attention will also power the spell to help your aim come to fruition.

✳ A SPELL FOR POST REMORSE

There comes a time when we post to vent our frustration, and once the feeling has been vented, we no longer need the rest of the world to see that we were vulnerable for a moment. Even if you choose to delete, screenshots are forever and once information is out there, it can have real-world consequences.

If you have post remorse, try this spell to help give Past You a little grace when you need it in the future.

WHAT TO DO: After changing your privacy setting on the post you'd like to see disappear, print it. If it isn't safe to print it, grab a piece of paper and write "POST" in the center of it instead. Fold the paper into three columns, place a small handful of salt into the center of the paper, and tuck one side over the third, so you have a narrow paper the width of one column. Take one end and fold the right topmost point to the diagonal corner, forming a small triangle at the tip of your column. Fold the bottom of the column up to the one-third mark of your paper and tuck the triangle into the tube made by your columns. You've just created a "pharmacy fold" that was used by compounding pharmacies to send powders home with patients. The salt can purify your mind, body, and spirit of the feelings of shame, loss, or confusion associated with the post. Now the work to remedy those feelings begins.

🖼 TAPPING THE WEB

Like a spider's web, algorithms are about connectivity, connecting one thread to the next. Pluck one thread and the whole web feels it. Use spider energy to connect to online algorithms so that they work better for you.

WHAT TO DO: Keep an eye out for spiderwebs, whether in nature or in your home. When you find one, snap a photo.

Share your image and ask friends to describe you in one word. (You'll return the favor.) Wait twenty-four hours or until you have three responses, whichever comes first. When you have a collection of words, select a favorite, and layer it as text over the web à la *Charlotte's Web*. (If you haven't already, read the book!) Post with this incantation: *Pluck the web, feel the vibe. / Look, comment, like, subscribe!*

Why is this significant? By weaving words in her web, Charlotte the spider taps into the collective empathy of the town (like social media posts tap into the collective empathy of the virtual web) to recognize, accept, and celebrate Wilbur the pig's uniqueness and importance. Put this energy to work for you!

BONUS POINTS for making a web for everyone who gave you a word and share them privately with a blessing of gratitude: *The web is a better place because of you.* ♥

@ 📠 BUILDING YOUR NICHE

Business connections are a great demonstrator of the axiom "It's all in who you know," as we never know where our contacts can take us. To capitalize on this idea, consider a business-oriented blog for your current or future career. If you don't already have the job of your dreams, now's the time to manifest it. By writing about your field, even on a blog you own, it establishes credibility in the minds of employers and customers alike.

WHAT TO DO:

★ Look into a small aspect of your work life and research ways to improve common concepts or practices.

★ Connect with like-minded industry contacts through business platforms and see what they're passionate about. You'll get a leg up if you can contribute to the conversation.

★ Blog posts don't have to be lengthy; you'll hold your audience longer if you can present complex concepts as bite-sized pieces.

★ Consult your tarot cards or other divination tools for blog topics. For example, a 3 of Pentacles might prompt a blog post about whether or not certificate programs are worth the cost in terms of added revenue later. No one needs to know where the inspiration came from, unless it's a part of your niche.

📹 MIND YOUR BUSINESS

You've been here before. Another situation where it's best NOT to get involved or devote your energy. Share this spell as a video to help yourself and others disentangle from interactions that are just not worth it.

WHAT TO DO: Set up your camera so that only your hands are being filmed, then turn the sound off. Take a length of black (protective) cord and think of your particular situation. As you do so, tie a loose knot and continue to visualize, embedding the thought in the cord. Make two more knots, again visualizing the situation as you tie them. Feel the complications, the stress, and the anxiety associated with it passing into the cord.

Feel the knots—and their tension. Even though they're loose, they're tangled and messy. That's what the situation is doing to you. Now, untie each knot, saying aloud: *Over and under / Tangled and torn / This is not worth it, / I am free, reborn!*

Post the video and keep it up until the situation is resolved—then delete it from all platforms and devices.

📷 🎥 YOUR BOOK OF SHADOWS

The *Book of Shadows* is named for the practice of hiding a "shadow" or falsehood in the book, so that if anyone were to copy your book without your consent, they'd have a mistake in their ritual. Magical recordkeeping can be a huge undertaking when you're first starting out—there's always the stigma of "is it good enough?" Magical recordkeeping isn't supposed to be a stick with which to beat ourselves up. It's supposed to be a record so that we can replicate our results when something works or change it up when something doesn't work. Movies and television shows depicting these incredible and ornate books are all well and good, but dedicating a regular notebook is just fine. We are going to make our own decorations for a composition book.

WHAT TO DO: Gather glue, magazines, tissue paper, pens, markers, paint, or any other art supplies you'll need, along with the book of your choice and wax paper. Lay the book with the cover side up on your working surface and cut a piece of wax paper slightly bigger than what you're decorating. Since we're using glue on the cover, we don't want to accidentally glue the pages together. Motifs of celestial bodies, stars, moons, and circles are all popular decorations. Record or take lots of photos of your progress for your feeds. (Make sure to allow adequate drying time!)

📹 Be Like Persephone

Persephone has it all: Goddess of Spring, Queen of the Underworld, all the pomegranates she can eat . . . Be like Persephone: she refuses to be defined as one thing. We're not one-dimensional, although sometimes it can feel like it. This spell will help—you'll need a twelve-sided gaming die (just one!).

WHAT TO DO: Set your camera to record. Hold the die in your hand. Each side represents a quality, skill, or aspect that you have inside you. The qualities assigned to the numbers on the die are based on numerology: 1. confidence, 2. balance, 3. creativity, 4. stability, 5. freedom, 6. intuition, 7. synchronicity (being able to recognize it!), 8. prosperity, 9. fulfillment, 10. gratitude, 11. connection to Spirit, and 12. self-value.

Roll the die. Know that you are capable of any one of the qualities associated with the numbers on the die; their development is part of your life's journey. Share the video on your platform of choice with the quality assigned to you as hashtags to seal the spell with words (for example: #creativitygoals, #iamcreative, etc.). Repeat this spell on days when you doubt that you can have it all. If you see repeating numbers, take it as a nudge from the Universe to focus on that particular aspect of yourself!

✦ MAKE YOUR OWN RULES

By now you have seen a few spells and gotten some magical experiences under your belt, and you're developing the discernment that's so important to magical practice. What's a genuine experience versus excitability? How can you apply the scientific method to your practice to make yourself a more effective witch? The thing is, while recordkeeping and research are important, never let a book tell you that it knows more about your culture, experience, and belief than you do. The world is full of beautiful, vibrant experiences, and no single book on witchcraft can encompass them all.

WHAT TO DO: Make a list of colors, flowers, herbs, or other tools in witchcraft and—WITHOUT looking them up—make a corresponding list of all the things you would use them for, things that you're sure no one else would. For example, for money spells, most people probably reach for a green candle, because green is a synonym for money—but what if you want your money spells to have some stability to them? If so, brown is a great color to use. It's time to make some rules of your own. Post a few examples to your profiles and ask your followers what theirs are.

STReeT-SMART PROTECTION

Community apps can be used to weave a protective spell around your neighborhood.

WHAT TO DO: Use your favorite mapping tool to get a visual image of your neighborhood, then print it. Place stones at the edges of the map in four directions so that they create a frame around the map. As you place the stones, speak the incantations that go with them aloud. Note that different traditions associate different elements with the directions—do what is right for you!

NORTH, Earth Element: Place tiger's-eye, smoky quartz, or obsidian. Say: *This space is protected! Our foundations are firm!*

SOUTH, Fire Element: Place citrine, bloodstone, or garnet. Say: *This space is protected! Electricity flows, no fire shall harm. We are warm and welcoming to all who come with good intentions.*

EAST, Air Element: Place iolite, sugilite, or celestite. Say: *This space is protected! We see all and welcome visitors and friends.*

WEST, Water Element: Place amethyst, moonstone, or selenite. Say: *This space is protected! There is clean water in plenty and floods are kept at bay. All feel safe.*

Post the image as your profile photo. Blur the map—the magical work and intention is already in it.

🖼 JUST DESSERTS

When unfair things have happened, and it seems there is no justice in the world, it can really benefit us to check in with our spirit guides, ancestors, or the divine. To do this, you'll need a deck of tarot cards.

WHAT TO DO: Find the Justice card. In the tarot the Justice card rules fairness, equity, and impartiality. Set up your camera to record and shuffle your deck thoroughly (especially if it's a new deck!) and say: *Cards divine, wander through time / show me the way for me and mine.*

Repeat three times while you shuffle. Now, turn your cards face up and fan them out so you can see all seventy-eight. Spot the Justice card? Don't pull it out just yet; also take the cards in front and behind the Justice card so you have three cards in your hand. The card that was in front of Justice goes on the bottom, then Justice in the center, and the remaining card on top. The bottom card is the root of the injustice. The top card is the remedy for the ills committed. If you need to draw any clarifying cards to suss out the details, gather the cards up and deal out eleven cards. The eleventh card is where you'll start your clarifying, as Justice is the eleventh trump in the Major Arcana. Share an image of your reading with friends and followers to gain further insights and boost the justice process.

🎥 DROP THAT HOT ROCK!

There's a lot of talk about the power of forgiveness—that it's about putting down burdens, that it has more to do with you than the person you're "forgiving." But let's be clear: You don't have to forgive ANYONE, and there is more than one way to move on from a bad experience. Sometimes you just have to drop it like a hot rock before it hurts you anymore. All you need is your camera, a rock, and a place of moving water.

WHAT TO DO: Find a stone that's big enough for you to write on and easy to throw. Hold it, and think about the wrong done to you: the perpetrators, how it made and makes you feel (feel it!). Write all of this on the stone with a nonpermanent marker (because all this is temporary) and see the stone sucking all of it in. Now, take your stone to a place of running water—a brook, lake, stream, the ocean . . . Set up your camera so that it is focused on the water. From a safe position, hurl the rock into the water with a one-word spell: *Bye!*

Capture the moment on video, sound on. Make sure you get that *ploop!* when the stone hits the water and sinks to the bottom where it belongs. Share your video to amplify this work. Set up your post as a temporary video that will disappear, along with, eventually, the anger and hurt. The water will wash away the writing, doing double duty to help heal you.

CLEANSING WITH SMOKE

People the world over have used smoke to renew their space, kill germs, and lift their prayers since before recorded history. Specific indigenous communities have smoke-cleansing rituals called smudging; don't do this unless you're a member of those communities and trained in smudging. If you're outside of those communities, look into botanicals that aren't a part of their religious traditions to make sure you're not co-opting cultural practices. Start with plants found in the spice aisle of the supermarket; these allies are considered open practice.

WHAT TO DO: Gather your incense materials and a notebook or your *Book of Shadows* and set up your camera to record. *Carefully* light an incense charcoal tablet, and once it's burning hot, add a pinch of rosemary to balance your space and give you courage and comfort. Close your eyes and record all feelings, memories, and experiences that come up for you when you smell it. You're building a body of experiences around plants that are your own and not the result of cultural appropriation. When the rosemary has burned away, using a spoon or other tool, add cardamom, which has the magic to strengthen unions, or another botanical you'd like to know. Your personal cleansing practice starts with how each ally makes you feel. Share a video or photo of your process to expand the experience.

PASSWORD PROTECT

Long ago people outlined their doorways with protection spells; doorways are portals through which people, animals . . . and other things . . . pass. Passwords, in essence, are protection spells; they allow us into our devices and (hopefully!) keep others out. When choosing a password, choose wisely!

WHAT TO DO: Of course, when you choose a password for anything, you should give a thought to the rules of encryption—using letters, numbers, and symbols. But why not make the arrangement of letters, numbers, and symbols magical? Make each password personally symbolic and unique; you can also create your own magical "words." Remember not to include information that you share publicly (e.g., magical dates, like a birthday or anniversary, or the name of your familiar (February 20). Keep these things in mind as you craft your password. When you set it, do so with intention: *Only I shall pass this door. / Only me, and no one more.*

@ MANIFEST WITH OAKMOSS

Manifestation might sound like a New Age buzzword, but it talks about a specific goal of magic: bringing something into your life that didn't previously exist there. One ally to use for this purpose is balm of Gilead. It's from the same genus as myrrh (June 5), so it's no surprise that they share magical powers like strength, protection, fire, and processing emotional pain.

The queen of manifestation comes in the form of a lichen (a gray-green moss-like botanical found on trees, rocks, and other structures) called oakmoss, a magical ally that is used often in perfumery because of the incredible depth of scent it produces. It makes a superb ally for manifesting your wishes, hopes, and dreams.

WHAT TO DO: Find your personal manifestation ally. Some options are balm of Gilead, camphor, dittany of Crete, fuchsia, lavender, laurel, myrrh, oakmoss, patchouli, sandalwood, and vervain. Whether you have essential oils, physical plant material, or just a photo printed from your favorite search engine, get to know the features of the plant, its aroma, color patterns, bark, and flowers. Research its associations with manifestation for a post on the plants you would like to develop a relationship with for that purpose. Record and organize these allies through photos and text in a bulletin board app.

HELP! I'VE BEEN HEXED!

There are times when nothing seems to be going right—or worse, when everything seems to go wrong despite your best intentions and efforts. You're not crazy. Consciously or unconsciously, others throw negative energy our way, and, if you're vulnerable and it happens at the right time, it can affect you. Try the following spell to lift that hex.

WHAT TO DO: Find a photo or image of yourself that you like (or you can use a symbol of yourself). Print the photo and frame it with dead nettle (this month's flower, and great for protection and hex-breaking). If you can't find nettle, try hyssop, rue, or sage. If procuring plants is an issue, you can also use crystals: jet, kyanite, amethyst, and hematite will also work for this spell.

Next, create an X over the image with herbs or stones to block the hex and protect you from further harm. As you work, repeat the mantra: *Dissipate all harm directed at me!*

Post this spell collage as your profile or background image and keep it there until you feel that things are normal again.

📹 ORANGE BLOSSOM SPELL

Orange blossom, along with many of the citruses, has a reputation for being uplifting, antidepressant, anti-anxiety, and sedative. The magic of orange blossom is solar fire (think about how much sun it takes to turn water into oranges) and it aligns with the sign Leo.

WHAT TO DO: Diffuse 1 drop of orange essential oil in 100 mL of water. If you'd like the slightly more floral version, instead look to neroli, the "other" orange blossom. Frequently paired with orange blossom, neroli oil is made from the flowers of the bitter orange tree, as opposed to the sweet orange tree. Because neroli is distilled from flowers as opposed to fruit, it has a more delicate scent and is more costly. However, both aromatics are calming, anti-anxiety, meditative, and soothing. If you'd like the magic of the bitter orange with a cheaper price tag, plus the addition of a gorgeous green note, petitgrain is an incredible ally, distilled from the leaves of the bitter orange. You'll find the magic of happiness, relaxation, emotional soothing, and the release of tension. For this post, think of the things you'd like to let go of before starting the diffuser, and then share a video of the diffuser running. This will produce a meditative sort of feeling for both you and viewers of the video, encouraging them to breathe.

@ THE OLDEST SPELL

You've probably plucked at a daisy and said, "loves me, loves me not." If that's not the oldest spell in the world, it's up there. Take it to the next level.

WHAT TO DO: When you have a question and need guidance, flowers are ready to give it to you. Ground and center and set your video to record. Choose a flower that corresponds to your question and start plucking. Don't be limited by two-answer choices—you just have to remember all of your options as you pluck your petals. Here are some examples:

★ Let daisies or peonies help name your new baby (furred/feathered/scaled or human).

★ Let chrysanthemum assist you if you're thinking about starting a new relationship—or for making retail therapy choices: this one or that one?

★ Loves me, loves me not? Reverse that question (love them or lust them . . . or not) with a red rose.

★ Which job offer should I take? Sunflowers and zinnia have some thoughts. . . .

Your question is your spell, and as flowers don't have a standard number of petals, that random wildness that is the essence of magic is very much at work. Share your video on your platform of choice with your question as the caption, or as a voice-over.

@ GET THE BIG PICTURE

While algorithms show us what they think we want to know at any given time, it's important to remember that they can only operate as they're programmed. Instead of feeling overwhelmed by a friends list that primarily features the same people again and again, try going to your list and checking in with some friends that you haven't heard from in a while.

WHAT TO DO: Sit or lie comfortably and close your eyes. Picture your region. Picture it highlighted on a global map. Now you have a starting point. Start to see small circles or points highlighted on the map, representing your friends. The more history you have with that person, the brighter the pin in their part of the map. As you zoom in and out of the map, friends' pins come closer into focus. Scroll around in the map in your mind's eye, paying particular attention to areas of the map that are highlighted in yellow, a warning color. These friends are likely to benefit most from your social check-in. Don't come at them with something dramatic like, "My psychic senses told me you needed me!" Try, "Hey, you're on my mind, and I thought I'd check in to see how you're doing." We all need a friend to check in sometimes, and even if they let you know that they're fine, you'll strengthen your connection to them by checking in.

🖼 OUROBOROS AMOROUS

Snakes symbolize so much: love, health, wisdom, and death (as well as renewal, when they shed their skins). The symbol of the snake (or dragon) eating its tail—*ouroboros*—can be found in mystical practices from ancient Egyptian magic to medieval alchemy and represents the eternal life cycle and infinity. Anything you put in the frame it creates is perpetual.

WHAT TO DO: Find an image of an ouroboros in the public domain or create one yourself. Place an image of yourself and friends, a loved one, a pet, your familiar, or your significant other within the frame of the snake's body. Post (or text or email) the image with the spell: *Our love is eternal / A circle unbroken / Ouroboros Amorous / Sealed with this token.* Post to celebrate friendship or love milestones, or just to strengthen bonds.

🖼️ 🎥 INTUITION CHECK-IN

Opal is such a diverse stone that there are eighteen currently known varieties of opal for your magical needs. Please note, opalite is not one of them—opalite is a colored glass that is attractive to the eye but not a naturally occurring stone, so it carries the magical qualities of sand or glass. The crystalline structure of opal, by contrast, is made of interlocking stacks of tiny spheres, which shows we have protections upon protections, making us invisible to those who wish to harm us and allowing us to embrace spontaneity. Part of the spark that opal offers is to awaken the psychic within us. Yes, everyone has intuitive abilities, and opal is there to nurture them within us.

WHAT TO DO: If you have opal, whether in jewelry or as a rough specimen, great! If you don't have a piece of opal handy, use your favorite video search engine to pull up videos to connect with the overarching spirit of opal. Reach down into your gut, where intuitive feelings can manifest, and connect them to the spirit of the opal. Think of plugging a power cable into a wall socket. Record any thoughts, feelings, memories, or awarenesses that arise. Once you establish this spirit connection, you can connect with opal at any time: for protection, an intuitive check-in, or a boost of happiness. Post images or videos of opal to share this magic.

✒️ ARIES, REBOOTED!

Today marks the beginning of Aries season and the astrological New Year. It's also one of those multiple shots at the second (and third and fourth) chance the Universe gifts us during the year to start over. And nothing says "begin again" like a reboot.

WHAT TO DO: Sometimes we need to shut down, unplug, and start anew for things to work properly. For machinery, this is true on a physical as well as a symbolic level. Take this day to do a cleansing reboot of all your devices.

Turn everything off, thanking each device before you shut down. Wait nine minutes (nine is the number of completion). As you power up your device again, fire up a text-based app and write an intention: *In the name of the Ram, / Reboot, refresh! / Begin again and work your best!* PS—you're also tapping into the energy of the spring equinox, which is upon us!

🎥 BANISHING THE ICK

Copal resins are light, sweet, and have the energy of antique lace: soft and strong enough to stand the test of time. There are over 300 varieties of copal to establish a relationship with, and they are found across the globe, so there is surely a species near you to connect with. Copal's magic is in hex-breaking, exorcism of nasty entities, and dispelling negativity. Burning this resin on incense charcoal tablets is a heavy-duty banishing spell full of Jupiter energy that leaves no stone unturned.

WHAT TO DO: Set up your camera on a tripod and record a time-lapse. Light an incense charcoal tablet and place into a fireproof container to burn. Add 1 to 2 copal tears to your incense charcoal and allow it to start smoking. If you know the direct source of the negativity—be it a person, place, or thing—write that on a gray candle to neutralize the source and keep it from finding you again. Anoint the candle with jojoba oil to overcome obstacles. Place it into a candleholder and burn completely.

 # secret gardens

What seeds (literal and figurative) are you planting today in the hope that they'll blossom in the future? Host a virtual ritual to create a garden of dreams.

WHAT TO DO: Have participants join your meeting platform of choice and record the meeting (make sure they're all aware that the ritual is being recorded!). Each participant "holds" a "seed," and will be given a turn to "plant" it. As the lead, you will have to call each person to participate before going yourself. When called, they say: *I plant [flower or plant of choice] / for [intention]!*

The participant should move forward as if they were placing the seed into a "pot" or "in the ground." After all the participants have had a turn, stop the recording. Create (or have one of the participants create) an image of the garden incorporating all the plants and flowers. Share the recording with all the participants. Only post publicly if everyone in the ritual is comfortable sharing.

📹 BENZOIN OIL FOR CALM

With the seasonal change can come some hectic energy. Benzoin oil adds a much-needed sense of peace to your life and your magic. Its creamy, sweet vanilla scent is reminiscent of summer frozen treats from childhood and the comfort they represent. The calming magic of benzoin also invokes the magic of harmony, inspiration, and peace of mind. It strengthens the mind and body against hexes and negative entities and inspires love: for the self, for others, and for humankind.

WHAT TO DO: Set your phone to record video. Diffuse 1 drop of benzoin essential oil in 100 mL of water for ten minutes and breathe slowly and evenly to release tension, anger, or other destructive emotions. Feel a sense of calm empower you and fill you up with cool, clean, refreshing energy. Either post the video to help your followers take a moment for themselves, or screenshot points of the video for photo platforms.

◀))) PROTECTIVE RINGTONES

In magic, bells are a means of communication. They clear space by driving dark energy away, they call to spirit, and they mark beginnings and endings. They warn. When your phone rings, it tells you that someone is calling—which can be exciting (an interview callback!) or dreadful (OMG, who is this?!).

WHAT TO DO: Assigning ringtones to announce who is calling is a mundane means of protection (identification protects and prepares you), but associations can also send out audible energy that surrounds the caller, and can set the vibe for clear communication:

★ Song snippets conjure good memories of the party on the line and create an aura of warmth and well-being.

★ Chimes banish negative energy.

★ Animal noises, bird calls, and insect songs bring the power of these creatures to your call.

When you assign the ringtone, do so with intent: *When I hear _____, I know it's you. / Our connection will be bright and true.* Relationships change with time—update and refresh as needed!

@  CRYSTAL eTHICS

The crystals we talk about in this book are a fun and inventive addition to your magical practice, but if you're not sure where your stones come from, you need to investigate. Like the chocolate industry, crystal mines have a dark history of forced child labor, among other issues. Blood diamonds aren't the only culprit in the labor wars over mining.

WHAT TO DO: Get to know the owners of your local shops. There are small, independently owned mines all over the world, and those owners advertise by driving around the country and stopping at small, independent witchcraft shops to sell directly to their wholesale customers. Research the history of certain stones, their mining locations, and the industry around them. At the writing of this book, there has been a controversy around lapis lazuli being mined in Afghanistan and the money potentially funding terrorist cells. The average stone consumer might not know the origins of certain stones and their purchase can be against their moral code, without their knowledge. Research some of your favorite stones and create a bulletin board post about their history and the mining practices that bring them to you. See what this rapidly changing industry is doing with your hard-earned money. Post your findings so that you and your followers can act within your ethics.

🎥 NESTING GRATITUDE FACE

Manifestation is a thousand times easier, faster, and takes far less effort when you're happy with what you already have. Let nature and some surveillance footage help you build and spread gratitude.

WHAT TO DO: Collect/recycle any kind of string you have on hand and are ready to part with—that includes ribbon, yarn, thread, etc. Cut into pieces that are about five inches long. Once you have a nice pile, scrunch them together with your hands and say: *Thanks for _____!* (What are you grateful for? Name as many things as you can!)

Take the pile and put it outdoors, then set up a surveillance camera. Focus it on your pile of strings and start filming. If you don't have access to this kind of technology, "before" and "after" photos will work as well. Eventually, the birds will come and take pieces to line their nests. Check the pile and the footage in a day or two. Post the video (sped up and edited) with the spell: *Thanks, feathered friends, for adjusting my attitude. / Manifest! Manifest! through sharing and gratitude.*

Every view adds strength to your powers of manifestation. The helping birds physically take your intentions into the Universe, spreading the expression of your gratitude far and wide!

PROTECTIVE CLOVE MAGIC

Clove is a botanical with a reputation for hex-breaking, but its ability to dispel negativity is also legendary. Its protective magic and solar and fire properties burn away anything nasty before it can get to you. The qualities can have a layered effect, carrying the magic of protection and mental powers to protect psychic development. All you have to do is let your intention do the talking.

WHAT TO DO: Make a simmer pot to banish negativity and bring happiness and luck into the home. Gather oranges (protection, joy), cloves, apple (attract contentment), and optionally add almond flavoring. Almond flavoring uses apricot seed, as bitter almond is toxic. Apricot carries the magic to defend against evil and open the mind. To a pot of boiling water, add 1 sliced orange, 1 sliced apple, a small handful of cloves or 2 tbsp of powdered clove, and ¼ tsp of almond extract. Don't forget to grab a few photos of your process to add some intention to your timeline. Maybe you'll inspire a few followers to tidy up their spaces as well. Allow to boil for a few moments before turning the heat to low and setting the timer for thirty minutes. An added bonus: the steam will hydrate the air and make it more comfortable—but you'll want to turn the heat off before the water evaporates and causes a fire hazard.

@ THE LOVELY LENORMAND

You may already be familiar with the tarot—but have you heard of (or tried) Lenormand cards? In the eighteenth and nineteenth centuries, Marie Anne Adelaide Lenormand dabbled in bookselling, cartomancy, and necromancy (talking to the dead). These two latter skills made her a go-to for advice by none other than the Empress Josephine herself (and other famous French folks of the age). Today we know her because of the thirty-four-card deck that bears her name, the Petit Lenormand (unlike the Grand Lenormand, which is a completely different and unrelated deck!).

WHAT TO DO: Unlike the tarot, Lenormand cards focus on thirty-six images, such as The Ship, The Bird, and The Ring. Major arcana cards in the tarot may seem to revolve around a single archetype, but they are filled with multiple layers of symbolism that tell an intricate story. Note that some Lenormand cards have playing-card references on them, but it's the central images that are key.

Play with a deck of Lenormand cards. While each card does have a traditional meaning assigned to it, go by the feelings and associations YOU bring to the images. Share a general one-card reading with your friends and followers to gain further insights and grow your knowledge.

see CLEAR WITH CORIANDER

Coriander is the seed of the cilantro plant, a fiery plant with a more aggressive flavor than parsley, though both carry lust and fertility magic. Use coriander's capacity for encouraging clairvoyance (clear seeing) in your divination.

WHAT TO DO: Take coriander seeds, a fireproof container, and incense charcoal tablets to a spot where you won't be disturbed. Using tongs, light your incense charcoal and place it in a fireproof dish. Once the charcoal is red-hot, place a pinch of coriander onto it. Sit or lie comfortably while closing your eyes. Think of clairvoyance as your own personal .gif library. Pick an area of focus—for example, travel. Start thinking of things that relate to the topic of travel and how they might show themselves to you. For example, if someone were to travel to a state park, they might see a brown and white state park sign with a four-wheel-drive vehicle driving over uneven terrain. With your incense burning, open a dialogue with yourself to establish these vocabulary words within your own mind, which will help show your inner self the best ways to communicate. Repeat often and expand your vocabulary together for best results. Post a video of incense smoke or write about the properties of coriander to strengthen your intention.

@ CHOCO-BUNNY MAGIC!

At this time of year, the world is filled with rabbits—the cute, fuzzy kind *and* the delicious chocolate kind. Rabbit is a symbol of abundance, awareness, and, of course, luck. Chocolate, besides being the best thing on earth, is a potent ingredient for love magic spells. It also promotes confidence and happiness.

WHAT TO DO: Send virtual chocolate rabbits to friends in need of their energy (see above) or just because. Buy a chocolate rabbit, open it, take a bite, and then take a photo of it. Make sure you savor the taste of the chocolate while you are doing this and feel the energy of rabbits and chocolate moving through you.

Now, send this energy out into the world. Email, text, or post the photo you took along with this spell: *Taste the chocolate on your tongue, / Know the magic has begun. / Sending love and luck your way, / Bunny magic saves the day!*

🎥 BANISH WITH DRAGONS

Dragons are fantastical beasts that soar through the air, breathe fire, and are associated with protection. They can use their incendiary breath to destroy anything that comes into your space as a threat, so why not ask them to aid you in your quest for peace?

WHAT TO DO: Given a dragon's natural ability to breathe fire, it only makes sense that they'd want you to use fire and air to deliver your request. Set up your camera to record video, then place a charcoal tablet into a fireproof container and light it. Once the tablet is glowing red, take a pinch of dragon's blood incense and carefully place it on the charcoal. This chalky red resin comes from the dragon-scaled palm tree, and has a musky, cherry-scented smoke; it's associated with protection by dragon spirits. Record a video of the smoke lifting your prayers to the spirits of dragons willing to aid you in your quest to rid yourself of unhelpful spirits. Visualize yourself calling to the sky in your inner landscape, asking for the aid of the dragons. Wait to see if a dragon (or many!) comes to aid you in your request. Ask if you can thank them by burning dragon's blood resin or accomplish some other task. Make sure it's something that you are ready and willing to do, as it would be bad form to go back on your word.

◀))) 🎥 CLEANSING WITH SOUND

To cleanse with sound, you can simply sing a note, or use a charm, talisman, or other objects to produce the noise of your choice. Don't worry if you don't like to sing. If you can whistle, hum, speak, or otherwise create sound when air passes over your vocal cords, this process will work for you. If you are not able to speak, sound cleansing with bells, chimes, gongs, or other instruments will also work. And don't worry about perfect pitch: the vibrations themselves are what will knock off any "dirt" such as negativity, jinxes, and the like.

WHAT TO DO: Step into the room to be cleansed and center yourself. Take all the scattered energies roaming your body and bring them to the center of your body. Send any excess energy from your body into the planet, where it can be used more effectively. Take three deep breaths in through your nose and out through your mouth. On the last exhale, sing a note, any note. Feel the vibrations of your vocal cords breaking down any negativity or other unwelcome feelings, or lingering sluggishness. If you aren't comfortable singing, find your favorite music and have a dance party in your space. The joyful associations will amplify the cleansing. Hang wind chimes around your home to allow for regular sound cleansing. Post a video asking your favorite music to clean your spaces.

📹 STOP-MOTION seed spell

To get through times of self-doubt, plant a lavender spiral: the purple flowers are the color of the crown chakra, and when they bloom in a spiral, they reinforce your connection to the Universe.

WHAT TO DO: Fill a wide, round pot with soil. Starting from the center, plant the seeds in a loose, outward spiral to the pot's edge. (You can do this outside if you're in a warmer climate.) Cover the seeds with soil. As you work, speak this invocation aloud: *A spiral dance of soil and seed / Earth and fire, water, and weed. / From earth's womb, up to the sky, / We are one, the Divine and I.*

Take a photo. Revisit the spiral each day, at the same time if possible. Repeat the invocation and take a second photo. Water as needed. (If your plants don't thrive, don't worry. They have absorbed your troubles. Scatter the earth and begin again.) When the lavender has bloomed, take a final photo, and create a video of the growth with the individual photos. Layer the video with the text: *I am divine and so are you!* Post publicly or share privately with those who need this message.

PROTECTIVE THORNS

The thorns we find along the stem of each rose are of varying size and provide different levels of protection. Remember, if something can protect itself, it can protect you. Obviously avoid plants you're allergic to, but learning about the spirits of these plants is a great step toward a cooperative relationship with protective allies.

WHAT TO DO: Document your process from beginning to end with photos or video. If you're getting your blooms from a flower shop, feel free to talk to the staff there to make sure you can get one with the thorns on. Place them in a paper bag to dry, shaking frequently to allow for even dry time.

Pluck the thorns from your roses by carefully grasping the sides of the thorn and bending it first to one side, then the other. Don't take thorns from a live plant, as this will create an open wound that can become infected and harm the plant. Write your name on a small piece of paper and, if you have some, anoint with diluted rose oil to consecrate and bring peace of mind. With white glue, glue the thorns stem-side down onto your paper. Now if anyone tries to mishandle *you*, they'll get the sharp poke they deserve. Share your video or photos to amplify the spell.

@  4 × 4 × 4 × 4

The number 4 represents personal improvement, love, and self-care. Use your favorite platform to engage with and spread the magic of this day.

WHAT TO DO: Set a reminder to take a screenshot of the time at 4:44 (a.m. if you're an early riser—if not, p.m. will work, too). Share the screenshot as a temporary post with the intention: *Four by four by four by four, / When I care for myself, I become more.* And do one or more of the following:

★ Post pictures of four things you want to let go of; they can be images or symbols.

★ Quietly unfollow or mute four accounts that do not spark joy; as you unfollow or mute, say "hail and farewell" to honor the connection (you followed these folks or accounts willingly at some point).

★ Send wishes of love and self-care to four friends.

Remember, four is more! Views, likes, and shares empower you to be your personal best!

SOUNDS OF THE SEASON

Each season has its own sounds, textures, and smells, no matter where on the globe you are. As we move through the seasons, it is important to mark the passage of time, whatever that looks like in your neck of the woods. Many books on witchcraft talk about four seasons, and the expression of those seasons as though they are universal, but they aren't. Not every climate gets snow. The Southern Hemisphere seasons are the opposite of the Northern, so December might be sweltering and August snowy. Even within the United States where I'm from, the northernmost border might be snowy well into the rest of the country having summer-like temperatures.

WHAT TO DO: Find a place to sit and appreciate what the weather is doing. You might record a post of the sound of the rain, or of the hushed patter of snow falling. If it's fall and the leaves are changing, you might post the sounds of leaves rustling in the trees. Set up your device to record, then once running, leave it to be in the moment. Connect with what's happening immediately around you. This may mean sitting outside—but use your senses to give you feedback. Don't just wander out into a blizzard without a coat for "likes." Share your recordings to immerse yourself and others in seasonal magic through sound.

@ SERENDIPITY SHARING

Ever check your phone, only to see the number 11:11 looking back at you? Or maybe you're out walking your dog and you spot a snake, a cardinal, or a butterfly. Perhaps you witness a gorgeous sunset, an image in a cloud, or a bright crescent moon. These are serendipitous moments of magic. Creatures, numbers, and symbols convey messages for those who see or stumble upon them. Why not share the wealth?

WHAT TO DO: Serendipity is important to this spell. It MUST be organic, which means you must have your phone or camera in hand to capture the moment. If you don't, it means that you were just meant to enjoy the moment. Snap a picture or screenshot and share, perhaps with a short message about what you are sharing. For example, capture an image of a monarch butterfly and send it out with the message: *Transformation coming your way!* or screenshot 11:11 with the phrase *Angel love for all!* Number combinations, animals, plants, etc., each have their own meaning—but as YOU are the witness, your message should be related to *your* experience, although viewers will bring *their* experiences to share (and so the magic takes on new aspects as it multiplies).

DIFFUSING ANXIETY

Liminal times between seasons drive people together, but they can ramp up the anxiety to eleven.

WHAT TO DO: Diffuse these essential oils if you're empowering your own space, both before stressful and anxiety-inducing events or after. Remember to be aware of allergies or other potential reactions when working with essential oils!

- ★ Lavender: balance, harmony, centering
- ★ Rosemary: confidence, happiness, release
- ★ Bergamot: attraction, strength, success
- ★ Ylang-ylang: harmony, balance, raises vibrations
- ★ Clary sage: manifestation, divination, clarity
- ★ Patchouli: hex-breaking, commanding, protection

Take a cotton insert and place it inside an inhaler tube, making sure the lid is tightly secured. Add 7 to 10 drops of an essential oil or synergy (a blend of essential oils that does not contain a carrier oil) to the cotton. Place the stopper into the bottom to hold the cotton inside the tube and lay it on its side to rest for ten minutes. Once the oils have been absorbed by the cotton, unscrew the cap, and lay the open end against one nostril, then gently inhale in through the nose and out through the mouth. Repeat on the other side. Replace the lid and secure tightly. Share video of creating the blend or inhaler tube.

 # @ VIRTUAL CARNATIONS

The carnation is a symbol of love. In their natural state, carnations are pink and purple; pink is the color of love and purple represents a connection to a higher power.

WHAT TO DO: Send a virtual carnation (a drawing or photo) to a specific person through a message, email, or text, or a general post that everyone can see. Use different colors to express different types of love and connection. (Note: color meanings vary from individual to individual. Use these suggestions as a guide.)

★ White: new friendship

★ Pink: familial love (not necessarily a blood relative, but the connection you have with another person)

★ Red: passionate love

★ Yellow: the joy love brings

★ Blue: the honest expression of feelings

★ Rainbow: the love of acceptance

★ Purple: divine love

★ Green: healing love

★ Orange: love through creativity

Accompany your carnation with the magical message: *Roses are red, but carnation loves, too. / Sending love from me to you!*

▶ THYME OF HEALING

The magic of thyme is that of compassion and consecration. It's an herb of the heart, and its rulership of Venus is readily apparent. The courage thyme gives us is a courage grounded in love of family and friends. It allows for the magic of healing and divination, so if you've had health concerns that aren't readily understood, perhaps it is time to do some divination with thyme.

WHAT TO DO: Dried thyme is best for this spell. There are a few ways to ask for thyme's assistance. This spell focuses on healing, but you can word it for any of the associations listed here. With your tongs, light your incense charcoal tablet. ("Windproof" lighters light the charcoal more effectively.) Set your camera to record, grab a pinch of the dried thyme, place it on the hot charcoal, and say: *Herb of courage, herb of healing / Show me the ailment I've been feeling. / Up to now, I've been dealing, / Release this ailment, banish the ceiling.*

Watch the thyme incense smoke and the shapes it makes. Softly focus your eyes on the smoke and allow images to come into your mind to show you what you might have missed. Release whatever ails you into the smoke and allow the smoke to rise to the Universe, gods, or spirits, carrying any ailments with it. Share your video of the smoke to boost healing for yourself and all who view it.

@ FOR ISHTAR, FOR LOVE

Ishtar is the Mesopotamian counterpart of Aphrodite, the goddess of love in the ancient Greek pantheon. She's also the goddess of war, but for this spell we're interested in her as a love goddess, specifically of sensual love. You'll need some ground cayenne pepper, rosewater (a spray bottle will come in handy), and a single date—try Medjool dates; they're supersweet. The date is a nod to Ishtar as "The Lady of the Date Tree."

WHAT TO DO: In addition to her love and war duties, Ishtar is also a celestial goddess; one of her symbols is an eight-pointed star. Set up your camera to record. Use the cayenne to form an eight-pointed star by forming two overlapping squares. As you form the star, visualize Ishtar: we only have stylized images of her, so think sensuality, sexiness, and what that means to you. At the center of the star, place the date. As you do so, picture that sensuality seeping into your relationship, warming it up, caressing it . . . then invoke the goddess: *Lovely Ishtar, heat up my love, fire the sweet spot, shine like a star!*

Spritz the star with rosewater, being careful to disturb the cayenne as little as possible. Share your video (or a still shot of the star) with the caption or voice-over: *For Ishtar, for Love.*

TAROT FOR CLARITY

In the tarot, The Hanged Man illustrates the epiphany wherein we realize the point of it all, the "light-bulb moment" where we realize we deserve better. The lone figure, hanging by the ankle, sees no hurry to change his situation, for he hasn't learned what he came to this place for. When he does, he'll get himself down, empowered, but it must be his choice. Consent is key.

WHAT TO DO: If you don't have a deck of tarot cards, but you have access to a printer, use your favorite search engine to look up images of The Hanged Man in different tarot decks and choose the one that speaks to you. You'll get a lot of traditional images, but don't feel you have to pick that one just because it comes up more frequently than the others. Print the image you resonate with. Gather a candle (and candleholder) with a corresponding color that feels appropriate. Place the tarot card under the candleholder (safety first!). Onto the candle, write "Clarity" with a ballpoint pen. Anoint with the oil of your choosing. (Olive oil is fine to bless candles with.) Place the candle into the holder and say: *The time for clarity is nigh. / Enemies don't have time to say "bye."*

Light the candle and allow it to burn completely. Make a video, or simply take a photo of the candle flame and share with friends and followers to boost clarity.

@ LIFTING THE SHADOW BAN

Most of the time, people who've been blocked by the powers that be on social media are given a "Go Directly to Jail" card and know why they've been banned (fairly or not). But there are just as many times where messages do not go through and you seem to become invisible, even for a brief time. Try this spell to lift the veil of a shadow ban.

WHAT TO DO: Many times, it's the unwitting use of certain keywords or phrases that put you in the time-out chair. Tap into the collective empathy of your platform of choice to reframe your profile. Get an image of a picture frame—make it beautiful, bold, and gold for success, or silver for mystery and magic (or a combo of the two!). Inside the frame, type the spell: *Blame. / Shame. / Ill fame. / Reframe! / Regain. / My Good Name. / XXX.*

Make sure you use strikethrough text on the words "blame," "shame," and "ill fame." Strike these words one at a time, visualizing these smirches disappearing from your account. Post whenever you feel you've been blocked or banned and keep it up until things return to normal.

 PINE PITCH SITCH

Pine has a huge list of magical correspondences from general magical assistance to banishing, creativity, growth, and inner guidance. Today's working revolves around strengthening existing relationships through pine. Pine is a fiery ally, being ruled by Mars, so it's the perfect plant for quelling adversity, strengthening bonds, and growing friendships.

WHAT TO DO: Name the friendship or relationship you'd like to strengthen, either aloud or on a piece of paper. The point of the spell is to show this person that you value their place in your life; we aren't negating anyone's free will. Place the piece of paper under your incense burner for safety. Using tongs, light your incense charcoal tablet and wait until it is glowing red. Place a pinch of pine needles or pine resin onto the burning ember and allow the smoke to bloom. Feel the threads of your friendship warm and become pliable, just like the pine needles thawing in the spring. Allow those threads to enliven your relationship and grow stronger. Keep the name of your focus or their face in mind as you are enveloped in the scented smoke. Post a video of the smoke rising to the heavens (the recipient of your spell is protected because their name is hidden under the incense burner).

✕⁄ BINDING TROLLS

We've all been spammed and trolled. Take the practical steps of blocking, reporting, and muting. As you do, bind those who phish, troll, create false accounts, or just have bad intentions for extra protection.

WHAT TO DO: Get three pieces of fresh rosemary; its highly protective properties and incredible scent will help you focus. Lay the rosemary on your device of choice, which should be open to the app that has potential or current troll issues. Take a piece of black (protective) string and carefully wrap it around your device so that it binds the rosemary to it, and chant:

★ 1st wrap: *I call to [name of account] and those who troll and bait, I bind you from harming others and harming yourself.* (Yes, just like in *The Craft*—those scriptwriters did their homework!)

★ 2nd wrap: *I call to [name of account] and those who phish and scam, I bind you from harming others and harming yourself.*

★ 3rd wrap: *I call to [name of account] and those with ill intent, I bind you from harming others and harming yourself.*

Leave the device for at least an hour. Do this with all the devices you use for accessing vulnerable accounts. Know that repetition may be necessary.

⚡ QUIET QUEST

Now that the spammers are gone, it's a great time to take stock of the accounts on your friends list that are no longer in use. Remember, not every "friend" on your list is a kind pair of eyes: some of them are surveillance cameras. Followers are one thing, even if they aren't yet friends. However, people who drain your energy through pedantic behavior and intentional psychic vampirism need to GO.

WHAT TO DO: *Before* you sit down with your friends list, grab a white candle (purity of intention), your favorite anointing oil or grapeseed oil ("I am worthy of love") or sweet almond oil (unconditional positive regard), and a candleholder. Carve the word "Silence" into the candle with a ballpoint pen and anoint with your chosen oil. Place into the candleholder and light. Post a video of the candle flame for a meditative/breathwork moment before diving into your friends list. The goal here is to attain your own bit of quiet in your brain. As the candle burns down, remove any old accounts, people you've hidden from your feed rather than deleting. It's time to delete them. If their being on your friends list costs you peace, the cost is too high. Delete them. If they've left social media, changed profiles, or let their account go fallow, delete. This is your haven: you get to decide who partakes in your space.

@ CRYSTAL FRENEMIES

All crystals are beautiful (as are people), but not all of them work well together. Be aware of crystals' various energies and that when working with them, these energies can cancel each other out, and so, not do much for you.

WHAT TO DO: Refer to a trusted resource for crystal uses and energies. Here are some crystal pairings that are widely agreed upon as no-nos:

★ Confidence-boosting tiger's-eye and empathy-enhancing smoky quartz or amazonite could cause sensory overload, especially for folks who are natural empaths or psychics.

★ Carnelian's or red jasper's high energy and go-getter natures don't mix well with calming and subtle amethyst or blue lace agate.

★ Gomed (hessonite) and cat's-eye or pearl have conflicting energies that conjure negativity.

Generally, stones with similar structures and colors and similar elemental and zodiac associations will work well together—but what feels right and good to you when you have the stones in front of you? Share and compare potential crystal pairings with friends and followers to get second, third, and fourth opinions.

🖼 THE DIVINE SPARK

The Empress is a card associated with the Divine Feminine and the bounty that comes from within. One of the facts of modern living is that we can go quite a long time ignoring the needs of our bodies: sleep, food, water, and more. It isn't healthy to do so for long stretches, but it can become a habit if we aren't in a secure place with our bodies and their needs. The Empress is associated with Venus, so an experience of the body and luxury is a great way to celebrate the Empress card in April.

WHAT TO DO: Set up your favorite Empress card in a place of honor and build an altar to yourself around it. Many fruits carry Venusian associations (January 29), such as apples, peaches, and raspberries. Find something from the list of Venus fruits that you have access to and hopefully enjoy. Use these and other fruits; use your favorite resource to learn the magical associations before including them to help tailor your experience of your senses in the way that best suits your needs. Set the scene with visually appealing fabrics and luxe textures. Consider snacking on cheese curds (Venus) drizzled in honey. Involve as many senses as you can. Feel free to take some photos to share beforehand, perhaps a panoramic shot of your space, before really diving in with all your senses.

@ MRX BACKUP!

Just about everyone knows about (and dreads) the arrival of Mercury retrograde (MRx). But there's nothing to fear. Think of it as a three-times-yearly reminder to do the things you should be doing anyway, like reading and understanding contracts (and negotiating!) before you sign them, watching what you say, backing up your data, and preparing for delays. Mercury retrograde tells us to be prepared, so let's do this!

WHAT TO DO: Look ahead and get the MRx dates for the rest of the year. Set reminders to back up data, change passwords, and clean up in the week leading up to the retrograde. Share on your favorite platforms to spread awareness. Set this spell to pop up: *Mercury retrograde is here. / Remember, there's nothing to fear. / Back up. / Pack up. / And prepare. / If you see this message, SHARE.* (Include the MRx dates.)

THE SPIRIT OF OLIVE

Olive is such a delightful presence in your kitchen, garden, or ritual space. If you ever have the chance to meet an olive tree, do it. They are such sweet spirits with kind souls. The magic of the olive is solar and fiery and aligned with Leo. The wisdom of olive is the kind, quiet sharing of an elder, rather than the boisterousness of youth and feigned experience. To work in concert with olive is to have the protection of sage wisdom, and the peace of connection to something outside yourself. The association of olive with prosperity doesn't hurt, either. Because there is a connection between prosperity, wisdom, and olive, if you're attempting to create a budget, leaving an offering to the spirit of olive is especially auspicious.

WHAT TO DO: To call on the aid of olive the spirit, find a brown (stability) or white (purity of intent) candle. Carve "Wisdom" into the candle with a ballpoint pen. Anoint with olive oil and place into a candleholder or a small cup or saucer with three olives on it. Say: *Olive be for me, the wisdom I seek. / Help my actions match the words I speak. / Blessings I ask from you, Olive. / I'll wait to hear the message you call of.* Safely burn until complete. Post photos or video of your candle to spread olive's wisdom.

MINT MONEY MANDALA

Tap into Taurean energy by creating and sharing a mint money mandala!

WHAT TO DO: Place a pile of coins in the center of a flat surface—we're talking silver here, quarters at the very least. Surround your pile with a fan of bills so that they look like rays coming out of the coins (don't worry, singles will work). Surround that with a ring of fresh mint. Pack everything tightly so that you can't see the surface underneath. Create an outermost ring of gold glitter.

Snap a photo of this mandala or create a video with a voice-over: *Cash for you! / Cash for me! / Minting money, / Set it free!* Post on your favorite platform with the spell to share and spread the wealth.

📹 🖼 CHEERFUL EXPRESSION

Sunflowers follow the path of the sun through its travels in the sky each day. On cloudy days when the sun is far from our view, sunflowers turn and face their sunflower friends. This is a reminder that even sunny personalities need to look to a friend once in a while when the sun is far from view.

WHAT TO DO: Sunflower magic is that of blessings, joy, and removing the blockages to creative expression. If you can find sunflowers at the florist or grocery store, great. If your post is an image from your favorite search engine, that works, too. Invoke the spirit of sunflower to bring cheer to otherwise dark days with a yellow candle, a brown candle, and sunflower oil (as long as you aren't allergic!). Into the yellow candle, carve the word "Cheerfulness" to use your will to find joy. Into the brown one, carve "Blessing" for stability in blessings. Anoint the candles and place them in a fireproof container. If you can find sunflowers, arrange them behind the candles so that any images you take will focus on the clarity of the sunflower, rather than the writing on the candles. Light the candles to help you find your way to other sunflowers to help you find your joy; allow them to burn down completely. Share a video or photo of your candles burning on your platforms of choice to boost the magic!

 **@** **RAINBOW-HEALING**

Use rainbow magic to send seven-layer healing to a place on earth you love.

WHAT TO DO: Capture a country, city, or area that needs protection or healing with a map app. Work with a place that calls to you. Make seven copies of the map and:

★ Layer the first map with a yellow filter and the text: *I send joy to [name of place].*

★ Layer the next map with an orange filter and the text: *I send solutions to [name of place].*

★ Layer the next map with a red filter and the text: *I send love to [name of place].*

★ Layer the next map with a green filter and the text: *I send healing and peace to [name of place].*

★ Layer the next map with a blue filter and the text: *I send clarity to [name of place].*

★ Layer the next map with an indigo filter and the text: *I send visibility to [name of place].*

★ Layer the last map with a purple or violet filter and the text: *I send justice to [name of place].*

Speak the incantations aloud as you layer each map. To post and share, stitch the maps together to create a video or post them one after the next so the entire spell can play over and over to send healing.

@ ISUA FOR STRENGTH

Isua stone was formed 3.8 billion years ago in alternating layers of iron and algae. Once you've made up your mind to do something, Isua will move mountains to make sure you complete your task.

WHAT TO DO: As we have worked to build the lives we are worthy of, and that are worthy of us, we are building the connections to the spirits of the natural world itself. So, if you can't find a piece of Isua stone, search for an image of Isua stone online. Once you have the image, connect to the spirit of Isua stone, and allow its primordial energy to wash over you. The strength of iron (ruled by Aries, Leo, and Virgo) brings emotional balance, invulnerability, and success in legal endeavors. Connection to the fossilized algae is balancing the mind, body, and spirit. Isua stone takes the chaos of our lives (think of how chaotic it was to form land on a planet of volcanoes and magma) and brings balance. Ask the spirit of Isua stone to center you in the storm of your life and bring calm. Post photos of Isua stone and discuss its properties, or videos of your experiences with its energies. Sharing the image also imparts a bit of its strength to all who see it.

04
23

🎥 @ AFFIRMATION STONES

If you've ever encountered a rock painted with an affirmation, then you know the joy that comes from such a serendipitous surprise. Of course, you only get to experience this when you physically encounter these magical treasures (these are spells, too!). But you can replicate and even amplify that magic by bringing your discovery to the web.

WHAT TO DO: If you encounter a painted stone, first, seize the moment. Feel and live the experience for as long as it takes with no phones or cameras. When you're ready, ground and center and set your camera to record. Retrace your steps approaching the stone; try to repeat every step exactly as you remember it.* End the video by focusing on the stone so that viewers can see and read it.

Share your video on your platform of choice with the hashtags #lookdown, #foundmagic, #sharingmagic, and #magicinthewild to seal the spell with words. BONUS POINTS for making your own painted stones and sharing them digitally. You can also leave clues for others who are in the area to find them such as map coordinates or images of the surrounding area.

*For safety and security, do not share details of the exact location if the stone is found near where you live or places you frequent often. #beawarewhatyoushare

🖼 🎥 BODY ACCEPTANCE

Our bodies are miraculous. It's time to give thanks to the vehicles that carry the weight of our soul around every day—especially on days when it feels like we have gotten a bad deal when "everyone else" has it so easy. Everyone has things they wish their body could do, even if they aren't disabled. Maybe you took a bike pedal to your shin when you were eight and now it aches when it rains. Maybe you never quite got the hang of jumping rope or whistling. That is a part of your story: who you are, and what makes you, you. Today we give thanks.

WHAT TO DO: If you have photos of your younger self, gather some. It's okay if you don't—not everyone does. Scan or take a snap of any physical photos that you'll feel comfortable sharing. If you don't have any, feel free to include a selfie that makes you feel empowered. Post something you are thankful that your body has allowed you to do, whether it is to create life, or make it to your best friend's birthday party. Everything you've accomplished to date has been with this body. It is a joy to inhabit this body today, even if that isn't the case *every day*. Take a few moments (whether for yourself, or in a video) to reflect on the amazing things you have accomplished and give thanks to your body for carrying you through it.

MUSIC MAKES THE MAGIC!

Looking at photos can give us perspective, because our emotional responses are based solely on the visual. Set that image to music and watch it change. You'd be surprised by how much a combination of audio and visual prompts can affect your experience.

WHAT TO DO: Use a video—one that you've made yourself or can access in the public domain—that represents your feelings. For example, you could use a tornado destroying a house if you feel afraid or not in control of a situation. Layer that video with music representing how you *want* to feel. Using the example above, you might want to play soothing, calming music, something that alleviates fear, to contrast with the raging tornado. The music could soften your fear, or make the fear seem silly or unreasonable (think of Professor Lupin's "Riddikulus" spell in *Harry Potter*!).

Meditate on the new combination, focusing on the phrase: "I want to go from [negative feeling] to [positive feeling]." Share your video-sound combo and add your intention as a caption, if you're comfortable sharing.

@  e-empowerment

The social webs that we've built over time can be called upon to help reinvigorate our business acumen and employment strategies, from finding a new job to hiring new employees. They are a living, breathing energy that can be called upon throughout our careers to celebrate accomplishments and to support others in their times of need as well.

WHAT TO DO: It's time to reach out to our connections, and do so with intention. Using your business profile or a profile on a resume-themed site, create a post talking about your work history and show how your social web has helped you shine. As you create the post, visualize yourself excelling in and enjoying whatever role you wish to play. If appropriate, tag colleagues to thank them for their assistance throughout your career. Tapping into this latticework of interconnected lives connects us to our personal history, our shared triumphs, and the ways in which we have supported each other. For new connections, this post will illustrate that you're someone who is willing to give accolades, someone who will remember and reward people who have stepped up to the plate. This kind of ability to give and receive gratitude is a great skill to have, especially if you'd like to move up to management in the future.

 **@ DIY HERO(INE)**

Today is Superhero Day! Unleash your inner heroic persona by creating and sending it out into the world to save the day (or at least make it a little better!).

WHAT TO DO: Ground and center, then take time to meditate or journal on what a heroic individual is to you:

★ What do they look like?

★ What are their powers?

★ What are their symbols? Their colors?

★ What is their name? (If you need inspo, there are loads of free name generators to play with!)

Once you have answers to these questions, create your character using your favorite avatar app. Going through this ritual makes what you have created *real*. In this case, you have created a visual representation of a piece of the Universe. This is important! Once created, send your images out into the world. Include messages to friends who need a heroic presence—or post for yourself when you need a hero in your corner.

EMOJIS FOR PROTECTION

Symbolism predates the written word. Emojis have taken centuries-old magic of symbolism and translated it to the common era with happy faces, sad faces, and any number of hand signals from a thumbs-up to praying hands or high fives. We can translate these symbols to any magic, with or without the aid of technology, and it still works: that is the power of magic.

WHAT TO DO: Define the situation that needs protection magic. By laying it out, we get a bird's-eye view of the issue and any potential pitfalls to be aware of. At that point, evaluate some potential remedies, magical and mundane, then translate them into emojis. Posting an emoji will strengthen the intention you've set as you work on a magical solution separately. For example, if your remedy involves divination, a crystal ball emoji will do just the trick. Moons are always helpful for magic both done at night, and if a disguise is needed to keep you safe. The neat thing about posting your string of emojis as a post on your chosen platform is that it doesn't have to make sense to anyone but you. Anyone reading it will lend you the energy of their attention for a moment or two, and might even ask you what's up, thereby giving it even more oomph.

 WALPURGISNACHT

Today we stand on the eve of Beltane, one of the two most powerful days of the year. Remember that with every day of significance on the calendar, the eve is just as important (Halloween is the "eve" of All Hallows' Day, and then there's Christmas Eve, and so on). These are times of great anticipation, excitement, and hope. In German folklore, on Walpurgisnacht (Night of the Witches), all the witches meet on the Brocken (the highest peak of the Harz mountain range in Germany) to dance with the Devil—sounds fun, right? Devils aside, tap into the power of the collective tonight with a virtual bonfire to mark the arrival of spring, a fresh start.

WHAT TO DO: Today, gather like-minded folks to post images of fire. Flames big and small, flickering or still, are welcome; fire cleanses, clears, and inspires. Be sure to post the images with this incantation, in text or as a voice-over: *On Witch's Night / We share this light, / Clear the shadows, / Cleanse the blight! / As the wheel makes another turn, / Fire to inspire, fire to burn!* Share as a temporary post (and share others' posts as well!), for the power of this night is short!

🖼 IT'S BeLTANe!

Your media feeds may be filled with photos of flower crowns and maypoles. Traditionally, people wash their faces in the dew of the first morning in May for clear sight, clear skin, and a fresh outlook on life. Take this magic to heart with an exercise in self-love.

WHAT TO DO: If your magical supplies include a spice rack, steep 2 tbsp of dried rosemary in boiling water. If you have fresh rosemary, you can use a little more. Turn off the heat and carefully (as you are working with heat and steam) tent a tea towel over your head to provide a nice steam facial that unclogs pores and inspires a dewy look. For an extra boost, consider hydrating your skin with moisturizer in the shape of sigils or symbols important to you, including hearts for love, stars for hope, or moons for peace. Once cooled, you can then use the rosemary infusion to rinse your hair and give it shine and scalp nourishment. While you engage in this self-care, visualize yourself feeling gorgeous and grounded. Post photos of your spa day, setting the stage with candles, incense, or all your moisturizers and lotions lined up. This sends a message of warmth and love. Each time someone likes or shares your photo, they carry with them the knowledge that there's never a bad time to remind yourself that you are loved, beautiful, and desirable.

🎥 BALLOON-A-MOON

Harness the full moon in Sagittarius that will happen within the next month. (The full moon in Sagittarius can take place anywhere between late May and late June.)

WHAT TO DO: We're looking at this spell now to give us time to prepare. First, find out the date and time of the full moon in Sagittarius. Because the full moon is in the sign of the Archer, which is ruled by the planet Jupiter, it's a good time to think about expansion. What do you want to see grow? Create a video of a balloon being inflated. Use a color that relates to what you would like to see expand (for example, red for love and relationships, green for health, gold for success, or blue—the color of the month, and a color that promotes clear communication of your ideas and desires). Layer the video with a brief statement of what you want to expand either as text or as a voice-over. Don't forget to express gratitude! Save the video and post it at the Sagittarius full moon and watch your wishes grow.

 WARDING FOR THE HOME

It's a new month and time to lay your wards if it's something you've been meaning to get to, or refreshing if you've had them up for a while. Calamus root is a flowering plant in the grass family, also called sweet flag. It grows in swampy marshes all over the Northern Hemisphere and lends its sweet aroma to perfume and medicine. This plant is easy to tell from its friend, bearded iris, by the sweet smell it releases when crushed or torn. Calamus essential oil is an easy-to-find ally that aids in protection magic, exorcism of evil spirits, and self-love. The latter two qualities make it an ideal ally for warding your home.

WHAT TO DO: Take a 2 oz. spray bottle and fill it one quarter of the way with rubbing alcohol or witch hazel. Add fifteen drops of calamus essential oil and swirl to incorporate. Fill the bottle the rest of the way with water (distilled is best) and roll between your hands to mix. Empower the spray with bells or your voice. Spray around the interior of your home to chase away any negative spirits or energy, or stagnancy; work counterclockwise to banish. Post a video of you making or using your spray to boost the banishing magic.

📷 MAY THE 4TH BE WITH YOU

It's a good day to think about the "Force." In the Star Wars universe, it's the inherent life force that exists in all of us (and that we just celebrated on Beltane). Remember, fiction is a reflection of reality with a fantastical twist!

WHAT TO DO: Capture the magic of the Force today with a selfie that your energy transforms. Turn on your camera and put it in selfie mode. Look at your reflection in the camera as if you were looking in a mirror. Look into your own eyes and know that you are the result of many generations past. Wait until you feel balanced and grounded—don't rush it! The cumulative energy of eons is reborn again and again. When you face the force . . . snap a photo! Share this image with a sparking star curtain to honor the story of the Force and your place in it. Repeat as a ritual (without taking a photo; you can use your phone on selfie mode, or a mirror) to reground and connect to the Universe.

STABILITY UNDER STRESS

The divine order knocks us off balance from time to time. We fall, and we learn to get back up. The building blocks for emotional stability revolve around ideas surrounding security and safety. One of the best ways to build resilience and deal with stress involves controlling our breath. Taking the reins and controlling your breath when under stress is a benefit to your entire system.

WHAT TO DO: Set up your camera mount to capture your breathwork practice. Close your eyes. Rather than working to blank out your mind, focus on numbers. Square breathing is a very helpful practice that gives you a) something to focus on, and b) a built-in pattern to make it easily repeatable. You're going to breathe in through your nose and out through your mouth for the entirety of your practice. Even if you only make it thirty seconds the first time, you're helping your nervous system. Breathe in and count 1-2-3-4. Hold your breath for 1-2-3-4. Slowly release your breath for 1-2-3-4. Hold your breath for 1-2-3-4. Then start the cycle over again. Share your video to inspire others and expand the meditative magic you've created. Doing this practice for a few moments a day helps your body understand that its job, even when you're under stress, is to take even, deep breaths to regulate your nervous system.

THE WISHING CUP

In the tarot, Cups carry the stories of our emotions in their depths. In traditional representations of the 9 of Cups tarot card, a jolly man sits in front of a row of perfect cups with his back to them. Clearly, he's happy—and so confident in what he has that he doesn't even have to look at it.

WHAT TO DO: Use the 9 of Cups as a talisman. Post a photo or image of the 9 of Cups on your page and invite friends and followers to lay their wishes and desires before the Cup Master (don't forget to lay yours there as well!): *In the cups, your wishes sleep. / Take a cup, drink slowly, drink deep. / Tell your desire to the Master, / That it may come to pass hereafter.*

Reply with a cup emoji to let them know that their message has been received. Send a fancy cup emoji and a blessing to anyone who reposts or shares: *May the cup of your life overflow with blessings!* All interaction adds energy to the spell and boosts your wish!

📹 DEATH BECOMES HER

Death in the tarot is the gateway to new life and a reminder that it is a change you need. The Death card lets you know that something is rotten and needs to go—an ending as a doorway to another reality or situation. Your life doesn't end because your situation has changed. You are merely occupying a different space.

WHAT TO DO: Find the Death card in your tarot deck of choice or print a picture of one that calls to you when you search online. A popular symbol found in many iterations of the Death card is the rose carried by the figure of Death, which symbolizes the potential strength and prosperity that follows change. It's time to prune your own "roses" so that you can flourish and prosper yourself. Everything dies at some point; it is our job to prune those dead limbs and renew ourselves for the challenges ahead. If you're using a printout, write along the border of the card, listing what is to be pruned from your life. If you're using a card, add a piece of paper under the card's border. Find a black (endings, the Void) candle and carve "Ending" into the surface with a ballpoint pen. Anoint with sweet almond oil (the blessings of nature), place into a candleholder, and burn completely. Post a video of the burning candle and request that your followers comment or share which things in their life need to come to an end.

⚡ THE NODES KNOW

The north and south nodes in your birth chart reveal your life's purpose (north) and the experiences of your past lives that inspire this purpose (south).

WHAT TO DO: Search for an online nodes calculator or birth chart generator that shows node placements, then plug in your birth date, time, and place. Look for these symbols: ☊ (north) and ☋ (south); they will always be opposites. For example, if your north node is in Pisces, then your south node will be in the sign on the exact opposite side of the astrological wheel, Virgo.

Once you know your nodes, explore what you think they tell you. For example, if your north node is in Pisces, look at Pisces traits to see if anything aligns. Pisces is known for healing—is your purpose to heal generational trauma (December 4) for yourself and your loved ones? If your north node is in Pisces, your south node will be in Virgo. Look to Virgo's qualities to discover the past-life qualities that have prepared you to be that healer. Earthy Virgos are pragmatic and detail-oriented—maybe you've karmically mastered grounding and stability, qualities that would aid a healer. Create a text post to share your nodes and interpretations with people you trust. Watch for opportunities to fulfill your purpose. Sharing magnifies awareness, and engagement will help illuminate your path.

◄ MISFORTUNE AVERTED!

Lemon balm, aka *Melissa officinalis*, is the bee's knees (in the sense that bees love it!). This lunar plant is a friend to anyone who works with the grieving or dying. The association of Melissa with the dead helps keep spirits of unwelcome dead away from your home. During the points of the year where the veil between the living and the dead is thinnest—like now!—refresh warding around your home that deals with unhealthy spirits.

WHAT TO DO: To make a Spirit Spray, you will need a 2 oz. spray bottle, 7 to 10 drops of lemon balm essential oil, 1 tsp of rubbing alcohol or witch hazel, and some water (distilled is best).

To the 2 oz. bottle, add the witch hazel first, then the lemon balm essential oil. Because lemon balm is distilled from the flowers of the Melissa plant, rather than the leaves, it's an expensive oil to make. The number of drops suggested above is a guideline for that reason. If you feel the scent is too faint, go ahead and add another drop or two. Swirl the mixture together to incorporate the oils, then fill the rest of the bottle with water. Spray the exterior doorway(s) to your home to cleanse it before walking into your space. Then proceed counter-clockwise (banishing) around the interior of the space to drive out any nasty spirit energy. Post a video of yourself making or using the spray to expand its potency.

📹 MELT A HARD HEART

Wounds can be hard to endure, but time can heal them. Give the process a little nudge with this spell.

WHAT TO DO: Freeze a flower in an ice cube—an orange blossom if you can get your hands on one. Part of the purpose of this spell is to cleanse and let go, giving yourself a clean slate to begin again. Orange blossoms are perfect for this work, but if you can't find them, any white flower will work just as well.

When the ice is set, place the cube on the ground and set up your camera in time-lapse mode to record it melting. Overlay the video with these words, spoken or typed out: *Anger and hurt, melt away, / That I may love again one day.* Share on your profile until you feel your anger soften.

◄ HOUSE MAGIC FLOW

Communication in the home is important. To keep communication flowing in all directions, burn some lavender! It calms chaotic energy, brings and protects peace, and helps with developing clairvoyance.

WHAT TO DO: You'll need a mortar and pestle, or other herb grinder, along with incense charcoal, tongs, a lighter, a fireproof container, a spoon, lavender flowers, and a white candle. Take a small handful of lavender and place it into the grinder. Lavender buds act more like a seed than a true flower, so if you place them onto incense charcoal without grinding first, they pop and spark and can be a potential fire hazard. When the flowers are roughly ground, light the incense charcoal. Once the sparks have died down and the coal is glowing red, sprinkle a small amount of ground lavender onto the charcoal to ensure it is burning evenly.

Take the candle and carve "Communication" onto its surface with a ballpoint pen. Anoint the candle with sweet almond oil for communication blessings or olive oil for healthy communication, place it into a candleholder, and burn completely. As the candle burns, add lavender to your burning charcoal and say: *Fire below / Air above / Help us communicate with love.* Allow the smoke to permeate the space, then post a video of burning incense or a candle flame to inspire your followers and expand your intention.

@ PERSPECTIVE POWER

Perspective can make pebbles seem like boulders, and a patch of grass a fantastic jungle. Being close to something distorts it so that sometimes situations can seem larger than they really are, or sometimes help you notice smaller details you wouldn't normally be able to see. When we get stuck on a problem, we get frustrated. We miss things. Use your camera to create a spell image to enhance your vision of issues and situations so that you can tackle them with grace.

WHAT TO DO: Go out in nature (which is already magical!) and see what you encounter. Flowers? Plants? Wildlife? Water? If you're drawn to something, go low. Safely set your camera on the ground and snap a close-up photo. Layer it with these words, visualizing your issue: *Zoom in. / Closer . . . closer . . . / What is missing? / Show me more!*

Post and share! Views and likes will bring you closer to a solution.

@ THANKS, KNIGHT OF CUPS!

Knights in the court system go out into the world and carry messages through their actions; they have the strength and stamina to see their objectives through. The suit of Cups is our spiritual center, filled with the knowledge of emotion, relationships, and connections. Acknowledge the things that you are thankful for today to add fire to your hopes, renew your spiritual center, and stave off the burnout that comes with pushing too hard for too long.

WHAT TO DO: Find the Knight of Cups in your deck, or search for one that speaks to you in your favorite search engine. If you use a ritual chalice, grab it; otherwise, use a glass and fill it with water. Place the glass in your magical working space with your card and think about the things that you are thankful for in the last week, month, and year. Imagine each thing on your list as a drop in the cup the Knight is holding for you. When the cup is filled, imagine drinking it—then drink the glass of water you set out. Once you've finished, refill the glass and leave it and your card on your workspace for three days to remind you of your gratitude. Take a photo of this mini altar, then pour the water out for a flower, tree, or potted plant. Share your photo with text or a voice-over about what you are thankful for to sustain the energy you've created.

@  CAPTION THIS!

Visual imagery inspires and embodies magic—and sometimes, more witches make for more detailed magic! Try this spell:

WHAT TO DO: Think about something that you are trying to manifest right now. Browse images of artwork—classical pieces that are in the public domain—and find one that expresses your desire. Post it on your profile along with this spell, asking others to describe the magic they see in it: *Art is magic, / Magic is art. / Caption this, / And play your part!*

Every response adds energy to your manifestation efforts and perhaps details you didn't consider before. Be sure to express gratitude to all who assisted you.

THE WITCHES' GARDEN

Garden shapes allow energy to flow so that it resonates with more intense energies, depending on the number of sides (or lack thereof) and where the energy "pools." This is true for one-inch flowerpots and acres of garden.

WHAT TO DO: Check out the list below if you'd like to align your magic to your garden beds. Once they're grown, they're doubly steeped in magic: for their natural alignment and their growing conditions.

STAR: A great shape for protective herbs.

CIRCLE: Emotional healing or personal empowerment.

CRESCENT MOON: Nurtures; plant herbs and flowers associated with your moon sign.

SPIRAL: Increases magic or banishes, depending on the direction of the spiral.

SQUARE/RECTANGLE: Brings stability for the home, reinforcing the foundation (especially of the group).

TRIANGLE: Brings strength to any magical goal.

Create a video walking the perimeter of your garden to immerse yourself, your friends, and your followers in the magic of its shape and the plants it contains. If you can, end with an aerial shot, turning your garden into a visual talisman. Caption with a mantra that suits the shape to focus its power.

@ PLAYING CARD ORACLE

Tarot's Cups, Swords, Wands, and Pentacles twin with playing card hearts, spades, clubs, and diamonds.

WHAT TO DO: Keeping symbolism, association, and numerology in mind, share a general one-card read on your platform of choice. See if friends and followers have any synchronicities!

HEARTS: guidance on emotions, love, and relationships • SPADES: guidance on ideas, thoughts, and the intellect • CLUBS: guidance on creativity, passion, drive, and purpose • DIAMONDS: guidance on money, wealth, and career • COURT CARDS: personalities; look at expressions and patterns to add nuances to your interpretations • ACES: beginnings; like the tarot, the essence of the suit • TWOS: partnerships • THREES: creativity and teamwork • FOURS: balance and celebration • FIVES: challenges • SIXES: renewal • SEVENS: luck • EIGHTS: working hard • NINES: wisdom, especially when gained through experience • TENS: completion

📷 🎥 KAMBABA JASPER

A sublime forest-green and black stone filled with whorls, voids, and incredible patterns, Kambaba jasper is a fossil made from cyanobacteria colonies that are some of the oldest organisms on the planet. Imagine the peaceful nature of that ancient version of the Earth: cooled enough to have standing water and algae, but no animal life, jobs, mortgages, or fights. Its long lifespan connects us all to our past, present, and future selves, because it has been here longer than trees and vertebrates.

WHAT TO DO: Find a piece of Kambaba jasper that speaks to you, or a photo of it. Feel the energy field around the stone, and record any sensations, memories, or feelings it provokes. Reach out through your energy field and allow the stone to enter your energy and record any sensations, memories, or feelings. If you are working with a physical stone, charge your stone through incense, energy, or sound. Salt and water are common cleansing methods, but they can damage soft stones, so a general rule is to avoid them if you don't know the stone well. Feel yourself drawing energy up from the earth and sending it into the jasper, like charging a battery. Never use your personal energy, as it can make you feel ill or tired. Share photos of the stone or videos talking about what you felt while working with it.

@ SHARE A LITTLE SMOKE

Spring means spring cleaning (we're still in it!), and that goes for energy as well. There's nothing like a good smoke-cleanse to clear the air—and you can share it.

WHAT TO DO: You can buy an herb bundle for smoke-cleansing but consider making your own using plants that are local to you. Ground and center, then turn your camera on. Set it up at an angle that will capture you (or just your hands) holding the herbal bundle. Using your hand or a feather, fan the smoke around the area, saying: *I banish the dark energy from this space. / Be clean, be clear, with love and grace.*

Share your smoke cleansing video to supercharge your intention; sharing will also allow others to benefit indirectly from the cleansing.

BONUS POINTS for using alt text to describe your spell for all five senses, for those who may not be able to experience your ritual visually, audibly, or olfactorily.

🎥 MATCHSTICK MAGIC

This fast-luck spell will remind you how lucky you are and restore your faith in yourself. Sulfur is a mineral that is aligned with the sun and the element of fire. It banishes enemies and obstacles with a surprising *flare* for the dramatic. Using sulfur in your magic is incredibly powerful because first it dissipates any hexes and then protects you from future attack. The spark that fires a match will speed your working into the Universe for a rapid return on investment.

WHAT TO DO: Use one match for each issue that might keep you from being the lucky, prosperous witch of your dreams. Set up your camera to record your process. Label each match with the name of your obstacles. Allow inspiration to spark your creativity. If you can write the word on your match, even better. Strike the matches against the strike plate on the matchbox and allow the spark to bring forth the light of your soul (in alchemy, the soul is represented by sulfur). Allow the match to burn for a moment to destroy the intention named on that match. Don't burn your fingers. If you have a cauldron or other fireproof dish that can be used outside, consider burning your matches in one small pile, rather than one at a time. Post the video of you burning the matches. Every engagement with the video will ease the removal of the obstacles in your path.

GET-IT-DONE SPELL

Need some motivation? When work piles up and you just need to get things done, it's time to tap into drone magic—not the camera kind, the bee kind! There's no worker like a worker bee—and today's World Bee Day, so there's that, too!

WHAT TO DO: Drones do it all; they build, they tend to the queen, they pollinate. Their buzz is the sound that drives the Universe. Use that sound (also a "drone") as a magical frequency. If you can, capture a bee in action—safely, of course. IMPORTANT: Capture image *and* sound. Share as a video or just the sound bite with this spell overlaid in text: *Droning / Honing / Focus / Growing / Bee a drone / Get it done / My tasks are whittled down to NONE.*

Post temporarily until all your work is complete. Repost or create another video or sound bite when motivation is needed.

OPEN YOUR HEART

Kunzite stimulates the emotional heart center by helping the body process energies that can be overwhelming to the heart, translating them into loving communication. With this empowering stone, we're going to help open your heart to beneficial feelings, allowing our hearts to release anything that doesn't belong.

WHAT TO DO: Anoint the center of your chest with olive oil or sweet almond oil for the blessings of nature. To do this, place a drop of oil on your finger and create a clockwise spiral over your heart to increase feelings of love, emotional support, and connectedness. Connect with a physical piece of pink kunzite, or search for a photo online to work with. With a physical stone, allow the stone to enter your energetic heart space, and record any feelings, sensations, or memories. If working from a photo of kunzite, feel your heart center's energy come to a point in front of your heart like an antenna to connect with the spirit of the crystal. Because you don't have the physical stone, the spirit will be easier to establish a rapport with. Say: *Spirit of Heart, how lovely thou art. / Feelings of [insert emotion] can now depart.* Share photos with text or videos about your experiences with this magical stone.

@ WORD-FIND WISHES

Games are magic! Try this one:

WHAT TO DO: What are the things you're wishing for RIGHT NOW? Make a list of all these words, then create a word-find puzzle to share. You can use a free word search generating platform to incorporate the words into a word search game, or a word-processing application to create the word search puzzle yourself. Share the puzzle on your feed and invite others to play: the first three words they see are what they will manifest in the coming month. Have them post their findings. Every time they post, it boosts those things for you as well as for them! Even if no one posts comments, or even likes your post, this still happens because people will see it. We don't always get to witness magic at work.

@ 🎥 see YOUR success

The benchmarks for success are different for everyone.
It's important to recognize what you consider to be
successful, then recognize the hard work that went into
achieving it for what it is.

WHAT TO DO: Sit down and make a list of your accomplishments, starting with the past year and working
your way backward. It could be personal, financial,
magical, emotional—anything you're proud of. On a
second sheet of paper, make a list of things you had to
succeed at to make the accomplishments happen.

ACCOMPLISHMENT	SUCCESS ORIGIN
1) Got promoted	1) Developed my brand online through an industry podcast
2) Started dating	2) Went to therapy to deal with anxious attachment style
3) Earned my black belt	3) Attended classes consistently, even when tired

Make a video diary discussing your successes and
encourage others to share their own. Share where
you're comfortable. How is making such a list a magic
spell? Recording makes things real (sometimes we have
to see things to really believe them, including our own
accomplishments—give yourself credit!) and it hones
our focus to encourage further success.

 **SPRING PANSY RING**

Lay some pansies flat on a piece of paper and apply pressure (with a hammer) and you'll leave a pansy-shaped impression on paper or fabric—the flowers and this action make for potent magic!

WHAT TO DO: Gather some pansies. Use colors that correspond with what you'd like to focus on: yellow for joy; purple for spiritual connection; pink for love and relationships; blue for peace; orange for creativity. If you wish to share the creation of your ring, set up your camera to record. Lay your pansies face down in a ring on a sturdy piece of paper. As you do this, think of where your energies need to focus. Create concentric rings of pansies to form a bull's-eye. Feel your focus getting stronger as you work inward.

Once all the pansies have been placed, cover the paper with another piece of paper or wax paper. Then using a hammer, gently tap each flower to transfer its image onto the base paper. As you hammer each flower, say the spell: *Focus, focus, fixed in flower, / Pretty pansy, pass your power!*

When all the flowers have been pressed onto the paper, carefully peel the top paper and flower matter away. Share your pansy rings as a single image or as a video with the spell as the caption.

◄ CLEAR THE WAY!

Now that the month is almost over, it's time to clear the air and make way for June with frankincense. It has the magic of banishing, and it's a heavy lifter in that arena.

WHAT TO DO: Gather incense charcoal tablets, a pair of tongs, a lighter (preferably windproof), some frankincense resin (those drops of resin are called "tears"), and a fireproof container for the charcoal (careful, it'll get hot!). Set them up in your workspace. With your tongs, carefully light the charcoal until sparks chase across the surface of the tablet. Once the tablet is alight, put it into the fireproof container and place a single tear on the surface of the tablet. That may not sound like a lot, but resins make a *LOT* of smoke, so proceed with caution until you've found your comfort level. As the smoke rises, you can turn on fans around the house to disperse it. PRO TIP: A cheap plastic shower cap will make a great cover for your smoke detector while you're burning resin so that the detector doesn't sing you the song of its people. Just remember to take it off once the smoke has cleared. Post a video of the incense smoke rising from the center, with a shout-out about that which you are trying to clear in order to give voice to the spell.

BANISH ENERGY VAMPIRES

It's World Dracula Day (in honor of the publication of *Dracula* on this day in 1897)—a good day to rid yourself of energy vampires. Sometimes they're not easy to recognize, but eventually you will feel them: just being in their presence drains the life out of you and interactions with them leave you feeling depleted.

WHAT TO DO: When you encounter an energy vampire, take a moment to meditate on what energy they're tapping into: Your emotions? Your mind? Then open that person's profile and place a piece of selenite for mental clarity and black tourmaline for protection on or near the screen of your device. Say the spell: *Vampire be gone, / Human, return! / Soften, evolve, live, and learn.*

Then mute that person's account—some people become vampires without even being aware of it. Let the moon go through a complete phase from new to full. If after this time you sense no change, unfollow or block the vampire. If you're unsure, keep them muted for another complete moon cycle and revisit.

📹 LABYRINTHINE LAYERS

The labyrinth (July 22) is a time-honored tradition that goes back four thousand years. Not to be confused with a maze, a labyrinth is a single path leading toward the center of the space. A maze is designed to confuse you, but a labyrinth is designed to show you the way. Because there is only one way in and one way out, it is a divine place to search for answers. It is just you and your time to think. If you'd like to visit a labyrinth, search for the "world-wide labyrinth locator" to find a sacred space near you. Many of the sites listed for labyrinths are churches, so do your research and decide how you feel about that before you go.

WHAT TO DO: If there are no labyrinths near you, you can search for labyrinth images on your phone to trace with your finger. At the start of your labyrinth journey, firmly state your question or the concern that you need to puzzle out. Mull over the pros and cons of your question, as well as where to find the missing pieces you might need to make your decision. The repetitive movement of the meditation gives you ample time to turn off your outside brain and turn on your inside brain. Post a video, if permitted, of your movement through the labyrinth so that friends and followers can take the journey with you. Any engagement adds energy to your own journey through the labyrinth.

✳ WITCH WAY?

The physical direction you face when you perform a spell or ritual is important in magical practice. Each direction—north, south, east, and west—is associated with an element and aspect of life.

WHAT TO DO: When you do magical work, check back to this day to add the power of direction and the elements to your work:

★ Face NORTH to add the element of AIR to your spells. Use for spells and rituals that focus on thoughts, ideas, and the mind.

★ Face SOUTH to add the element of FIRE to your spells. Use for spells and rituals that focus on creativity, passion, and power.

★ Face EAST to add the element of EARTH to your spells. Use for spells and rituals that focus on stability, money, and growth.

★ Face WEST to add the element of WATER to your spells. Use for spells and rituals that focus on love, emotions, and change.

How do you know which direction you're facing? Just about every phone has a free compass app you can use. Note: associations for directions differ from culture to culture and tradition to tradition. Do what works for you.

▶ RELEASE WITH BAY LAUREL

In the realm of social media, there are friends we've known our whole lives, and then there are the ones we've known a week—and that was six days too long. In the realm of the digital, there is a potential for just "hiding" the profile and coming back to it, or ignoring those people for a bit, but the reality is that no one is entitled to access to you. While "delete"—with or without the block function—is a perfectly acceptable answer to the problem, let's make sure the trash is taken out for good.

WHAT TO DO: Get a bay leaf from the spice cabinet, a lighter, tongs, and a fireproof dish. Set up your camera to record, then grab a pen and write the name of the one to be banished on the leaf. Don't add the name of the banished to the bay leaf, as we don't want any lurkers sending word back to the banished person. In that case, you can write "exorcism" or "banish" onto the leaf. If you have no bay leaves but you do have bay laurel essential oil, feel free to diffuse a drop in 100 mL of water. Bay leaves are a peace-loving magical ally that purifies space and gives us permission to release anything from our lives that no longer serves us. Holding the leaf in tongs, light the tip of the leaf and allow it to burn like incense. Say: *I release anything that no longer serves me.* Share your video to boost your intentions.

🖼 BACKGROUND MAGIC

Wallpaper. It's the first thing you see when you power up your device. Tap into the magic of wallpaper and background images every time you open your technology.

WHAT TO DO: You can cast a spell every time you open or power up your devices through your wallpaper. It's all about the choices you make and the intentions behind them. Here are some examples:

★ Have a dream destination? Use wallpaper with a beautiful image of your special place with the intention: *I shall go there.*

★ Need healing? Use an image of a natural space with lots of green (a healing color!) and water (cleansing and healing) with the intention: *I am well and whole.*

★ Want to bring romance into your life? Choose a piece of beautiful artwork that shows what love means to you with the intention: *I deserve love.*

Make image boards of possible wallpaper selections, then share your top pics and intentions with your friends and followers to help you choose. Once you post your wallpaper, every time you open up your device and it comes up, remember your intention—the magic is released, and the spell is recast! Switch up your wallpaper as wishes come true.

ANGELIC(A) PROTECTION

If you'd like to get to know an angelic energy without needing an introduction to it, angelica is the step that you might be looking for. Its name even gives a hint to its magical parentage, *Angelica archangelica*. The archangel associated with fire, Michael, is invoked for protection. For those of us who have a hard time asking for and accepting help, angelica can help you do that!

WHAT TO DO: To create your amulet of protection, gather a small bag (black for protection, or blue for protecting your emotional well-being), a piece of angelica root or cotton balls and angelica essential oil, and a white (purity of intent) or yellow (protection of your thoughts) candle. Place the angelica root into the bag along with a few cotton balls to protect the root. If there is no root, just add a drop of angelica essential oil to the cotton. Angelica has a very earthy aroma, so if it's too aggressive for your nose, feel free to add a drop of another protection ally like lavender (reveals secrets); benzoin (reveals treachery); or cloves (dispels hexes). Carve "Protection" into the surface of the candle with a ballpoint pen and place the charm near the candle (not close enough for a fire hazard!), then burn until complete. Post a video of you making and using the charm to expand its power and share protective energy.

🎥 ROSE DIVINATION

Rose is associated with love, but it's also attuned to the future and psychic communication of all kinds. For this reason, a single perfect rosebud makes a great pendulum to ask questions about spiritual awakening, transformation, fidelity, and harmony.

WHAT TO DO: Find a rosebud—the flower you're looking for will have a firm, closed bud. If it's closed but feels soft or mushy, it's overblown and will wilt quickly and may lose petals during your divination. You'll also need red thread, scissors, and a sewing needle. Using the scissors, cut the stem just below the receptacle (the fleshy bulb below the petals). Thread the needle with your red thread using a piece about twelve inches in length. You'll want it to be long enough to swing freely. Using the needle to pierce the receptacle, draw the red thread through the flesh of the rose and tie a knot in the string so that it has a handle. Pendulums work on *ideomotor function*. This means that your mind, body, and spirit know the answers, and the pendulum is a way of bypassing your conscious thoughts and getting to those answers. Ask obvious yes and no questions to help you interpret its movements. Hang up the rose to dry and with care: you can have this loving ally for years to come. Create a video of yourself making or using the pendulums.

🖼 STRAWBERRY SUCCESS

Strawberries are magical for so many reasons. Their heart-shaped fruits exude love and courage. Their seeds (on the outside of the fruit) can germinate even when there is no soil. Strawberries are self-sufficient and giving, and great for fertility and success spells—a good thing to keep in mind next time you eat a strawberry. But how can you tap into her magic digitally?

WHAT TO DO: Go to your grocery store or fruit stand and buy a carton of strawberries. If you can pick your own, even better. Cleanse your strawberries. One at a time, pick up each berry and imbibe it with this spell: *Abundance and fecundance: / Edible heart, do your part!*

Snap a photo and send it to a specific person who needs it with the same wish. Once this is done, say: *And for me, too!* If you don't have allergies, eat the strawberry. Repeat for as many people as needed.

📹 BASIL DEBT BANISHING

WARNING: AVOID BASIL OIL WHILE PREGNANT, AND DON'T USE BASIL ESSENTIAL OIL IF YOU HAVE A HISTORY OF SEIZURE OR CHRONIC MIGRAINES. Use basil's banishing power to help restore your finances to working order. This will right a wrong, like unscrupulous banking practices (including predatory overage charges), but it won't fix a long-term or systemic issue.

WHAT TO DO: Use dried basil for this spell. If you don't have access to dried basil, you can chant an incantation over your next slice of pizza, or diffuse some basil essential oil while working on your budget. You'll also need a fireproof dish, tongs, a lighter, dried basil, and powdered clove (exorcism of curses, prevents astral spying). It's an interesting combination; blend to your nose rather than a given "recipe." If you don't like it, you won't want to use it, and then it can't work. Light your charcoal and place it into the fireproof dish, then add a small pinch of basil and allow it to start smoking before adding a pinch of powdered clove. While the incense is smoking, say: *Basil, basil, herb of fire, / Bring to me, my heart's desire. / Banish all debt now for me, / Banish debt so thoroughly.* Talk about the debt you're hoping to discharge. Share videos showing the blending process and burning the incense to increase efficacy.

📹 LUCKY LADYBUGS

Ladybugs symbolize luck in many cultures. And they're helpful in keeping pests away. Perform this spell after sunset. This will give the magic time to percolate overnight—and it's a good time to release ladybugs as the dark and cooler (not cold) temperatures are good for them to get used to a new space. You'll need a container of ladybugs (easy to order online or purchase at a garden center) and your camera.

WHAT TO DO: Go to a green, outdoor area. Place your camera on the ground and set your container of lady-bugs next to it. Prop the camera up slightly with a small rock so that it will capture the ladybugs coming out of their container. Adjust for the light as needed. Start your video to record in time-lapse mode and release the ladybugs with the spell: *Bless this space with good luck! / Bless me with good luck! / Bless all who see this with good luck!*

Share the video—all or in part, depending on the length—overlaid with the text of the spell or as a voice-over that says: "The further it spreads, the greater the luck for everyone!"

🎥 MANIFEST WITH MYRRH

The solar fire of myrrh is nurturing, nourishes the soul, and carries blessings of all kinds. It helps with the acquisition of material objects, especially ones with a luxury attached. The centering, calm, and comfort of myrrh brings an increase in focus. Myrrh is there for you anytime there is a requirement for success or uncrossing.

WHAT TO DO: Myrrh comes in a few preparations, most commonly essential oil and dried resin. You can work with either for the magical aims above. For manifesting desires, consider using a "hot" method, because the additional heat will help speed the magic, just as if you were to add a hot element like cinnamon, cardamom, or clove. Take a fireproof container, incense charcoal tablets, tongs, a spoon, a lighter, and myrrh resin. If you can only find frankincense *and* myrrh, that's fine, as frankincense has the magic of removing obstacles from your path. Light the incense charcoal and add the myrrh to the tablet. (Use the spoon so you don't burn your fingers.) State your wish out loud or write it on a piece of paper you can place under your fireproof dish. Sharing a video of the myrrh smoke will boost your intention and purpose (which you can keep to yourself, if you wish).

@ NUMBER OF THE BEAST

The Book of Revelations rockers, and of course Hollywood, have forever colored our perceptions of the number 666. But don't be fooled. Six is the number of renewal, so a triple 6 is the ultimate do-over. (Plus, pun intended, when you add 6 + 6 + 6 you get 18. Add 1 and 8 together and you get 9, the number of completion.) When you encounter 666, it's a sign that you need to make some adjustments or begin again before you complete whatever it is you're pursuing.

WHAT TO DO: Take advantage of the numeric magic of this day: at 6:00 a.m., pull out your phone and take a screenshot of the time, then overlay it with the text: *666 / I must fix / [problem]*.

Send the image to yourself and post it on your platform to get support for this magic. Views, likes, and shares increase the energy behind your fresh start!

06

06

🖼 @ BEFORE AND AFTER

"Before" and "After" photos are stunning and startling, but in reality it took many steps to get there. Try this spell to spark the transformative process.

WHAT TO DO: Before you start your transformation, examine your feelings:

★ Frustration: Your hair is driving you crazy because you're growing it out and it's in that odd "in-between" stage, so you cut it all off.

★ Fear: You go to the doctor and your blood pressure is up, so you change up your eating and exercise habits.

★ Excitement: Walking down the street, you spot an amazing piece of furniture, but it's a little beat-up. You take it home and give it a stunning makeover.

Once you feel that you are in charge of the emotions that are sparking the desire for change, snap a "before" photo of whatever it is: your space, your object, yourself. Take whatever time you need to make your transformation, then take an "after" picture.

Share both images, one after the other, with the spell as caption to honor your process and inspire others: *Cease to scroll and you shall see / The change that's right in front of thee. / To make it was no little heft, / Prepare for change, and swipe to the left.*

📹 ☎ NEW JOB COLLAGE

This spell is a visual altar of your intention and desire—in this case, to secure new, satisfying employment, but it can be adapted for other purposes! You'll need some glue, base paper (see below), and printed paper materials that you're willing to cut up (magazines, greeting cards, invitations, catalogs, etc.).

WHAT TO DO: You may have a very specific job in mind. If not, think generally: what kind of job are you looking for, and what are *you* looking for in a job? Flexibility? An intellectual challenge? Fulfillment? Great coworkers?

Set up your camera to record in time-lapse mode. The magic of this spell is the collage *and* the process of its creation. Write a statement of your intention along with your ideas and desires on your base paper—which should correspond to your desire with color: gold for success, or green for growth, or even the colors of your dream company's logo. For example: *I will get an offer of the employment I seek* or *I will get a generous offer from [company]*.

Cut out words, images, and symbols from your magazines, catalogs, etc., and arrange them in patterns on your base paper. Let yourself be guided. Glue everything down and admire your magical work. Post the video, ending with the finished collage.

📹 STRUT YOUR STUFF

It's time for the magic of the strut. This movement isn't about walking: it's about attitude. You can have a strut with a wheelchair, a cane, prosthetics, crutches, any mobility device, or none. Your attitude is one that says, "I know I'm awesome."

WHAT TO DO: For this working, all you need is your favorite music and your phone's camera. Before it's time to record, go through your playlists until you find some music that just screams, "I'm awesome" and make a playlist. If you're using a streaming platform, many have sharing options that allow you to share them directly to your social media streams. Once you have the music that makes you move, practice your strut. If standing tall makes you feel sexy and powerful, do it. If you want to decorate your cane, do it. The magic in this exercise isn't walking, it's *GLAMOUR MAGIC*—showing the world that you're incredible and anyone would be lucky to know you. EVERYONE IS SUBLIME, GORGEOUS, AND DESERVES TO BE SEEN.

Once you've got your strut perfected, it's time to set up the camera and show your debut to the world. If you want an extra flair, set your recording speed to 0.3 or one-third to feel like you're walking in slow-motion in an action movie. Now set your timer and shake what the gods gave you.

🎥 @ CRUSHING IT!

When you're crushing it, you own it, you got this, whatever it is. You are the master—though you might not always feel like it. It's times like these when you have to "fake it till you make it." Try to share this spell to help you capture that *I can do this, I got this!* feeling. You'll need an aluminum can, a camera, and a dream.

WHAT TO DO: Set up your camera to record. Hold the aluminum can in your dominant hand. Why aluminum? As a magical metal, aluminum promotes invisibility—not so much like Harry Potter's cloak, but the kind that will help you hide things that you don't want other people to see, such as self-doubt and fear. Aluminum also preserves and offers light protection, which is perfect for this work.

Visualize what you're trying to accomplish. BONUS POINTS for seeing the colors on the can assisting you in this work! Hold this in your mind and say the spell: *I am crushing this!* Then squish the can. Say the spell again as you throw the can upon the ground. Then say it a final time as you stomp on it. Share your video with the spell as a caption or a voice-over and keep it up until you've completed your task.

🎥 @ HYPERSTHENE SPELL

Hypersthene is a dark, banded black crystal that is similar to silver sheen obsidian in appearance. It helps silence overly critical voices in your head by standing up for what is right and increases cooperativeness, including from within. Connection with this stone helps us truly listen to our inner voice without the clutter of outside influence, doubts, and concerns, as it cuts right to the heart of the matter at hand.

WHAT TO DO: Connect to the energy of the stone, or search for a photo of hypersthene online. Allow it to come into your body's energetic field, and record any thoughts, feelings, or memories that come up. Close your eyes and begin your journey to your inner landscape (February 5). Once there, call to the spirit of hypersthene to get to know it and have a few interview-style questions to ask the spirit of this stone of insight, such as: "How can I best work with you?", "Do you prefer to work with me during a certain moon phase?", "Do you have any crystal allies that you enjoy working with?", and "Are there any things that you'd prefer I not do when we are working together?"

Post a video or text discussion about the qualities of this magical stone and your experiences with it.

 @ AURA CAPTCHA!

Kirlian photography shows the energy flow around your body; there are special cameras for this. Get an in-person aura photo session if you can, but in the meantime, there are apps that will give your mobile phone Kirlian abilities so that you can take and share aura photos yourself.

WHAT TO DO: Use your aura photo app of choice to take images of yourself and your loved ones. You'll be capturing the head and neck area—and most of the image you get will be taken up by the colors, which have specific meanings:

★ Yellow: inner joy, happiness, contentment

★ Orange: creativity, boldness, adventurous

★ Green: healing, recovery, being close to nature

★ Purple and White: spiritual, connection to a higher power, the Universe

★ Blue: clarity, honesty, ideas are flowing!

★ Red: passion, anger, high energy

★ Muddy: low energy

Auras are not forever; energy fields change. You can be surrounded by creative orange one day and healing green the next. Share your aura photos where you are comfortable; ask friends and followers their thoughts about where you need to focus.

 **YES . . . OR NO?**

Sometimes all you need is a yes or no answer. Playing cards can help.

WHAT TO DO: Give a deck of playing cards (May 16) a shuffle. Ask a yes/no question. A red card will indicate a yes, a black card will indicate a no. If you'd like to get more in-depth information, start with the cards being drawn as suits of the tarot.

Wands are clubs (fire, adventure, risk), Pentacles are diamonds (earth, prosperity, home), Cups are hearts (water, feelings, and relationships), and Swords are spades (air, communication). Aces are new beginnings, twos are balance, threes are your network, fours are foundations, fives are challenges, sixes are our hopes, sevens are a mystery, eights are movement, nines are growth, and tens are the end of a cycle. Jacks are messengers, queens are growth and healing, and kings are authority and control.

Post a video of yourself doing a sample one-card reading or offer to do them in a live video stream for friends.

▶️ 👥 PROTECT PRIDE!

Capture the crafting of this candle as well as its burning to increase its magic.

WHAT TO DO: You'll need eleven sheets of beeswax (see colors below); candle wicking; a black Sharpie; and some jet, obsidian, or tourmaline chips.

Clear and dedicate your space, then set your camera to time-lapse mode. Lay the wax sheets out in a line so that they overlap slightly in this order: black, pink, gray, light blue, red, orange, yellow, green, blue, purple. Press the overlapping edges together so that they bond; the heat from your hands should be sufficient. Using your Sharpie, write this spell across the beeswax sheets, then sprinkle them with the stone chips: *I pledge protection to all people, wherever they may be. / And to the principles of equality, inclusion, and love, / For all humanity in the Universe with acceptance and justice for all.*

Lay the wick along the edge of the black sheet so that a tail sticks out at either end. Then carefully and slowly roll the candle, keeping the wick in the center and the edges as even as possible. When the candle is completely rolled, press the loose edge into the body of the candle to bond.

Post the video of the process to inspire others. Create a separate post to burn the candle. (February 2 = group ritual inspo!)

FIND YOUR VERTEX

If you've ever felt like the Universe sends you the same garbage on a different day that you didn't ask for, you might want to discover your vertex.

WHAT TO DO: In astrology, your vertex can show you the things that happen to you in life that are beyond your control—and the role you may feel thrust into because of these things. Plug your birth date, time, and place into a Vertex Calculator. There are two points you want to take note of:

1. *The sign in which your vertex lies:* This marks important turning points in your life. When someone has a sun or rising sign (see January 6!) that's the same sign as your vertex, it's very likely that person will have (or had) a big impact or influence on your life.
2. *The house in which your vertex lies:* These are areas of fate and will show you significant life events to look out for.

Encourage friends and followers to find their vertex—then compare and contrast. Because astrology is personal, #beawareofwhereyoushare—private sharing may be best!

📷 STEP IT UP!

Some of the most effective spellwork is accomplished when it is combined with physical action; you're expending and dedicating kinetic energy. If you wear a pedometer, you're capturing the data of that energy— why not have it do double duty? (If you don't wear a pedometer, most phones have health apps with step counters built in.)

WHAT TO DO: While elaborate ritual is filled with mystery and majesty, the simple act of walking can amplify your magical work. Couple the physical energy you'll expend today with what you are trying to manifest. Start in the morning. When you put on your pedometer or access your health app, begin with a mantra: *With every step I take today, I am closer to [what you are trying to manifest].*

Share with friends if you share stats—swapping steps and mantras will multiply the magic! Try to remember to repeat the mantra every time you move. At the end of the day, screenshot your stats with the spell.

📹 SANDALWOOD WISHES

Sandalwood is a gorgeous tree that has been used in religious ritual for its divine fragrance since before recorded history. Unfortunately, sandalwood has become overharvested to the point of vulnerability; vulnerable is the rank just before Endangered on the conservation scale. To continue to enjoy sandalwood in an ethical manner, Australian sandalwood is the preferred cultivar due to the conservation laws of the country.

WHAT TO DO: Create a petition to the Universe, gods, spirits, or ancestors with your manifestation desires. Try to keep your goal specific but succinct: a raise, a new job, a car with fewer miles on it, you name it. Write it on a piece of paper that will become your petition. Decorate your petition with symbols, colors, and anything else that strikes your fancy. You can set up your camera to record you creating and decorating, without showing what you're working on if it's a private matter. Anoint the four corners of your paper with sandalwood essential oil for stability in your wish fulfillment. Place it somewhere you'll be able to see it for the next few days or weeks while you work on making your goal a reality. When your desire manifests, burn your paper, or tear it up before throwing it out. Post your video to amplify your spellwork.

@ GONE FISHING

We spend a lot of time fishing for information. Search engines are all very well, but sometimes the best and most important data comes directly from people. The fish is an ancient symbol for wisdom. In Celtic mythology, the Salmon of Knowledge held the keys to existence. This spell will help you seal your emails with the wisdom of fish.

><((((°>

WHAT TO DO: Why is the fish talisman so powerful?

★ The tail is formed by the "greater than" sign—showing that you seek to expand your knowledge.

★ The open parentheses that form the scales suggest a lack of closure . . .

★ . . . but they are enclosed by "greater" and "less than" signs, which indicate completeness.

★ A degree symbol forms the fish's eye—how much information do you need?

Start your convo and add a fish at the end. Before you hit send, whisper: *Go fish, tell me what I need to know!*

▶️ @ CORN MAGIC, AIR MAGIC

Corn carries the magic of prosperity, fertility, and mental acuity, so it's a great talisman for those who own their own businesses. Corn also carries the magic of agreements (and holding parties to them), evokes nature spirits, releases tension, and promotes luck, love, and air magic. It's this air magic that we're going to harness today, with a fun twist.

WHAT TO DO: All we need for this spell is a bag of microwave popcorn and a marker, rather than something pointy that can poke a hole in the bag. Microwave ovens use electromagnetic waves to excite the molecules inside the microwave, heating them up. That's a lot of "free" energy for your spellwork that you didn't have to sing, dance, or chant for. If you're looking for a quick prosperity spell, draw your favorite money symbols on the bag. If you'd like to bless the bag with some incense before placing it into the microwave, that's okay, too. When you hit start on your microwave, also hit record on your phone. Follow the directions on the bag for your microwave, and don't forget to stop the microwave when the pops slow to one every few seconds. Accept the bounty of the earth with knowledge that your desire is coming. Post your video with or without revealing your intentions (your choice!) to make your spell pop!

DANDELION WISHING SPELL

Nothing says "Make a wish!" like blowing a fluffy dandelion head. (Okay, *maybe* a birthday candle—but you only get one of those a year!) Use your platform of choice to increase your wish-making power across the metaverse with this quick spell.

WHAT TO DO: Take a video of yourself blowing away the seeds of a dandelion head and post it on your platform of choice. That's it? Not quite. It's important to know *exactly* what you're doing.

First, you're helping the dandelion to propagate. You are literally planting seeds, and each potentially carries your wishes to fertile ground. How do your wishes get there? By your will, and your breath. Your breath comes from inside you; it helps power your body by oxygenating your blood. Breath has power. Three deep breaths can calm a panic attack. Shallow breaths can help you work through pain. When you blow on that cluster of fluffy white seeds, know this. Feel this. Visualize the power of your body and the desire at the heart of your wish passing into each seed. As you do this breathwork, chant to yourself: *From my core I send this desire. / Find fertile ground to bloom and inspire.*

Remember—don't reveal your wish. That part of the spell is for your eyes only!

🎥 @ LITHA LESSONS

The summer solstice has arrived! (If you're in the Southern Hemisphere, it's the winter solstice!) In many spiritual traditions, the summer solstice is a time to reflect on the blessings received throughout the year as well as bless you for the dark half of the year to come. Gathering herbs like Saint John's wort, which blooms around this time of year, and having bonfires and cookouts—these all have their place in celebration of the longest day of the year.

WHAT TO DO: The longest day of the year also means the shortest night of the year, reveling in the warmth of summer (whatever that looks like in your region) and savoring the warmth for the long, cold nights to come. The gathering of herbs is a Litha tradition because the herbs and flowers are at their peak during this time. If you're able to grow garden herbs, the morning of Litha (from *liþa*, an old Anglo-Saxon-derived word for "gentle or calm") is a great time to harvest them, after the morning dew has dried to reduce chances of mold. Flower crowns are a popular craft for the summer solstice season, as they are a celebration of nature's bounty. Your summer solstice post can talk about all of the amazing things you've been able to put into action this year, like a magical gratitude journal entry.

SMASH BEAUTY STANDARDS

Forget what anyone else thinks about what is "beautiful." What is beautiful to you?

WHAT TO DO: Meditate on what beauty means to you. You may default to what others say is beauty. Once you're comfortable with *your* definition of beauty, you're ready.

You'll need paper images of the beauty standards you want to smash: images of products and their promises; clothes tags; size guides; a fireproof dish; a lighter; and some dried sage, rosemary, mugwort, lavender, or bay leaves, or any combination of these herbs. (We'll be burning this, so do NOT include images of people.)

Set up your camera so that it's focused on your dish and start recording. One by one, take each beauty standard image or word, tear it up, and put it in the dish. As you work, say how these things make you feel, and what you'd like to change. Mix your dried herbs into the ripped paper. Do this with your hands, visualizing the herbs clearing away any criticisms, insults, or bad feelings associated with beauty. When all is mixed, set it on fire; light and relight as needed until only ashes remain. Cast those to the wind.

If you're comfortable, post the video with your voice. Alternately, you can always overlay it with an appropriate song or sound effect—chimes and bells also chase negative energy away.

🎥 CRYSTALS TO WIN IN COURT

Dealing with a court case? You'll need the right tools:

CITRINE boosts self-confidence and self-esteem. It screams, "You deserve to win!"

HEMATITE helps quell anxiety related to the proceedings and enables you to defend yourself with a clear head and even speech.

RED JASPER protects against negativity, balances emotion, and promotes rational thinking. A great way to do this and provide balance is to wear them as earrings (two stones confer balance in the hemispheres of the brain).

Tiger's-eye, red jasper, and hematite got together and made a crystal baby—TIGER IRON—just for this exact moment. It is the ultimate balance of all three stones: the stability and confidence of tiger's-eye, the protection and courage of a red jasper, and the brain-processing power of hematite.

WHAT TO DO: If you're currently undergoing a court case, any one of these stones is great to have in your corner. Once you've found the stone you need, it's time to let it know how to help! Set your phone to record and cleanse your stones by passing them over a candle (don't burn yourself!) through incense smoke or sprinkling them with a drop or two of water and sand. Post a video of your crystal cleansing to let your followers know you're ready to fight!

🎥 SUMMER TRAVEL CHARM

Share this spell to ensure that your trips are fun, safe, and as glitch-free as possible. Remember—if you encounter delays, you're being protected from something. Take it as a blessing!

WHAT TO DO: You'll need some squares of yellow cloth (yellow for joy!) and some dried herbs in equal amounts:

★ Mugwort: good for keeping awake and alert

★ Comfrey: for protection

★ Mint: all breaks should be refreshing, and mint will boost this!

Set up your camera and start recording. Add each herb to a bowl one at a time. Blend the herbs, speaking this incantation aloud: *By road, by air, by rail, by sea, / Adventure, joy, and marvels see! / By foot, by plane, by train or car, / Safe journeys for us, near and far!*

Make bundles of the herbs with the yellow fabric squares. Post the video, ending with your collection of charm bags. Include your voice or overlay the video with the incantation to share the spell to send safe travel vibes to everyone who sees it and is on the move. BONUS POINTS for leaving the bundles in random places for others to find or giving them to specific people for their travels.

📷 FILTERED POTENTIAL

Filters are a lot of fun to play with. From kitty whiskers to fairy wings, anyone can choose how they show themselves, and their avatars, to the world. Selfies have never been more fun to take and use to engage with a wider audience than ever before. Remember, a filtered photo isn't *really* you, so using your filtered photos makes you a little less of a target, and a little more secure in your personal life.

WHAT TO DO: Find your favorite photo app and open the selfie option. Find a few different spots to take a handful of selfies. Apply filters as appropriate. Snap away! Start using your filtered photo as an avatar or user photo as soon as possible and change the privacy settings on any old user photos to "Friends Only."

📹 SLOW OR SPEED UP TIME

Try this spell when you need a little more "control" over time. What you're really doing is reframing your perspective.

WHAT TO DO: Speed things up or slow things down:

★ If you find that time flies by way too fast when you're having a great time, try this spell, which you can prepare beforehand to share. Go to a beautiful place that gives you joy; it can be outdoors or in. Stand in the middle of it (as accurately as you can) and point your camera outward to capture your surroundings. Start recording and turn in a complete circle. Move counterclockwise as if you were winding a clock backward. Post the video in slow-motion with the intention, spoken or overlaid as text: *I live in the moment, I savor every second!*

★ On the other hand, if time seems to go so slow that it almost stops, try this: Go to a place that is boring for you. Stand in the middle of it (as middle as you can) and point your camera outward to capture your surroundings. Start recording and turn in a complete circle. Clockwise this time. Post the video sped up with the intention, spoken or overlaid as text: *I'm not distracted by time—I make every second count!*

Use these spells when you need to slow things down or speed them up!

🎥 DRAMA BE GONE!

Dragon's blood is a popular resin from the *Dracena draco* trees found in Yemen and Morocco (March 31) and is named after the bloody appearance of mature trees when they are injured or lose a leaf. (No dragons were harmed in the making of this magical ingredient!) Dragon's blood is highly protective and the perfect ally to quash gossip and drama stirrers. No one wants those people in their lives. Banish them.

WHAT TO DO: You'll need a fireproof dish, a lighter, a spoon, tongs, and incense charcoal tablets. Make a petition with a piece of paper. In the center of the paper, write the name of the person causing problems. Next, draw the air of drama that surrounds them. Whether that's action squiggles, stars, or glitter doesn't matter, as long as you can recognize what is supposed to be represented. Anoint the four corners of the paper with dragon's blood oil or take a piece of resin and draw an X at every corner. Place the paper under your fireproof dish to aim the power of the dragon's blood at their harm. Say: *Drama be gone, no one hears your scorn. Drama be gone, leave [target's name] forlorn.* Post a video of incense smoke purifying your space of anyone who'd rather talk smack about you than be an authentic part of your life.

🎥 🔊)) SYN SLAMS THE DOOR

In Norse mythology, Syn is the goddess of refusal. Her job is to guard the great hall of the gods. Basically, Syn slams the door in the faces of unwanted visitors. She also does double duty as a justice goddess, and so can judge when the door needs to remain open. We can all use a little Syn energy in our lives. Invoke her when you need to shut a door.

WHAT TO DO: This spell relies heavily on action and sound. If your living space is communal in any way, do this at a time when it won't disturb others. Go to a space in your home where there is a working door; make sure that it has no issues shutting. Set up your camera to record, and ground and center. Take some time to visualize the situation where you want to shut the door. Keep in mind that refusal isn't cord cutting (July 16). It's merely a separation that can be as temporary or long-term as you need or want it to be. You may be shutting the door to gain time, or silence. When you have your intention solidly in mind, slam the door, saying aloud or to yourself: *Keep out!* or . . . *I refuse!* or . . . *Not now!* . . . or whatever meets your needs.

Share the post (you don't have to include the words of the spell; as always, you don't have to share every detail of your work) and keep it up until you are ready to open the door again.

📹🖼 RETURN TO SENDER

Chicory is a proliferate seeder that LOVES any soil, especially if it's bad. You'll find this member of the sunflower family in your favorite Louisiana coffee, too! (Served the French way, with hot milk. ☺) Its colorful indigo flowers are perfect for "return to sender" spells and a great ally for making sure that your protection magic sticks where it's supposed to go, without raining down on innocent bystanders. Its solar influence warms and cares for you when you are too sad to do it for yourself.

WHAT TO DO: For an unreasonable boss, offer to make them a cup of coffee. Chicory coffee can help sweeten their opinions of you and gain their affection. It's a bitter coffee, so make sure to ask if you can sweeten it with some honey. It's the Leo energy of this purple flower that melts hearts and gets stuff done. If you think you have someone working magic against you, grab that chicory coffee or an herbal tea containing chicory. PRO TIP: Chicory can also boost your powers of intuition, so consider a cup before your next video doing free one-card tarot readings for practice. Share videos or photos of your coffee-making rituals to magnify the strength or heart healing of this magic.

@ HOOK 'EM AND HOLD 'EM

Hand gestures are ancient charms that say so much. Fold your middle and ring fingers into your palm and extend the pinkie and index fingers. What you do with your thumb is important: tuck your thumb over your middle and ring fingers, and you form "the horns," an old symbol across many cultures that wards off evil curses. Extend the thumb, and the gesture forms the ASL symbol for "I love you."

WHAT TO DO: Select your identity tone and grab the Horns or Love handle to add strength and protection or love (or both!) to any spell.

★ Hook 'em with some strength: A friend has posted that they just went for a job interview—comment with the Horns to boost their chances.

★ Hook 'em (or yourself) with protection: You're about to do some long-distance traveling to a place you've never been before. You post a travel protection spell (June 24, November 22, and December 16); tack the horns onto it, or add it as a comment.

★ Hold 'em with some love: A loved one posts that they're down after going through a bad breakup. Comment with the Love handle and the text: *I'm here for you.*

🖼 RELEASE WITH SUNFLOWER

The spirits we're releasing with sunflower today are the spirits of relationships past, the friendships that are no longer a part of our lives. We recognize the joy they may have brought to our lives, and the fact that their time has also passed. Let us wish them well on their way, while we release those spirits to go on to other joys, other opportunities.

WHAT TO DO: Buying sunflowers for yourself is the spiritual expression of meeting your own needs. Remind yourself that they're a gift for releasing yourself from the pressure of unfulfilling relationships. Finding sunflowers should be a snap in the warm summer months, but if it isn't, you can release them with the following spell. You'll need: a yellow candle, sunflower oil, a pen, a lighter, and a candleholder. On the surface of the yellow (thought, intent) candle, write "Release." You may have released the person or the friendship a while ago, but did you release the *spirit* of the friendship as well? If it still hurts, or you still miss them, likely not. Anoint the candle with a drop of the sunflower oil to call to the magic of the sunflower. Place it into the candleholder and light. Allow to burn until complete. Best if done on a Saturday. Post photos of sunflowers along with joyful memories to amplify the spell.

 @ VIRTUAL SCARECROW

Scarecrows are an icon of the fall, but really, their purpose is to protect crops and keep pests away when things are growing. What's stopping your growth? There's a scarecrow for that!

WHAT TO DO: The first thing to do when creating a virtual scarecrow is to determine your "pests." What's nibbling away at your creativity? Your confidence? The answer may be inside you. It could be another person. Or it could be a situation—perhaps something happened in your past, like a past failure that may make you afraid to try again. What would frighten that fear away?

Scarecrows are human—the "predators" for crows and other vermin. What is the predator for your pest? Assign an image or symbol that will be your scarecrow. Maybe it's an animal, or maybe it's yourself. Post the image with this spell: *Away, pest, away! / You won't bother me today. / I grow, I thrive, / Restore my drive. / I stand tall!*

Repost whenever your "pests" decide to make an appearance. (They always do, but you'll be ready!)

@ GINGER BEER SUCCESS

Sodas, even fermented ones, are magical, just like the constituent ingredients that went into making them. The trick to turning a bottled soda into a magical potion is energy. Because ginger's magical associations are with love, passion, courage, and strength, all those forces are driving your success spell, especially if you like *spicy* ginger beer.

WHAT TO DO: Take the lid off the soda bottle and hold it between your hands, at chest height. You're going to say this with your whole chest. Take a photo, then say the spell: *I am successful. I breathe success, I am success.* You have to FEEL it when you say it, or this isn't going to work. Reach down into the earth and pull the energy up from the planet, into your feet, your legs, hips, stomach, chest, and into your arms, down into the bottle of soda. Enough energy that you can feel it vibrate through your fingertips. Send it all down into the bottle of soda and feel it change the makeup of the soda. Every air bubble is filled with the energy you raised. Say it again: *I am successful. I breathe success, I am success.* Drink in the success you earned, then post your photo with the spell to sustain the energy.

WRITTEN IN FIRE!

Firework energy is explosive and spectacular—short-lived in its brilliance but long-lived in our memories. Tap into this energy tonight, whether in the skies or on the ground, with this spell.

WHAT TO DO: You'll need some sparklers, your camera, and an intention to rocket into the Universe. If something's lagging, fireworks energy (fire, inspiration, passion, etc.) will give it a liftoff.

Get your intention, project, or wish down to one word. Like the big fireworks, sparklers have a short life span. They'll last long enough for one word, so make it count! Once it gets dark, set up your camera to record, adjusting for the light as needed. Having a friend help with this one may be a good idea! Ground and center, then, keeping your one-word wish in mind, light up your sparkler. Use it to write out what you are trying to accomplish or manifest in the space in front of you. Speak your intention aloud as you write: *Spark up my [one-word intention].* It's okay if you need to do a few takes. Post on your favorite platform as a temporary post to give your efforts a boost!

📹 SECURITY IN ROSEMARY

Rosemary bestows a calm that is both grounding and confidence building. A magic rosemary bath will give you a whole system upgrade.

WHAT TO DO: Fill a saucepan with three cups of water and place it on the stove. Place a handful of fresh rosemary (dried will work, too) into the water *before* it boils, not after, to tease the volatile oils out of the herb. Pop a tight-fitting lid on the pan to keep the oils from escaping or you'll have water without much scent. Allow the water to boil for five minutes, then cut the heat, but don't be tempted to peek! Once cooled down, charge it by drawing energy up from the earth and into it. Now, run a bath and add your rosemary potion to it, or pour the potion over your head in the shower after shampooing and conditioning. Feel the energy of rosemary place a protective cloak of green energy around you, keeping you safe and secure. Post a video of yourself making your potion and/or discussing the results of your rosemary bath to sustain its energy and inspire others. PRO TIP: If you feel shaky or anxious after a spell, you need to ground again, because there is still too much energy in your body. If you feel desperately sleepy or starving after you've worked a spell, you didn't ground well enough before the spell and you used your own life force to power it.

 RECLAIM INDEPENDENCE

Declare your independence from what's holding you back with a tarot spell.

WHAT TO DO: You'll need a tarot deck that resonates with you. Pull out The Lovers and The Devil cards. Both images tell stories about choices—can you see the differences and similarities? An overlord (an angel in The Lovers and a demon in The Devil) looks down on two humans. In The Lovers card, the couple stands in a blooming garden, free to do whatever they wish. In The Devil card, the people are chained to the pedestal on which the demon sits—not exactly free, but not so chained down that they couldn't escape if they wanted to. What holds you captive?

Turn on your camera and start recording. Lay down The Devil card. This is you now: full of potential but not feeling free enough to take the next steps. Overlay this part of the video with a single hashtag that says what you would be freed of.

Now, place The Lovers card on top of The Devil card—this is where you want to be: blessed by the Divine and free to choose your own destiny. Overlay the spread with the hashtag #[issue]hasnopoweroverme (whatever you chose as the hashtag for The Devil card). Share as a temporary post and let it run until it expires.

🎥 ALMOND APPRECIATION

Almonds are alive with the feelings of joy, life, and all that comes with it. This Venus tree is happy that you're here as it carries blessings.

WHAT TO DO: Since almonds and other tree nuts have a high instance of allergens, we'll work from the inner landscape (February 5). Close your eyes and center your breathing in your diaphragm. Relax your body muscle by muscle, starting with the feet and working up to the top of your head. Starting from your place of power in your inner landscape, call to the spirit of almond. Introduce yourself as you would during any other first introduction. Include a relevant connection, like, "I love your work with chocolate" or "I'm very allergic to your physical energy, and I hoped to see what we can learn from each other in the spirit world." Once you are comfortable with the exchange, ask Almond if you could request the blessing of self-love and peace. Because they are their own entity, they may say no. They could say yes. They could ask for something in return—you don't know until you ask. The rebirth offered by almond is there for the asking. Make a video post about your convo with almond and your magical experiences with it.

📹 ENERGY BUBBLES

It's true that control is an illusion, but you can temporarily contain situations, emotions, and energy to give yourself the break you need to carry on. All you need is your breath, your phone, and some bubble solution.

WHAT TO DO: Ground and center, then meditate on what is overwhelming you. Really think about it. Journal if it helps. It's essential to get as close to the root of your discomfort as possible. (Many of us have deep-seated wounds; much of what happens day to day are merely triggers.) When you feel that you've captured it (this helps make it real), grab your camera and bubbles and go outside.

Record yourself blowing a bubble (or have a friend help if it's awkward). Use your breath to transfer all the things that are overwhelming you into the bubble. As you do so, think or say aloud: *Be contained, if just for a bit; / Let me rest—I won't quit!*

Some situations may require multiple bubbles. Some may burst bubbles. Keep trying until you feel that you've exhaled all of it. Share your video on your platform of choice. Capturing the moment of containment, even if that containment is brief, maintains that containment for a little longer. If you wish, caption the video with your situation. Likes and views strengthen the containment.

🖼️ 🎥 THE EARL OF ASKING

Earl Grey is a staple in tea cabinets all over the world. The sharp citrusy flavor that accompanies this black tea is bergamot, which carries the magic of commanding and compelling, attraction (both sensual and financial), and psychic protection. It is strongly associated with success, strength, and wealth (both in material objects and cash flow). Bergamot's greatest quality is its ability to answer calls for help. Asking for assistance—whether due to childhood trauma, people-pleasing, or any number of factors—can be hard. Trying to do it all yourself is harder and ultimately leads to disappointment, feelings of alienation, and burnout. Turn to the Earl of Asking for assistance. You'll be glad you did!

WHAT TO DO: To ask for help, boil water in a tea kettle (heating your tea water in the microwave can be dangerously explosive!) and gather a mug and tea. This spell works whether you're asking a person for help and need emotional support, or you're asking for help from the Universe/Spirit/Gods/Ancestors. While the water heats say: *Water within, water without / Bergamot send help, Spirit's about.* Pour the water over your tea and allow it to steep according to directions. Sweeten if desired and drink while working out where that help can originate. Post videos or photos of your tea-making process to boost this magic!

 @ IMMORTALITY SPELL

Whether we know of them or not, we all have ancestors and loved ones who have passed from this world. As Ernest Hemingway said, "Every man has two deaths, when he is buried in the ground and the last time someone says his name. In some ways, men can be immortal." Use this spell to keep the memory of those who live in spirit, and who have had a positive impact on your life, alive.

WHAT TO DO: Post an image of your loved one, or an object that belonged to them, or even a photo of their last resting place. Caption the image with: *This is [Name], [your relationship]. / He/she/they [complete the sentence with your connection]. / Please, say his/ her/their name aloud and speak of your loved ones. / #WhatIsRememberedLives.*

Likes, views, and comments amplify your message. Be sure to encourage others to participate by saying the names of their loved ones who live in spirit. BONUS POINTS if someone shares the name of their loved one and you say it, too, aloud or in the comments.

◄ᐱ PSYCHIC PROTECTION

People either love or hate patchouli. But it lends itself to the magic of commanding and compelling, so reaching for it when hex-breaking is a benefit.

WHAT TO DO: The realm of psychic protection is one that doesn't get enough attention. This work enables us to keep our thoughts, ideas, and goals to ourselves and protects the integrity of our intuition and passions. If you're in the camp of "patchouli stinks," work with the dried herb, as it's much less fragrant. To manifest psychic protection, you'll need patchouli, a candle (purple for psychic protection), a candleholder, and a lighter. If you are working with the dried herb, place a small circle *around* the candleholder to avoid causing a fire. If you're working with essential oil, place one drop in a 10 mL roll-on bottle, and fill the rest of the way with the carrier oil of your choice. Place the roller ball and cap, then roll between your hands to blend. On the surface of the candle, write, "Psychic Protection" with a pen. Anoint the candle with your oil. Place the candle into the holder and light. Feel patchouli's power keeping prying eyes away from your head and heart. Create a video of you making your patchouli roller and share with your experiences working with this herb to expand its power for you.

✳ THE PART OF FORTUNE

What if you could get a hint of what you need to do to find happiness, success, and love? Discover the Part of Fortune in your birth chart to unlock your personal best.

WHAT TO DO: As usual, you'll need your birth date, time, and place. Plug these into a Part of Fortune Calculator; you can find several for free online. You can also use a birth chart generator (look for this symbol: ⊗), but not all birth chart generators will show the Part of Fortune in your chart. Its placement will give you some insights on how you can better chase success—it's where your best luck and prosperity live. Look for:

★ Zodiac signs and houses: Each sign has its own direction on how to find success. If the Part of Fortune is in your ascendant, you're lucky (literally)!

★ Planets: The ruling planet for your Part of Fortune will tell you what kind of energy will best serve you. (What is the ruling planet of the zodiac sign of the placement of your Part of Fortune?)

★ Aspects: Aspects in your Part of Fortune will reveal your native skills and your potentially most fulfilling career path.

Share your findings with trusted friends and loved ones and encourage them to find their Part of Fortune. Look for the synergies and connections in your lives.

🖼 @ PYRITE FOR LEADERSHIP

Pyrite, also called "fool's gold," is a brassy gold–colored crystal that forms in cubes and masses. It helps you overcome shyness and anxiety, while boosting your self-confidence. It helps you prioritize problems for efficient problem-solving. If you are deadlocked and can't see a way forward, pyrite will help make one. Keep your head up, you've got this. If you decide to purchase a piece of pyrite, cubes are great for stability and staying grounded. Masses of pyrite will radiate that energy all around like a tumbled stone. As always, if you don't have a piece of pyrite, center yourself and connect to your inner landscape (February 5) and ask to meet the spirit of pyrite to ask for these blessings.

WHAT TO DO: With your piece of pyrite, center your thoughts and feelings and bring the pyrite into your body's energy field. Write down any thoughts, feelings, or memories. Connect with the energy of the stone and tell it exactly what you hope to get out of this relationship. "I want to be a more confident leader." Share photos of this magical stone and your experience with it—have others had similar experiences?

📷 @ FIREFLY MAGIC

We're a few weeks out from the summer solstice. This means we lose two to three minutes of daylight every day. With the growing darkness comes the twinkle of fireflies looking for friends. Whether you're looking for love, friendship, or companionship, firefly energy can help.

WHAT TO DO: The firefly population has diminished in some areas. You don't have to physically capture them to share their energy.

Wait until it's dark, then go outside with your camera; adjust for the light as needed. To increase your chances of seeing fireflies, go to an area that's wet and green. Fireflies like moisture; if it's a humid night, it's a prime firefly environment; green spaces like tall grasses provide shelter, food, and nursery space for firefly eggs—they're also particularly fond of pine trees. As they start to light up, begin recording. Stop when you have about a minute of footage.

Share the video with some background music or sound (glittering chimes pair nicely with the flickering of the fireflies—plus, they do double duty in banishing negativity), and this spell: *See my signal, / Love, I send. / Let's connect, / Let's be friends!*

@ 🎥 BLACK PEPPER SPELL

Black pepper is the final form of the peppercorn. The physical energy of this herb is unbelievable. It inspires courage and is useful for uncrossing spells. The spicy nature of all peppers makes it a protector of your space, agency, and bodily autonomy. Its banishing magic makes it a popular ingredient in powders and oils used in inspiring a nasty neighbor move, or a nasty coworker getting a different job.

WHAT TO DO: Take a sticky note, and on the *back* of the note (just under the sticky strip) write the situation that requires banishing magic. The Office Gossip set their sights on you? Banish them. Internet trolls making your day hell? Write it down. If you have nothing to banish? Give yourself a hug for your hard work and honor your courage. Take a pinch of black pepper, or a drop of diluted black pepper essential oil, and place it in the center of your banishing target. Fold the bottom up to the bottom of the sticky area, just *barely* touching it. Fold the two sides in, and finally fold the top down to seal your "envelope" of black pepper. Place it in the heel of your dominant foot's shoe. Keep it there until the situation resolves itself or the paper wears a hole in it. Throw the packet away in a public trash can rather than one at home. Share your experience with black pepper on your platform of choice.

🎥 @ A SPELL FOR BREAKUPS

Endings aren't easy, especially when it comes to relationships. The ties that bind can sometimes tangle us in relationships that cease to work. When this happens, it's time to cut cords.

WHAT TO DO: You'll need some blue string; blue is calming, and facilitates clear communication, which will be essential in this work. Set up your camera to record. Take up the cord, run your hands over it, and then:

★ Tie a loose knot, thinking of how and when the relationship started and how it made you feel.

★ Tie a second loose knot, thinking of what went amiss, how you tried to resolve it, and where you stand now.

★ Tie a third loose knot and meditate on why things must change, and the cords must be cut. If you still feel that things must end, proceed to the next step.

Untie your knots, run your hand over the cord again, and say: *Together as we are no longer serves us, / Cut the cords and be free to start anew.*

Post the video with the caption: *Cutting the cords for peace. Cutting the cords for freedom. Cutting the cords to regain my equilibrium. Cutting the cords for me.* Watch how your relationships change. Cord-cutting may also present opportunities for a fresh start.

@ FOMO: OH NO!

Writing things down (repeatedly) makes them real. Making lists of wishes and dreams brings them steps closer to reality and achievement. Take this concept to a new level with this spell. Just be aware of what (or, perhaps how, where, and with whom) you share.

WHAT TO DO: The first part of this work is offline. Ground and center. Boost your focus with ascent that makes you feel happy and relaxed. On a loose piece of paper or in your journal write out all the things you want to do right now: places you want to go, things you want to buy, events you want to attend, people you want to see. Include prices when applicable, especially if you're saving up for something. While it may take time, don't be surprised if the funds materialize in the form of refunds, cancellations, a new gig, a bonus, or a gift. Keep doing this ritual on repeat. Once you feel that your list is somewhat complete, you can move onto the next step.

Post your list on your platform of choice. IF you're comfortable and feel safe sharing your list, do so in straight-up text; you can use an app to make it pretty. You can also share your handwritten pages, blurred so that the text cannot be read (it still counts!). Seal it with the hashtags #mywishlist and #itshallcometopass. You can also add some power emojis (April 29, June 30, November 21) to magnify the spell.

@ 🎥 RANSOM NOTE

Magical spells draw on our senses. Sometimes all of them, sometimes just one. This spell draws on the visual connotations of a ransom note that can conjure up feelings of helplessness, violation of privacy, and anxiety. We often hold ourselves hostage to emotions, feelings, and expectations. Use this spell to help set yourself free.

WHAT TO DO: Record the creation of your note in time-lapse.

Use a piece of sky-blue paper as your base; this color is clear, peaceful, and healing and is a reminder to be gentle with yourself. From newspapers, catalogs, magazines, greeting cards, and other paper matter you don't mind cutting up, gather letters and words to form the spell: *Remember, you are enough.*

You can choose another word if you have a specific situation in mind that is holding you hostage. Share the creation of the note and the final work with the caption: *For all who need to see this, including me.*

07
18

🎥 TIME OF THE SEASON

Stay in tune with the cycle of the seasons by taking some time outside (if safe to do so). It's easy to miss if you don't make time for it. If you'd like to develop a relationship to your local land spirits, bring them offerings such as coffee, foods that would be safe for local wildlife, alcoholic spirits, brightly colored candy not found in nature, and more.

WHAT TO DO: Set up your camera, close your eyes, and connect with the land around you. To your viewers it'll look like you're taking a moment to breathe with the land. Instead, what you're doing is feeling your shielding, or energetic body armor, and increasing its size. You need to make it big enough to encompass the ground underneath you, as well as yourself. Seek to grant the ground underneath you access to your spirit to get to know you as a person. Pour offerings if you choose. Developing a relationship with your local land spirits has a host of benefits such as warning of impending weather and earthquakes, or they can head off home repairs or warn you of big expenditures. Get to know your home spirits.

If you can't venture outside, use a red candle (action) to ease you into a trance-like state by watching the dance created by the flame. Open your heart to the land. Post your video to encourage your viewers to take a moment to breathe, ground, and connect to themselves.

◉ @ 🖼 WAX AND WANE

It's National Moon Day here in the United States, so why not do a moon spell? Full moons are for gratitude and new moons are for intentions, but what about everything that happens in between?

WHAT TO DO: Waxing and waning moons are all about preparation—preparation to manifest, or preparation for new beginnings. Go online to find out what phase the moon is in today (or any day). Snap a screenshot of the phase and share it with the appropriate spell.

★ If the moon is waxing (waxing crescent, one-quarter [half-moon]), or waxing gibbous (three-quarters full), think about what baby steps you need to take to manifest your desire. Layer your screenshot of today's phase with the spell: *One step closer to my goals, step by step fulfill my soul!*

★ If the moon is on the wane (waning gibbous, one-quarter new, three-quarters [half-moon]),or waning crescent, think about what you need to clear away to make room for something new.

Layer your screenshot of today's phase with the spell: *I clean, I cleanse, I clear. / I'm ready to intend at Luna's dark sphere!* Share on your platform of choice as a temporary post (the moon is always changing!).

🖼️ 🎥 @ SQUIRREL POWER!

No matter where you travel, you will probably end up spotting a squirrel. What message is the Universe sending when a squirrel crosses your path?

WHAT TO DO: Be on the lookout for squirrels as you go about your day. If it is safe to do so, snap a photo or short video of them in action. Observe what they are doing at the moment. Squirrels may be telling you that:

★ You need to have more fun in your life (at play—especially with other squirrels).

★ You need to change direction (when the squirrel changes direction).

★ Great abundance is coming your way (if the squirrel is carrying loads of nuts and acorns).

★ You need to be more careful with your resources (if the squirrel is dropping acorns all over the place).

★ Be adaptive (if the squirrel is leaping from branch to branch or skittling across a wire).

★ Keep your eyes open for opportunity (if the squirrel is discovering a nut or acorn).

★ You should consider if you're being fair to others (if the squirrel is stealing from bird feeders).

Share your video or photo with your interpretation. Do friends and followers agree with your interpretation? Squirrel says to be open to all ideas!

LABYRINTHING

Labyrinths (May 27) are symbols of protection, the life path, and ritual roads, and an amazing tool for grounding and meditation.

WHAT TO DO: If there isn't a labyrinth in your neighborhood, you can make one: Go outside. (You'll need a large, accessible area like a playground, basketball court, or parking lot.) Draw a large spiral on the ground with chalk. Start in the center and draw outward, keeping in mind that when you walk inward you want to be walking clockwise to invoke. Take your time and keep the space between the lines as even as possible and about two to three feet wide. Make the spiral as large as your space will accommodate without cutting into the pathways.

When you're ready to step into your labyrinth, start recording a video; show the whole labyrinth first, then start walking so that your viewers walk with you. Show yourself or the path, whatever you're comfortable with. As you walk, chant: *Every step I take brings me closer to my desire.* At the center, take three deep breaths, then turn and walk back out, chanting: *Every step I take removes obstacles in my path.*

This ritual is all-purpose, so you can adapt it to whatever you want to manifest. If you're not mobile, you can draw your spiral labyrinth and use your fingers. Post on your platform of choice until your wish comes to pass.

 PEANUT MAGIC

WARNING: DO NOT TRY THIS SPELL IF YOU HAVE A PEANUT ALLERGY—SOMETIMES JUST TOUCHING OR BEING NEAR PEANUTS IS ENOUGH TO HAVE A REACTION! What magic can you make with peanuts? Lots.

WHAT TO DO: If you are okay with handling or being around peanuts, here are three spells to try to share.

★ Burn peanut shells to regain your equilibrium, especially if you've been shaken up by unexpected challenges! Post images or a video of the fire to amplify, and seal with the hashtags #peanutpower and #peanutsforbalance.

★ Peanut butter on a pinecone rolled in birdseed is a feeder that will attract birds to you. Each carries its own magic: cardinals are messengers who embody the spirit of loved ones who have passed, blue jays bring good luck, robins represent renewal and fresh starts, and swifts encourage multitasking. Post images or videos of birds and animals that visit your feeder with interpretations to amplify and share their messages.

★ Record the making of a millionaire sandwich: Peanut butter brings wealth and orange marmalade adds success. Post your video with the spell: *Humble beginnings yield abundant winnings!* to amplify and share the wealth.

@ 🔊)) CICADA SONG

Cicadas make appearances throughout the world in the late summer. In French lore, the singing cicada was sent to keep people awake and alert during the warm, long summer days. But the music had the opposite effect as it induced restful sleep! We hear cicadas more often than we see them. Capture their sound to cast a spell for a good night's sleep.

WHAT TO DO: Keep your phone handy and be ready to capture the cicadas' song when you hear them singing. Before bedtime, share this sound bite on a plain black background (add sparkling stars if you wish) with the spell: *Summer's lullaby, / Cicada's song, / Sends restful sleep / All night long.*

Likes, views, and comments will help boost the spell for you and for all who engage! BONUS POINTS for boosting the spell for yourself with a spritz of lavender water on your sheets and pillowcases if you are certain that you have no issues or allergies with this plant.

07
24

📹 HARMONY HELPER

Jasmine helps with the gaining of material objects as well as happiness, harmony with the people around you, and sleep. If you're concerned about pernicious spirits, a cup of jasmine green tea will help banish them beyond your responsibility. If you're interested in trying smoke scrying (divination), burning jasmine seeds has been known to help banish negativity, for as divine as the scent is in the flower, burning jasmine leaves and flowers have a certain "eau de cat box."

WHAT TO DO: Set up your phone to record. To increase the harmony in your life, grab a jasmine green tea of your choice. Heat your water in a kettle (microwaving plain water can be dangerously explosive) and over the heating water, say: *Jasmine brew, see me through, banish naysayers from my view.* See the heat generated by the stove as empowering your beverage, turning it from a standard tea into a magical potion. Repeat as you pour the heated water over your tea. Brew according to package directions. Sweeten if desired. Repeat a third time before drinking. As you drink your tea, see the cause of disharmony moving away from you, further and further until they're a speck on the horizon, and then gone. Know that they will disappear from your life, off to live their own life. Post an image of your steaming tea cup to boost this magic.

ANYTHING ALTAR

You can create an altar out of anything—tap into the magic of the moment and whatever you have in your home. Right. Now.

WHAT TO DO: Gather five objects wherever you are (home, work, in the depths of your bag or backpack). Don't overthink it, and work fast with whatever you have on hand. The purpose of this work is to recognize the magical properties of everyday things.

★ Earth is comforting, and can be represented by food of any kind, money, or actual dirt.

★ Air rules the intellect, thoughts, and ideas; it can be represented by books, games, and technology.

★ Fire is creative and can be represented by matches, lighters, "hot" foods, and all warm colors.

★ Water is emotion; any liquid or actual water can represent it, as well as vessels such as cups and bowls, greeting cards, and other sentimental gifts.

★ Spirit is the essence of the Universe. It can be represented by ancestor photos, religious objects, and objects with a history.

Snap a photo of it or record a video of yourself setting each object in its place. Share your post on your platform of choice with the caption: *Earth, Fire, Water, Air, and Spirit, / My wishes, desires, and dreams are in it!*

📹 LEMONADE LIGHTNING

Lemons carry the magic of emotional well-being, friendship, security, fidelity, and healing, while being aligned with the moon and water.

WHAT TO DO: Amplify the powers of any spell by wishing on a lemon peel!

WITCHES' PERFECT LEMONADE

> 1 cup lemon juice (fresh is best; if you need bottled, avoid the ones with lemon essential oil added as it's hard on the body, especially the liver)
>
> 3 cups cold water (divided)
>
> 1 cup sugar

Boil 1 cup of water and add 1 cup of sugar when boiling, then cut the heat. Stir until the syrup turns clear. Allow to cool while you juice your lemons. Add ice to a pitcher and pour the simple syrup over the ice. Add the lemon juice and stir. Add the remaining two cups of cold water. Chill in the refrigerator for two hours. Pour a glass and envision your desire. Ground your energy and bring up energy from the earth and into your hands, sending it into the lemonade you just made. Allow the lemon to increase the power of your spell, amplifying your message to the Universe. Drink and take into yourself all the power you have raised. Post a video talking about the powers of lemon magic, while making lemonade. No one needs to know what your spell was for. ☺

▶ @ HOLD YOUR OWN HAND

None of us are ever alone; there is *always* someone who cares. There will be times when that seems like it's not true. When that happens, believe, and know that you have the strength to get through this finite period. You got this.

WHAT TO DO: Set up your camera so that it records your hands. Ground and center and take a moment to meditate on your situation. Visualize yourself getting through it. As you do so, clasp your hands together. If your mind wanders into negative territory, clasp your hands tighter. Breathe, and say this spell: *I am not alone, but I hold my own hand. / I have the strength to face anything. / I can. / I can. / I can.*

Share your video with the caption: *Strong enough to hold my own hand when I need it.* Views (which you may not see), likes, and comments amplify your strength.

NEMESIS FOR JUSTICE

The Greek goddess Nemesis hands out just punishments. You may never get to witness justice being done, but invoking Nemesis may ease the process if you've been wronged.

WHAT TO DO: If you're a victim of injustice, ask Nemesis to assist you. Get a narcissus (or an image of one), a flower that is heavily associated with Nemesis. If you can't find a narcissus, a daffodil will do as well; they're in the same family.

Ground and center and think of how you were wronged. Then, the hard part: separate your feelings from what happened. This is what Nemesis calls us to do—go strictly by the facts. Set the flowers in your sacred space, then state the facts about what occurred, aloud. Do not include how it made you feel, just stick with a timeline of events. Only say those things that you absolutely know are true and are not hearsay, gossip, or opinion. This is not to doubt yourself or how it made you feel—those things are also completely valid but separate from this work. Once you have stated all the facts, say: *Lady Justice, avenge all wrongs!*

Snap a photo of the mini altar that you've made and share it on your platform of choice with the hashtags #fornemesis and #forjustice to seal the spell.

🖼️ 👁️ MONOGRAM MAGIC

When you add your name or initials to anything, you claim it as yours. Use your initials to get your own back—and serve yourself some justice.

WHAT TO DO: It's yours, right? Maybe you're in a disagreement with a friend or engaged in litigation. Whatever your dispute, find a symbol or image of what is in question. Cover the image entirely with your initials in gold text (success) with a black outline (protection). When you share this image, do so with the intention: *Justice is mine!* If you are able and are comfortable, post this image captioned with your situation. (Note that some cases require silence—by court order or common sense.) Leave the post up until your issue is resolved.

🖼 @ DIVINATION WITH RUNES

If you think runes look like cryptic writing out of *The Lord of the Rings*, you'd be right! J.R.R. Tolkien based all the runes he created for Middle Earth on real runes, writing systems that were used thousands of years ago. There are Anglo-Saxon runes, and Celtic ogham runes, futhark runes (Elder and Younger from different periods), and medieval runes. These figures were used for writing, but we can also use them for divination. Work with runes just like you'd work with tarot cards (although runes are usually carved on wood, tile, or stone): mix them up and randomly select pieces for interpretation. Each rune has a meaning associated with it. Let's give it a try!

WHAT TO DO: If you don't have a set of runes, make your own by looking up the symbols and drawing them on separate pieces of paper. Or, if you want to get fancy, try painting them on buttons (buttons make awesome runes!). You'll notice that many runes symbolize everyday things such as animals and plants. Magic has always existed in our workaday life; you just have to be open to it. Keep in mind that the meanings you'll find are super simple and just a beginning. They may also vary slightly from resource to resource. Share a general one-rune reading on your platform of choice and see if friends and followers have any synchronicities.

@ LAVENDER DOES NOT LIE

Lavender is a messenger of Mercury, god of communication, messages, and knowledge. Because of these associations, lavender is aligned with the element of air. It lends its magic to balance and harmony; protection through knowledge (after all, "forewarned is forearmed"); and divination, including clairaudience (sound waves travel through the air).

One of the most intriguing magical benefits of lavender is the magic of secrets, both the retention of and the discovery of them. There are several ways to uncover secrets hidden in our lives—just check in with yourself that you can live with what you find.

WHAT TO DO: To work with lavender, for any magic, you can turn any sweet recipe into a lavender recipe by adding 1 tsp of dried lavender buds per cup of sugar in the recipe. So, sugar cookies become lavender sugar cookies. Lemonade becomes lavender lemonade. Vanilla scones become lavender vanilla scones. You can add the lavender directly to the sugar for a pretty floral decoration, or you can grind the lavender into the sugar for a uniform texture. As you grind the lavender, tell it what you're looking for. Once you consume it, it can get to work. Share your lavender recipes and your experience with this magical herb.

BURNING MAN

It's August—which means it's time for Burning Man—not the party in Black Rock, Colorado, but a *real* (okay, *almost!*) burning man. This spell is all about creativity, inspiration, and passion. If your project is stuck, Burning Man can help!

WHAT TO DO: Get a piece of recycled cardboard and cut it out in the shape of a human figure. Ground and center, then think: for what do you need inspo? Write all your thoughts down on the front and back of the figure with a red Sharpie (for passion!). Outline the figure with cinnamon oil (revitalization and change), then glue on some chili flakes (to light a fire under your project!). Clear and dedicate your space and set up your Burning Man so that he's standing up (a couple of bricks or stones will help). Set up your camera so that it's focused on him and start recording. Light him up in a safe place (outdoors in a firepit or bowl) and keep a fire extinguisher close by in case it's needed. Say: *Light a fire in my heart, fire inspire and passion impart!*

Burn until only ashes are left. Make it a group ritual! Film the creation of your Burning Man to be inspo for others. Set a future date and time for burning. Have everyone participating tag you (and us) and add the hashtags #almostburningman and #socialmediaspellbook.

▶️ ORANGe OVATION

Citruses comes from the rue family, so protection magic is a given. Rue was planted to ring the temples of Hestia and Vesta in ancient Greece and Italy, respectively, to protect the virgin priestesses inside the temples. ("Virgin" meant a woman who was responsible for herself; no man had rulership over her.) The sun and fire associations are a common theme among the rue family; as rue protected the priestesses with the power of the sun, its citrus descendants can do the same. Oranges are one of the most popular citruses because they're inexpensive and their essential oil is not photo-toxic, whether it is expressed from the peel or distilled from it. We'll be using orange oil for today's spell.

WHAT TO DO: To align yourself with the protection of the sun, take a 1 oz. dropper bottle, and add 3 drops of orange essential oil, filling it the rest of the way with the carrier oil of your choice. (That's a 2 percent dilution rate, so it's very gentle.) Roll between your hands to gently mix the oils. Place 3 drops on the tips of your fingers, anoint your chest or diaphragm with the oil, and say: *Protection born from the orange fruit, watch over me during my pursuit.* Post a video of yourself making the oil or about your experiences using it.

@ QUEEN OF EVERYTHING!

You ARE a queen: strong, nurturing, powerful, and wise. Create a magical flower crown for everyone to see and use.

WHAT TO DO: This crown is crafted from live herbs and flowers with magical value. Use plants that have queenly qualities. Here are some suggestions:

- ★ Marigold: justice
- ★ Basil: royalty
- ★ Fennel: courage
- ★ Chamomile: strength
- ★ Elderflower: leadership
- ★ Rosemary: fidelity and love
- ★ Mugwort: protection

Find an image of yourself. Color the background gold, and fill in your face, hair, neck, and shoulders in black—this is protective; you are in shadow so that you can share this crown. Place your shadow portrait on a flat surface and place the flowers à la Frida Kahlo around your head. While you work, say the spell: *I wear the crown, I share the crown. / Queens, we got this!*

When the crown is complete, snap a picture of it and share the image on your platform of choice with the spell as the caption, inviting others to crown themselves.

📹 TIGER'S-eye INDePeNDeNCe

Tiger's-eye crystal comes in red, brown, green, blue, gold, and cream. It is especially attuned to leadership qualities as it releases fears and encourages stability. The practicality of tiger's-eye is especially important if your independence drives you to leadership positions within a large corporation, as it pairs well with the grounded reality that helps you see the whole picture, including finances. Don't look to this structured stone for a quick fix for the cash-strapped. It's going to amplify the energy you bring to the table, so if you're having a hard time summoning the energy, or the executive function to make change happen, pair it with clear quartz.

WHAT TO DO: Connect with the stone by holding the tiger's-eye in your nondominant hand; they're better for receiving energy from outside sources. Open your heart's protective barriers to allow the crystal's energy to contact yours. Record any thoughts, feelings, or memories that may come up. In connecting with the spirit of the tiger's-eye, tell the stone how the independence granted by the stone could make your life better. Ask it to help keep your goals in mind for the future. Post video recordings discussing the properties of tiger's-eye and its associated magic.

📹 @ 🔊 MANE MAGIC

We're well into Leo season, and Leos love their manes! So much is wrapped up in the strands of our hair. It's part of our identity; it carries our DNA; it is an extension of ourselves. And while it can sprout anywhere on or in the body, that in which we revel most comes from the crown. If your crown is bare, then that chakra shines brightly and unveiled.

WHAT TO DO: When you brush your hair or scalp, you stimulate your crown chakra. Short or long, sparse or silver, or any color of the rainbow, tap into hair magic with this spell: Set up your camera to record yourself brushing your hair or scalp in whatever manner you feel comfortable sharing. As you brush, visualize your crown chakra glowing bright violet with every stroke. Feel the Universe flow through you from the top down. Picture that energy extending beyond your body, reaching out and touching others. When you feel the process is complete, stop recording.

Layer the video with a purple filter or purple glow around your head to emphasize the crown chakra. Share on your platforms of choice with appropriate sounds or music (try the sound of a gong, which has been said to sound like recordings of outer space!) and this caption: *I feel the strength of the Universe within, / I am the Universe, its strength is mine.*

 @ COUNT ON PEARLS

It starts with a grain of sand that gets inside a living oyster. This causes irritation and the oyster coats the grain with a substance called nacre; coat after coat, the pearl is formed. Through experience—sometimes painful—something beautiful is created. Think of trials in your life as that grain of sand and use some pearl magic to help you through challenging times.

WHAT TO DO: If you have a strand of pearls, awesome! If not, you can use pearl buttons for this spell—you'll just need some thread to string them on. Before you begin, meditate on the challenges that you're facing. See them as grains of sand; they may be uncomfortable, but not insurmountable.

Ground and center, and set up your camera to record. Take the string of pearls in your hand and one at a time, touch each pearl and think of your challenge. Say the spell: *Grain of sand, become the pearl. / Your inner wisdom will unfurl.*

See yourself overcoming each hurdle and glowing with bright radiance. See each trial lose its edges and soften; it no longer troubles you. Repeat until you reach the end of the strand. If you are using buttons, touch each button and say the spell until you have strung all the buttons you have. Repost or repeat this meditation whenever you're facing a challenge.

@ 😊 FeRAL CAT PROTeCTION

Giving back is part of magical work. Feral cats roam our neighborhoods, quietly keeping vermin at bay and dodging cars, local wildlife, and the weather. Provide practical aid such as providing food or a sheltered area to sleep or hide when you can, but you can also weave a spell of protection. Note: animal control may provide services to spay/neuter and release.

WHAT TO DO: When you encounter a feral feline, snap a photo if it's safe to do so. Share the image with the words: *Feral friends, find safety, food, water, and shelter. I thank you for your presence.*

Seal the spell with a cat emoji, remembering that these text-drawings are magical sigils:

>^..^<

★ Greater than (>) expresses a greater purpose.

★ A period (.) indicates a stop (stopping the presence of vermin in your area).

★ The carat (^) means "to the power of" in algebra. This symbol denotes quick, exponential growth; feral kitties are quick because they have to be, and, without human intervention, they increase infinitely and exponentially.

★ Less than (>) expresses how these creatures are often perceived.

📹 MONEY MAVEN OIL

Benzoin is an airy resin that is responsible for uplifting prayers to the gods, the Universe, spirits, ancestors, and those helping spirits that guide us. The energy of Venus that rules benzoin makes sure that when we have the extra to spend on luxury items, it's still going to a good cause: those we love. It improves concentration for days that you're up late strategizing the best way to bring your ideas to bear. It's determination in a bottle. Let's create a soothing prosperity oil that reminds us of what we are working toward, especially in the realm of emotional comfort.

WHAT TO DO: Take a 10 mL roller bottle and add 1 drop of fir essential oil and 2 drops of benzoin essential oil. Fill the rest of the way with a carrier oil of your choice; jojoba and fractionated coconut oil are best for shelf life versus cost of materials. If you have meadow foam oil, it has three times the shelf life, but it's harder to find, and will cost a little more—but it is worth it in the long run for a prosperity oil. Place the roller ball and cap. Roll the bottle between your palms to mix. Apply to petitions, candles for prosperity spells, and long-term bills such as credit card debt or medical bills. Post a video making the prosperity oil or talking about the herbs used in it.

@ 📠 LOOK AT ME!

Using magic to boost business, career, and cash flow is a concept that is as old as time—BUT REMEMBER, magic is not an answer, but an *aid*. Magic teaches us to be thoughtful and deliberate about our actions. It also teaches us that, while it is good to be transparent, we also don't always have to show our whole hand. You can make magical business posts—with you being the only one who knows the magic behind them. Try the following method the next time you make a post about anything that must be seen (taking for granted that we'd like every post to get some attention).

WHAT TO DO: When you need an extra boost, utilize some word and color magic and a bit of visualization to help you get some attention. Post the word *"LOOK!"* before you copy and paste your link, image, etc. Use shouty all caps.

"Look" is a call to action. If you have the apps to do it, post it as white text on a red background like a stop sign. Red draws attention. It is also a confidence color, the shade of the root chakra, in fact, which rules our foundations. While you are making your post, visualize people scrolling through their feeds—people you know and don't know. Picture them stopping, looking, reading, and sharing.

📹 BANANAS FOR LUCK!

Bananas carry the magic of Venus, as they're quite phallically shaped. That Venus energy shines through in their ability to inspire resilience during times of great change. When the world is shaking under your feet, hold onto your hats and reach for a banana. The prosperity magic of bananas is quite evident if you've ever seen a bunch of bananas on the stalk. The yellow flesh of the banana tells us that it's great for magic in lifting the symptoms of depression and that it is tops when it comes to magic for inspiring good luck!

WHAT TO DO: Slice three ripe bananas into 1-inch chunks. Place a piece of wax paper on a plate or cookie tray and lay out each slice on the tray before moving the tray to the freezer. Freeze about two hours to make sure they have some structural integrity for the next step. Take 1 cup semisweet chocolate baking chips (chocolate is an herb! It carries the magic of prosperity, fertility, love, and hex-breaking.) and a teaspoon of coconut oil into a bowl. Microwave on medium in fifteen-second intervals, stirring in between. Dip the banana slices in chocolate with a fork and place them back on the paper to freeze again. Share them with friends and dream of all the things that your newfound prosperity will help you find. Post a video time-lapse of making this luck-bringing dessert!

@ WORDS TO LIVE BY

Who doesn't love an inspirational quote? Give yourself a boost and inspire others with this magical trick.

WHAT TO DO: Add a motto or phrase to your email signature or description to emphasize your overall message of the moment. Ground and center before starting your search. Take your time to find just the right words. They can be from anyone or anything that inspires you—just remember to give credit and post with intention. As you add your quote to your signature or profile, think or say: *These words are guiding my path; / I am finding and achieving what I seek.* Change as needed or when inspired!

🎥 @ BLESSED NEMORALIA!

It's the Feast of Diana, goddess of the Moon. Celebrated in Nemi, Italy, since around 6 BCE, this feast was originally held during the full moon in August rather than on this fixed date. Traditionally, the head of the family would cut fatwood from apple trees and craft a torch out of it to ward and protect the home. If the family made it around the house without having to stop to relight the torch, Diana would ward and protect the home and all who dwelled in it, as well as the land itself from thieves, curses, and hexes. Diana and Hekate (August 15) have been linked together during this festival for over two thousand years.

WHAT TO DO: To celebrate these goddesses, you can bake treats for them. To petition for the safety of your home and family, light a citronella torch or candle and carry it clockwise around the outside of your home, or carry a candle around the inside with the lights low. Post a video of burning candles or a retelling of the history of Diana. Telling the deity's story shines her light on all who hear it.

🖼 RECLAIM POWER WITH FIGA

The *mano figa*—a hand gesture where you form a fist by tucking your thumb between your middle ring fingers—is an ancient symbol with many meanings. The one we're most fond of is its association with the Divine Feminine and the reclaiming of that power: let's take it back, Queens!

WHAT TO DO: Like the extended middle finger represents the male essence (and other things), the figa represents the feminine (and all that goes with it!). The gesture is equally powerful, though more subtle. It wards off evil and brings the bearer luck.

Post an image of a figa on your platform of choice to banish negativity and shower luck and abundance on all who view, like, comment, and share. Post with the intention, and luck and protection will also bounce back to you! And haters, they get what they deserve.

🖼️ 🎥 HEKATE'S HARVEST

Hekate's bread is an offering to Hekate on her deipnon—a religious or devotional food offered on her feast day, the new moon. However, she is also celebrated with a bread offering to her today. People would petition Hekate to heal injured body parts by offering her loaves of bread shaped like the injured part. So, if you broke your arm, you'd bake Hekate an arm-shaped loaf of bread.

WHAT TO DO: To take part in this celebration, here's a quick sourdough-flavored flatbread.

TWO-INGREDIENT SAVORY BREAD

  1 cup self-rising flour

  1 cup Greek yogurt (You can substitute vegan Greek yogurt or vegan sour cream.)

Preheat the oven to 350° Fahrenheit. Into a mixing bowl add one cup Greek yogurt. Next, start adding the self-rising flour into the Greek yogurt a bit at a time. When you have a cohesive ball of dough, spray a cookie sheet with cooking spray and roll the dough to the desired thickness. (It will rise a bit when baked, so expect it to almost double in thickness.) Bake twenty minutes until golden brown. (For pizza, add tomato sauce, spices, and favorite toppings before baking.) Don't forget to share a portion with Hekate! Post a video of you making the bread, or photos of offerings after sundown.

 # HEALING ONIONS

For this spell, you'll need your camera, an onion, and a box of tissues (optional).

WHAT TO DO: Set up your camera to capture your hands. Hold the onion and start recording. What kind of healing do you need? Do you have a broken heart? A broken spirit? Are you recovering from or dealing with an illness? Visualize whatever it is you are going through and see it embedded in the layers of the onion.

When you're ready, peel away the first layer. As you do so, say: *I feel my pain, I peel it away.*

Smell the onion, and tears may come; saltwater purifies. Peel away the second layer, continuing the visualization. Again, say: *I feel my pain, I peel it away.*

Continue, shifting your focus from any pain you are feeling to how you want to feel. As you peel each layer away, the burdens should start to feel lighter. If nothing else, you are putting them out there, facing them, and dealing with them. With each layer, continue the incantation: *I feel my pain, I peel it away.*

Keep working until you get down to the core of the onion, then stop recording. Share your video overlaid with the incantation and appropriate music. If you're comfortable with sharing personal information, caption your video with your situation.

📹 FIERCE FIERY FUMES

Cedar's prosperity-specific properties are geared toward the gain of material objects, success, and wealth. It carries the magic of fire and Jupiter—that means *protected growth* for your ambition. We'll use the smoke of burning cedar, which is great for magic for strength and endurance. You deserve all the support you can get!

WHAT TO DO: Gather your incense supplies, incense charcoal tablets, tongs, a lighter, and a fireproof dish; additionally grab the cedar. Hold the charcoal with the tongs as the saltpeter that lights the tablet moves quickly (and safety first!). Once the charcoal is burning hotly, ground and center yourself. Connect yourself to the energy of the cedar, the warm, red, hot smell of the volatile oils in the wood, and the sprays of the needles. You can see where the association with fire comes from! Explain the need you have to remove any blockages to your prosperity from your home, that you need wealth and success to attain your dreams. Talk about what your dreams are; the spirit of the wood can help you in ways you hadn't foreseen. Lay some of the cedar on the charcoal and allow it to start smoking and enveloping you in a fog of the sacred. Post videos of incense smoke pushing out all blocks to your success.

🖼 @ 🎥 URANUS FOR CHANGE

The planet Uranus is the seventh planet from the sun. It takes about eighty-four years for Uranus to make a complete orbit around our star, and when he shows up, it's usually with startling change, which for us can be very uncomfortable. When change turns your world upside down, ask Uranus for help.

WHAT TO DO: Ground and center, then set up your camera to record the creation of this spell (or you can just repost the finished piece). Grab some blue and green watercolors and paint a picture of Uranus (go for progress, not perfection!). When it's dry, write this spell in protective black ink inside the planet: *I've been shaken, / I've awakened! / It's time to move, / Restore my groove!* Post and repost whenever you experience a surprising shift.

📹 FAMILY LOVE SPELL

There are many types of love, not just the romantic love between sexual partners. Today we'll focus on familial love for parents and among siblings—the kind of love that can be expressed by spending time around the table for game night, but also inspires siblings to ask for or offer help to each other.

WHAT TO DO: Apple is the perfect fruit for familial love because not only is apple a Venus fruit (just look at the pentacle hidden inside the apple), but it is also fed by the watery energy of emotion. Apples are great for blessing your garden and asserting yourself and your boundaries. Apples attract contentment. While it might be a bit early for apple cider, if you're somewhere that gets chilly in the evenings, feel free to warm up apple cider with some cinnamon sticks in it for protection of those you love, and clove to bring luck into the home. If it's too hot for mulled cider in your part of the world, cut a ripe red apple in half crossways to show the pentacle inside it. Sprinkle with ground cinnamon and cloves and leave near where the family spends the most time to remind them to love each other all year long. Post videos talking about the love of family and how that contributes to your magical practice.

@ SALT CIRCLES

Sometimes the movies don't lie—salt circles help create sacred space and keep negative energies at bay. In magical circles, salt often represents the earth element, so it's good for grounding, too. Use this spell to cast a veil of protection over something or someone dear to you.

WHAT TO DO: Do this spell on a cleared tabletop. You'll need a good amount of salt—it doesn't need to be expensive pink salt; plain table salt will do. Slowly and carefully form a circle with the salt. While you're pouring the salt, say: *All is safe within the circle.*

When the circle is complete, place objects, photos, or symbols of that which you would protect inside. Say the spell again: *All is safe within the circle.*

Now, take out your camera and snap a photo of the full circle and its contents. Share with the spell for a third and final time: *By the power of three times three, all are safe within the circle. So mote it be!*

Keep the post up for as long as the protection is needed.

◄ PEACE BE WITH YOU

Petitgrain essential oil is created from the leaves and small twigs of the bitter orange tree. The magic of this tree includes joy, the banishment of anxiety, and an increased awareness of the emotional welfare of those around you. It's a confidence booster, too. Petitgrain essential oil also carries the magic of transformation, purification of the self, and an increase of physical energy, so it's a great ally for days when you feel like you're carrying yourself around in a wheelbarrow just to get going in the morning.

WHAT TO DO: The oil of petitgrain is going to allow us to work some magic for the peace in our lives and get our emotions in order, so that we can process them, instead of relegating them to a shoebox under the bed. Add 2 drops of petitgrain essential oil to a 10 mL roller bottle and fill it the rest of the way with carrier oil. Roll between the palms to mix the oils. When you feel stressed, frantic, anxious, or low vibration, roll this oil onto your pulse points to bring that right up. Post videos of making this magical perfume oil.

🖼 @ TAKE CONTROL

Success is achieved through many steps and actions, including how you deal with challenges and failures. This tarot meditation can help you stop, assess, and revamp so that you can move on and achieve your dreams.

WHAT TO DO: From your tarot deck, pull the 6 of Swords, the 8 of Cups, and the four Aces, Cups, Wands, Swords, and Pentacles. Ground and center, then snap a photo of the 6 of Swords. This card represents you being challenged. Post the card with the incantation: *I survived.*

Next, snap a photo of the 8 of Cups. This card represents you moving on from your challenges (which may have been emotionally draining—Cups!). Post the card with the incantation: *I move forward.*

Lastly, lay out the four aces—Wands, Cups, Swords, and Pentacles—in a cross formation. These cards represent the potential of all the fulfillment that lies ahead of you: creative, emotional, intellectual, and earthly. Post this image with the incantation: *Next, success!*

Recreate this post (don't simply repost) each time you encounter a challenge or failure and need help bouncing back.

@ CRYSTAL BOUNDARIES

Having good boundaries is especially important online, as many people feel that they can behave in ways they never would in person. Here are some stones to help you stay true to your own personal boundaries.

WHAT TO DO: Before you run to the crystal shop or dig through your collection, try to make a list of at least one boundary per type so that you know how to recognize a potential problem before it arises.

★ Black kyanite: "Return to sender" stone. This is going to watch your back for you, and it will keep any nasty spells directed your way back where they came from.

★ Black tourmaline (included in quartz): Banishes negativity and grounds ill intent. Black tourmaline comes in columns with very clear cleavage or layers. It also "invades" or is included in quartz so it can act as an energetic net. Think of it as a rete, or net, used by ancient Greek gladiators.

★ Lapis lazuli: Sets clear expectations and reinforces your own established boundaries.

★ Obsidian: Absorbs negative intentions and burns them away before they can harm you.

Post video or photos of the crystals you used and how, or if, they helped.

THE FEMININE FIRE

Fire is inspiration and creativity, the essence of the Goddess in whatever form she takes: maiden, mother, or crone. Record their crafting as well as their burning to give them more potency.

WHAT TO DO: Set up your camera to record your crafting. Bundle and bind your herbs with a straw or twig base. Each bundle is dedicated to a different face of the Goddess. Incant as indicated:

★ MAIDEN: Bind lavender and lemon balm with lavender thread and the incantation: *Childlike empress, fresh and new, show me your unblemished view.*

★ MOTHER: Bind rosemary and roses with red thread and the incantation: *Oh, queen of caring and gentle face, swathe me in your protective embrace.*

★ CRONE: Bind cinnamon with black and amber threads and the incantation: *Keeper of wisdom that comes with time, your presence is a gift divine.*

Share the videos overlaid with the incantations as text or a voice-over. Make it a group ritual: Post your crafting video to inspire others to tap into this energy and set a future date to burn bundles as a group. Light up the bundles in honor of feminine energy or women you admire or wish to honor, or when you need to draw on these qualities.

BLACKBERRY SPELL

Blackberries are the bomb—of flavor, utility, and magic. They're a wonderful ingredient for abundance and success spells. They're also protective (wild blackberries have wicked thorns) and promote good health. Spread some blackberry magic with this spell.

WHAT TO DO: Blackberry juice can be used as an ink. Set up your camera to record. Place a handful of blackberries in a bowl and gently crush them with a spoon. As you work the fruit, say the incantation: *Blackberry ink to write success / Bring my needs and desires, more, not less.*

You can add a bit of water to the fruit if it's too chunky to write with. On a clean sheet of white paper, write or draw your desires. Fill the paper. Flip it over if you need to. You may not be able to read or make out everything you've written, but that does not matter; your thoughts and intentions have soaked in. Allow the paper to dry completely. Roll it up, then place it on a fireproof dish and burn it, saying the spell once more.

Share the video of your spell's creation and burning, or still pictures of the whole process or any part of it. Post with the incantation as a caption and sealed with the hashtag #blackberrymagic.

@ REGARDING REPLY

"Re" carries many connotations. "Re" relates to or regards, and it also means "reply." Purposefully placing "Re" in the subject of an email is part outright intention and part glamour. Use sparingly when you need a response!

WHAT TO DO: Use this spell when you absolutely *need* (not just *want*) a response. Enter "Re:" before the subject of your email in the subject line. Compose your message, and before you hit send, speak this intention aloud (or mouth the words if you live in cubicle land): *An answer to this I must receive, / Please respond; my need relieved.*

The glamour aspect? Glamour magic takes many forms, one of which is the blurring or softening of reality. Placing "Re" as the start of a subject line refers, but it also directly addresses the person from whom you want a response; it asks for a response—a bit blurry, but that's what glamour is. Use sparingly!

# @ CRYSTAL SHAPES

Every crystal has its own unique power—but their shapes add to the potency of their energy. Decisions, decisions . . .

WHAT TO DO: Some guidance on crystal shapes: CRYSTAL CLUSTERS have many points and so scatter energy in many directions. If you're looking to saturate an area with that stone's energy, a cluster is for you! DOUBLE-TERMINATED CRYSTALS are energy conduits, and great for centering. EGG-SHAPED STONES symbolize newness and beginnings, so if you want to start something, an appropriate egg-shaped crystal can help. OBELISKS (also known as "generators") are wands that can direct energy. Where will you point yours? What do you want to focus on? The PYRAMID CRYSTAL's broad flat base tapers to a point that directs energy upward. Because of this, they're awesome magical partners for stability spells. CRYSTAL SPHERES are complete and encapsulate the energy they carry. Crystal spheres or balls are amazing meditation and scrying tools. And of course, crystals are available as intricately carved statuettes of animals, deities, plants, and more. Keep in mind that the stone also carries the energy of its shape! Create spell images of your crystals and seal them with hashtags that share your intention and the stone's powers.

🖼 CATS FOR COURAGE!

The ancient Egyptians loved their cats. They believed these familiars (February 20) protected their homes, had magical powers (truth), and brought luck. On a practical level, cats took care of vermin and, like now, made a house a home. All this cat magic is wrapped up in the sleek and fabulous feline goddess Bastet, who was invoked for good health and protection. Bastet sees everything. Tap into her energy when you need a little courage.

WHAT TO DO: For this spell we'll create a Bastet talisman with a chrysoberyl, or cat's-eye, which embodies practically all of Bastet's qualities including confidence, a positive outlook, and protection. Clean and change your cat's-eye with salted water, then carefully pass it over a candle flame and through incense smoke. Myrrh is a great choice for this work. It rhymes with "purr" and is protective, too! BONUS POINTS: if you have a special cat in your life, gently pass the cat's-eye through their fur to add their energy to the talisman. Now, hold the stone in your hand and invoke Bastet: *Bastet, see all, / Send courage, protect / And hear my call!*

Share an image of your cat's-eye on your platform of choice to expand Bastet's gaze on all who seek and find you.

📹 PUMPKIN SPICE BANISHING

At this time of year, everyone's a little fall-hungry. Every ingredient in pumpkin pie spice is a magical powerhouse.

WHAT TO DO: Recipes like this usually start with equal parts of the mix until you establish your own tastes and change as needed. Blend with your nose. Start with a small measurement like ¼ tsp. Then mix and see what you need more of. You have to like it, or you won't reach for the magic of this blend:

Allspice carries the magic of sex, lust, physical attraction, courage, and good fortune.

Cinnamon protects, promotes creativity and love, and boosts other magic.

Cloves dispel negativity, break hexes, protect, and purify.

Ginger is energizing, increases strength, and improves luck.

Nutmeg is calming, encourages fidelity, and is strongly aligned with justice magic.

Black Pepper is great for uncrossing, justice magic, and increasing mental alertness.

You can use this blend and add it to ice cream, coffee, steamed milk, or anything your heart desires; you don't need to wait for a special occasion. Post a video of the mixing experience to boost the magic.

🎥 @ ALTAR IN A BOTTLE

Altars can take all forms. Bring all the elements together with this spell; you'll create an altar as well as a magical tool to turn just about anything—including yourself—into sacred space.

WHAT TO DO: Set up your phone to record the creation of your altar. Fill a clean spray bottle with water (water element). Add three pinches of salt (earth element) that has been mixed with three drops of frankincense oil (spirit element). Add a small crystal, like fluorite, that embodies the element of air. Add a crystal that carries the element of fire, like garnet; again, use what will fit in your bottle. If you wish, add a quartz crystal to your altar as it will magnify the qualities of all the other elements you've brought together. Swirl the bottle in a clockwise direction to invoke the elements. Share the video on your platform of choice with the caption: *Altar in a bottle, wherever I go / Is sacred space. Now you know.*

You can turn an entire room into an altar by spritzing each corner and all the windows. Turn yourself into a living, breathing, walking altar by spraying yourself. You can also change up the formula depending on the season. Just be sure that if you're using essential oils and spraying yourself, or anyone else, you have no allergies or sensitivities.

🖼 @ WATER MEDITATION

Try this ritual spell to strengthen your water connection. (People with water sun and ascendant signs—Pisces, Cancer, and Scorpio—may find this comforting.)

WHAT TO DO: If you are able, visit a body of water. Have a bottle of water and a flower offering handy. You won't be going in, you will just be near the water's edge—but be sure that you are in a safe spot! If there is no body of water near you, you can do this meditation with a bowl of water. Ground and center, then safely stand at the water's edge and focus on the surface. Do the same if you are working with a bowl of water. When you feel comfortable, chant aloud or to yourself: *Under the surface, under my skin, / Is water, my kin.*

If you are working with a bowl of water, place the flower in the bowl. If you are near a body of water and it is safe to do so, dip your hands in the water and sprinkle it over your head three times, then toss your flower in as an offering. If you cannot safely touch the water, use your water bottle. If you performed the meditation with a bowl of water, dip your hands in the water and sprinkle it over your head three times, then place your flower in the bowl as an offering. Snap a photo of the body of water you visited or your bowl of water with your flower offering with the meditation as a caption.

@ ACACIA IN THE KITCHEN

Acacia trees have symbolized immortality for thousands of years. They're hearty and evergreen, and their wood is incredibly durable, which makes it a great material for magical tools used for stability spells like this one!

WHAT TO DO: Considering that the kitchen is one of the most magical places in the home, it's an ideal place to cook up some stability. Acquire an acacia wood spoon and clean it lightly with salted water. Bless it with olive oil which will infuse it with luck and health energy. In the bowl of the spoon, trace a circle for stability: circles represent the never-ending cycles of the year, the certainty of change, and the turning of the world. You can also use a symbol that says "stability" for you. If you're handy with wood-burning tools, you can score the symbol on the spoon so that you will see it every time you use it. When you're ready to prepare food, use your spoon to imbibe every bite with the energy of your home's firm foundation. If you're preparing something you can actually stir, do so clockwise to invoke stability. Say the spell: *In the hearth of the home, our foundations are firm. / By wood, oil, and circles, this I confirm.* Snap a photo of your new magical tool and share it on your platform of choice with the spell as a caption to draw communal energy into it.

📹 @ 🔊 FERTILITY CRAYONS

Carrots are remarkable vegetables. In many cultures, they're symbols of luck, abundance, and, because of their shape, virility. All these qualities—not to mention their bright orange color—make them great for fertility spells like this one! And a little statistical magic: nine out of the ten most popular birth dates worldwide are in September. This month has its own special fertility magic—use it!

WHAT TO DO: Work on the sidewalk or stoop in front of the door you use to go in and out. Ground and center, then set up your camera. Record yourself using your carrot like a crayon. Draw a heart on the ground. Then from the heart, draw a spiral. Work clockwise to invoke. While you're working, chant: *Draw a spiral on the ground, / Abundance in the womb abound! / By hand, by root, by all who see, / Such is my will, so mote it be!*

09
02

If you have any carrots left, leave them outside as a gift to the Universe. Bunnies, spirit animals of fertility magic, love carrots! Post your video with the sound of your voice chanting or overlay it with the spell in text and music.

HONEY LOVE SPELL

If you're ready to make a commitment, try this spell to sweeten the moment (and make sure that all parties involved are aware of this magic!). PS—this spell also works for family love, so just adjust your intention!

WHAT TO DO: Have a lovely meal together—you make dessert. Ground and center and set up your camera to record. You can share the creation of the spell or a photo of the finished working. Whatever sweets you're serving, add a bit of honey! Start with a blank dish; then, in honey, draw:

★ A heart in the center to symbolize love.

★ A circle around the heart to symbolize commitment.

★ Bees (one for each person in the relationship) to represent the honey, but also the work that goes into making relationships successful.

When you've finished creating your sigil—because that is exactly what this is—say the spell: *Our love is strong, our love endures. / Our love is sweet, our love is pure.*

Place or arrange your dessert over or around the sigil and serve—make sure everyone gets a bite! Share the creation of the spell or just an image of the finished working with the spell as a caption. Seal the spell with the hashtags #honeylove, #honeyforever, and #myhoney or #myhoneys.

🖼 @ A LITTLE BIBLIOMANCY

Try this spell to see what guidance any book can offer you.

WHAT TO DO: A good part of the magic of this spell (and many spells) is the randomness and unpredictability that exists in the Universe. Go to a bookstore, library, or any place where you can handle a physical book. Take a moment to ground and center, and then wander.

★ What are you drawn to? Enter the stacks, and snap a picture of the section you're in.

★ Let your mind wander as you peruse the shelves—when you're drawn to one, snap a picture.

★ When you find a book that you're drawn to (again, let your mind wander—don't "look" for anything specific!), pull it out and take a picture of the cover.

★ Hold the book, turn it over in your hand. Flip through the pages and feel the paper. When it feels right, open to any page—snap a picture.

★ Now, read. What paragraphs, sentences, groups of words, or even a single word stand out? Snap a photo.

Share your series of photos as a single post, captioning it with: *In this image is your message for the day—what do you see?* Comments, views, likes, and shares grow the magic and expand the divination.

🎥 @ RAYS FOR DAYS

Every sunflower has the potential to produce two thousand seeds, which makes them wonderful partners in fertility and abundance spells (like this one!).

WHAT TO DO: Get a half dozen sunflowers; if you can pick your own, even better. Six is the number of renewal, and, while this is a spell for abundance, renewal is a part of the process—you renew your faith and your trust that all will be well. You'll also need a green vase, for growth, healing, and love.

Set your camera to record. Record the entire process: unwrapping your flowers, trimming the stems and leaves. With every step of preparation for putting the flowers into the vase, visualize where you need abundance. Then, one by one, place each flower carefully into the vase. Think about its position, its unique stature. Take this into consideration as you create your arrangement. Say the spell as you work: *Abundant health, abundant wealth. / Creative power in every flower, / From stem to seed, fulfill my need!*

Share the video (or a photo of your finished arrangement) with the spell as a caption, or as a voiceover. Participation, even that which is unseen by you, magnifies the energy of abundance that surrounds sunflowers.

📹 DREAM CANDLES

Objects carry spirit; the older they are, the longer they've survived, and the more things they've seen. Incorporate something old into your magic to create something new—a portal for your dreams. You'll need some old teacups; wood candlewicks; candle wax; a dream-boosting oil such as patchouli, rose, or jasmine; and any combination of dream-boosting, spirit-communicating crystals (try moonstone or selenite).

WHAT TO DO: Before you begin your spell-post, cleanse the cup with salted water and pass it through the flame of a candle and incense smoke to remove any lingering energies that might be attached to it. Before inserting the wick into the tab, write the spell "Speak to me" on it. Center the wick tab in the bottom of the cup, then secure it in place with a few drops of melted wax. Pour in the wax and let it thicken before adding the oil and stones, then let the candle set completely.

When your candle is ready, about an hour before you go to sleep, set up your camera to record, then light the candle. Say the spell: *At night when we walk in the spirit world, speak to me, you will be heard!*

Share the post with the spell overlaid as text or a voice-over to increase its efficacy. Extinguish the candle and sleep. Write down any dreams in as much detail as you can remember.

🖼 @ IN THE GARBAGE

Whether it's a bad habit, a toxic relationship, or anything that is just not serving you anymore, it belongs out of your life. People aren't garbage, but the context in which they are in our lives can certainly go there—or in the compost pile if you are keeping or can contribute to one (and that is a better use of the energy!).

WHAT TO DO: Think of things that need to be binned. Ground and center and take some serious time to think about this. Write it down and journal if that helps—and don't feel like you must do this all TODAY. Simply starting the process is good.

When you throw something away, take a photo of it. Overlay it with the text describing what you want to pitch. Every time you bin something that has an association, say the spell: *We're done, goodbye, into the bin / Our parting is a win!*

Add this line if you're composting: *Break down and cleanse for a better beginning.*

Share your collection of images on your platform of choice with the spell as a caption, or seal with appropriate hashtags like #lifecleaning, #magicalcleansing, and #cleansingnegativity to boost the spell, your resolve, and your newly cleansed life!

🖼 @ A LOST PET SPELL

It's heartbreaking and terrifying when a beloved pet, a family member, is missing. Do the practical work, then boost your search and signal with this spell. You can do this spell for yourself or for others in this situation.

WHAT TO DO: Ground and center, and begin with a visualization of your pet. Picture them home, safe and sound. Next, print out a favorite image of your pet and set it in your sacred space. Surround the image with cinnamon sticks, hematite, and tiger's-eye. This is not to beautify the image, but to surround your pet with protective energy: the cinnamon sticks emphasize passion and love for your pet and will keep the fires burning until they come home, hematite's magnetic powers will draw them back, and tiger's-eye supports a successful search. Snap a photo of the assemblage once you've completed it.

Keeping your initial visualization in mind, create a post with practical details about your missing pet; make sure to include multiple images of the animal so that it is easily identifiable. Make your protective spell the last image in your post. Post and repost until your beloved returns.

🖼️ 🎥 AMAZONITE KNOWS

Amazonite is soothing to the heart, making it a great ally for communication, because it knows what's in your heart, as well as the hearts of the people you're talking to. The clear informational categorizing makes it well suited to magic aimed at success. One of the principal building-block stones of the moon's construction, amazonite is a great "antenna" for the emotional regulation that people need to communicate effectively.

WHAT TO DO: Sit or lie comfortably with your stone in your nondominant hand to receive information from the stone. Open your heart center to allow the stone's energy to communicate directly. If lying down, consider moving the stone to the breastbone. Once you have connected with the stone, talk about the communication you are looking to incorporate or activate. Discuss what it would mean to you to have access to effective communication, whether it be with doctors, friends, coworkers, intimate partners, and more. Ask the stone if it can provide the assistance you need. It's still autonomous even without a body. Consent is key.

Record any thoughts, feelings, or memories that arise. Post a video or photo using this magical stone, and if you're comfortable, share your experience with it in voice or text.

PAUSE FOR MENTAL HEALTH

The semicolon has become a symbol and sigil for depression and suicide awareness; it indicates that it's time for a pause; depression and suicidal thoughts require a pause to work things out before continuing on. In boosting these signals and sharing information we are alchemists, potentially turning despair into HOPE, loneliness into LOVE, and desperation to RESILIENCE.

WHAT TO DO: Get to know and share these resources:

★ Do regular wellness check-ins with all your loved ones. NAMI (see below) has great resources for how to approach the people you care about on these sensitive topics.

★ 988 is the new three-digit suicide and crisis hotline in the United States (lists of international hotlines are available online). Nine is the number of experience and wisdom—the person on the line when someone calls. Eight denotes continuation, in this case, of life. The fact that there are two of them shows that no one is alone.

★ NAMI, the National Alliance for Mental Illness, provides support for people living with mental illness and for loved ones who are supporting people living with mental illness. If you are outside the United States, look at the website This Much I Know for similar resources worldwide.

@ HEALING FOR TRAGEDY

Tragedies often leave us feeling helpless. Time seems suspended and traps us in the moment. If this happens to you, remember this small ritual that will, we hope, help.

WHAT TO DO: First, make sure that you, and anyone you care for or for whom you're responsible, are safe and out of any danger. Meditate on what you have just experienced or witnessed; let it and all the associated feelings wash over you. It's important to deal with it and give it the time it needs. When you feel that you have the energy to share, surround the situation and all the people involved—whether you can see them or not, or know them—in blue light. Boost this healing by tapping into the energy of the web.

★ If the tragedy you experienced directly or indirectly is public or global, create posts or repost information with the hashtag #sendinghealing. Add a blue filter over the post to surround the situation and victims with healing. Offer practical support or share valid opportunities when and if you can.

★ For tragedies closer to home, choose an image or appropriate symbol for the situation and people involved. Remember to respect privacy; you do not have to reveal all or any details of what happened. Focus on sending healing rather than telling the story; that is different work for another time.

 @ SHARE, SCRY, AND SEAL

Incense embodies the elements of air and fire plus the qualities of whatever herbs and resins go into its making. Magically, incense can be used in many ways—try the three mini spells below.

WHAT TO DO: Ground and center, then light up your favorite incense and make and post video spells of the smoke (each should be a minute or less).

★ Share the air element: focus on the smoke and its movement. Post with your voice or caption: *Behold the element of air. May the sylphs bless your ideas and carry them where they need to go!*

★ Scry through the smoke: Post with your voice or caption: *Gaze into the wavering veil . . . what do you see, what does it tell?* Ask viewers to share their visions—each view, comment, and like expands the divination.

★ Seal an intention: Post with your voice or caption: *By air and fire, idea and inspiration, carry my message and my intention.* Ask to support your intention with symbols (June 3 and August 14) and words.

🎥 @ CHAI TEA LOVE SPELL

The magical properties of everything that goes into making chai (February 3) make it the perfect love potion: cardamom (aphrodisiac), ginger (passion), cloves (protection), cinnamon (raises the spiritual vibration between lovers), black pepper (heat), black tea (stamina and endurance), milk (nurturing), and sugar (sweetness).

WHAT TO DO: Set up your camera to record, ground and center, then take a moment to focus on love. Once this is solidly in your mind, start making your tea. You'll need about a cup of water for each cup of tea you're making. Put this into your saucepan and let it come to a simmer. While you're waiting, add sugar to your cup(s). When the water is simmering, add your spices. Stir the mixture. After about a minute, add your tea leaves (1 tsp to 4 tsp). Use Assam or Darjeeling or a combination of the two for the traditional chai. Let the mixture boil for about two minutes. Add your milk of choice to the tea. You'll need about ¼ to ⅓ cup, depending on how milky you want to go. The more milk, the more nurturing love will be.

Take your potion off the stove and strain it into the cup. Allow to cool a bit, then sip and savor love. Share your video with the caption: *Potion, tisane, elixir, drought, nurture love, romance, come fast!* Seal the spell with the hashtags #teamagic, #chaimagic, and #lovepotion.

@ MAGIC WORD OF THE DAY

Exercises, spells, and rituals where you work directly with nature's chaotic aspect do more than just work magic. After you practice these for a while, your expectations soften. Expectations can be necessary, but in many instances, they limit our powers ("expect" to fail, or "expect" to win!—and what happens when neither of these things happen?). Use this spell to find your magical word of the day. Record the entire process or just share the end result.

WHAT TO DO: Make a salt circle (see August 20). Take a bag of Scrabble tiles and place it in the center. Set your camera up to record if you wish. Mix up the tiles, then draw out five for the number of the day (9 + 1 + 4 = 14, 1 + 4 = 5). Create a word or as many complete words as possible with the tiles (it's okay if you have one or two leftovers).

Share a video of the process or just an image of your word. Caption the image or video with a request to friends and followers to give their insights on its meaning (don't be surprised if others resonate with the word(s) you created!). BONUS POINTS for adding up the numbers on the tiles until you get one digit, then use your favorite numerology resource to interpret what that means for you for today.

@ A SPELL FOR LATENESS

Oh no! You're late! What do you do? Everyone's late for something at some point in their lives. Whatever the reason, it happens. Try not to sweat it and use this spell to do a little damage control.

WHAT TO DO: You're already late, and in most cases, a few more minutes won't make much of a difference. BUT—first and foremost, focus on getting to wherever you're going safely. And know that as frustrating and disappointing as delays and missing things can be, obstacles are put in your way for a purpose. If you are able to safely, snap a quick screenshot of the time and chant this spell aloud or to yourself (depending on where you are and who else is around): *Arrived as I could, arrived when I could, / Those who waited, understood. / All is well.*

Note that the spell is worded as events turned out in your favor. Keep that in mind. When you can, post the screenshot with the spell as a caption.

✦ WOUNDED HEALER MAGIC

Chiron's placement in your birth chart shows your deepest wounds. Become aware and heal them.

WHAT TO DO: Plug your birth date, time, and place into a free online Chiron or natal chart generator. Look for this symbol ⚷ to see where Chiron lives in your birth chart. His placement may explain why you might:

★ . . . feel invisible (1st House)

★ . . . need to feel safe to be happy (2nd House)

★ . . . lack self-confidence (3rd House)

★ . . . fear abandonment (4th House)

★ . . . take life too seriously (5th House)

★ . . . obsess over health issues (6th House)

★ . . . feel heavy rejection with relationships (7th House)

★ . . . feel loss through endings (8th House)

★ . . . are spiritually hungry (9th House)

★ . . . feel you must prove your worth (10th House)

★ . . . feel rejected for being unique (11th House)

★ . . . are psychic and empathic (12th House)

Share your findings with trusted friends and loved ones. Compare, and help each other heal.

🎥 TEAM TAROT!

Use the tarot to help manifest the team you need.

WHAT TO DO: Set up your camera to record. Have incense or a candle burning: try jasmine and ylang-ylang to break down barriers that inhibit collaboration.

Pull out the threes from each suit from your tarot deck: Wands, Swords, Pentacles, and Cups. Three (February 14) is the number of creativity and teamwork and will be at work in this spell through the symbolism of the tarot. Set out each card, one layered on top of the other as you say the words of the spell for each card:

★ Lay down the 3 of Wands and say: *I seek assistance with [name the skills and qualities you're looking for]!*

★ Layer the 3 of Swords over the 3 of Wands. Say: *We face challenges and support each other through difficult times.*

★ Layer the 3 of Pentacles over the 3 of Swords and say: *Our work is superior, we are recognized for our talents. We take pride in our work.*

★ Finally, lay down the 3 of Cups and say: *We revel in each other's talents. We celebrate each other!*

Share your video with your incantation or simply sealed with the hashtags #teammates, #teamwork, and #groupmagic to magnify your request to the Universe.

STEP INTO FAIRYLAND

Subtle changes in temperature that take place at this time of year create the perfect conditions for mushroom (fairy) rings. Mushrooms are like icebergs; the caps and stems are the little bit you see, but there's a lot going on beneath the surface, much like Fairyland, which also exists underground. Mushroom rings form when the soil is rich with the nutrients they crave (many times from a rotted tree stump); well-fed spores pop out of the ground in a ring, a sacred space.

WHAT TO DO: You're likely to find a fairy ring where mushrooms find food: pastures, well-fertilized lawns, or in clearings in the woods or a park, especially where trees have fallen. Make sure to bring a present and a request. Once you've found your ring, ground and center, start recording a video, then step inside; this sacred space has already been set. Walk clockwise around the circle to invoke the fae, then say this spell: *Faeries, fae in your underground world, hear my voice, hear my words. / By the power of three times three, grant my wish, so mote it be!*

Place your gift in the center and think of what you want the fae to help you with; no need to say it out loud. Walk around the circle counterclockwise to seal it and stop your recording. Share your image or video with the spell overlaid in text or with your voice.

@ 🖼 BE YOUR OWN ADVOCATE

Being your own advocate is believing in your own truth while setting emotions aside and remaining calm while you go through the process of getting what you need. Try this ritual on repeat to train yourself to regain and maintain your equilibrium.

WHAT TO DO:

★ GROUND. CENTER. BREATHE. Taking three deep breaths is quick and you can do it anywhere: three times, in through the nose, down to the belly, and out through the mouth.

★ USE SCENT. Especially something personal like your dog's shampoo or your favorite aunt's perfume; scents like these bring the presence of someone who cares about you immediately to your side. You're not alone.

★ HAVE A TALISMAN. A visual or something you can hold is grounding. It can be anything, like a photo, a coin, or a piece of jewelry. Hold your talisman and pass your intention and request for help into it.

If you choose to share your talisman, a simple image of it or a part of it sealed with appropriate hashtags (#immyownadvocate, #findingmyvoice, #findingmyagency) will boost your intention and need without having to tell the whole story or reveal details.

@ BUTTERFLY-MOTH

Tap into the unique powers of butterflies and moths on the threshold of the autumnal equinox (upon us at this part of September). The equinoxes mark the two days of the year of equal darkness and daylight. Butterflies (for the most part) are day creatures, and moths (again, for the most part) embrace the night. Use the time and these spirit insects to help you embrace change.

WHAT TO DO: Find or create two images—one of a butterfly, and one of a moth. Note the colors of and markings on their wings. What do the colors and shapes tell you? (For example, brown is grounding, yellow is joy, blue is peace, black is protective; round shapes denote wholeness and completeness.) Next, create two separate posts:

★ Between sunrise and sunset today (or on the equinox—the day shifts from year to year) post your butterfly image with this spell: *Day angel, butterfly / Pollinate and flutter by! / Plant the seeds of transformation, / And in me see your creation!*

★ Between sunset and sunrise today (or on the equinox) post your moth image with this spell: *Winged soft friend, find your light. / Do your dance of change tonight. / Ease the shifts that I may meet, / When I transform, the change is sweet.*

▶ SWEETS FOR THE SWEET

People employ everything from sugar and honey to agave sweetener to improve the dispositions of the people around them, from sweetening the boss's coffee to bribing young children with rewards for good behavior. To restore some of your own happiness, we're going to use some baking magic to bring back some joy and happiness to your space. The magic of sugar centers around love, including lust, mood elevation, and battling depression. So, charge the ingredients with love to remind yourself that you are loved and a valuable member of your community, online and IRL.

WHAT TO DO: Make sweet bread.

SWEET BREAD

  1 cup of softened ice cream (vegan or just sweetened Greek yogurt works, too) in any flavor

  ¾ cup self-rising flour

  1 tbsp sugar

Preheat the oven to 350° Fahrenheit. Place flour in a bowl and add ice cream and sugar; stir. Spray loaf pan with cooking spray. Transfer mixed dough to the loaf pan and place in the oven. Bake for 30–35 minutes until a toothpick comes out clean when inserted. Place on a wire baking rack to rest for fifteen minutes before removing from the loaf pan. Post videos that explain the recipe and do a taste test!

@ WORD CLOUD MAGIC

Word clouds show us magic at work through our communications; what is emphasized says the most. While word cloud generators use programming and AI to create the cloud, all they really do is count our words, which create the magic. The generator merely shows us what we've done, and that magnifies our words' power and potency.

WHAT TO DO: We are three-quarters of the way through the year. Where has your focus been? What are, or have been, your deepest desires? Ground and center, then methodically go through your social media posts from January until now (not just spells!) and copy your words into a word cloud generator. When all your posts have been copied, take three breaths, and say the spell aloud: *The year is coming to an end, / To what purpose has my will been bent? / Words like mirrors reflect the soul. / What do I need to make me whole?*

Press the generate button. Examine your most-used words. What do they say? Update your cloud with colors and fonts appropriate to your desires. Share on your platform of choice with the caption: *Behold this year. Next?*

▶ MAGIC SUNFLOWER SEEDS

The sunflower's energy can help remove blocks to creative expression, increase happiness, and banish loneliness. Today, however, we're going to focus on the sunflower's magic of wish fulfillment.

WHAT TO DO: Grab a bag of sunflower seeds from your favorite local shop. If you're not feeling the shells, feel free to grab shelled seeds, or even candy-coated sunflower seeds—the magic is in you, not the seeds. If you are interested in flavors, they can also flavor your magic. For instance, dill seeds can grant wishes of awakening your magic within you. They can avert aggression toward you, and help you attract your desires. Buffalo-flavored sunflower seeds contain cayenne, which is great for banishing spells and uncrossing spells if you think someone has hexed you. Candy sunflower seeds carry the magic of joy and happiness. Decide the wish you want granted and state it firmly. Take the bag in your hands and summon energy from deep within the earth and draw a bit of it into yourself. Send that energy down into your hands and into the bag and feel the warmth and glow. Then start to eat and enjoy your seeds. With every seed you eat, think about the ways that your wish can come true: visualize it, feel it, know it. Post a video of your process and virtually offer your bag of seeds so viewers can take a seed and make a wish.

 @ FOUND FEATHERS

While walking in green spaces or even around your neighborhood you may encounter feathers dropped or shed by passing birds. Besides embodying the spirit of the animal to which they were attached, feathers are symbols of the air element and can assist in the direction of thoughts and ideas.

WHAT TO DO: When you find a feather, snap a photo of it before you pick it up so that it can be seen where it landed. Pick it up, and take another photo or video of it, turning it in your hands so that it can be identified. BONUS POINTS for bird identification—what message does your particular bird carry? Take a moment to think about what feathers do for birds; they protect, insulate, and help with lift—feathers can help you with these things, too. Lastly, hold the feather outward like you're pointing a magic wand (you are). Ground and center, then start a new video, capturing your hand and the feather. Slowly, turn clockwise in a full circle. Say aloud or to yourself: *Feather waiting on the ground / A sacred message to be found. / Protect and inspire as I turn around / With divinity I am crowned.* Share your images and videos together with the spell as a caption.

📷 @ BODY TEMPLES

Our bodies come in all colors, shapes, and sizes, and they are all equally lovely. It's our job to care for them so that they serve us well as shelters for our souls while we're here on Earth. Use this spell to tend your temple so that you can worship the Divine within.

WHAT TO DO: Sometimes it can be difficult to see beauty, inner or outer, at least as a whole. When this happens, start small. Everyone has something about their body that they like, despite what they may dislike. What about your body do *you* like? Let's say it's your hands. Look at them, and see that they're connected to your wrists. The beauty of your hands spreads to your wrists . . . then up your arms to your elbows . . . then to your shoulders and neck . . . It spreads over your face and down to your chest, and on and on. Everything is connected, so that it's not just one part, but the whole that is magnificent.

Snap a photo of your chosen body part. Look at the image and say the spell: *Beauty starts here, but does not stop / Outward it spreads, to every part / My size, my shape, my heart, my tone, / My body, my temple, my gorgeous, sacred home.* If and when you're comfortable and able, share the image with the spell as a caption to celebrate your temple and inspire others to tend and celebrate theirs.

ACCIDENTS AND AFTERMATHS

Seeing an accident happen, or the resulting wreckage, can be traumatizing, especially if you've been in a similar accident yourself. If you are a witness, first get practical help to the scene as soon as possible and send immediate energy. (Visualize a blue light surrounding the scene of the accident and send peace and healing to all those involved—including all witnesses.) Once you are away from the site, take time to ground and center, and try this spell. (NEVER take photos of the scene of an accident.)

WHAT TO DO: Find or draw an image of a praying mantis. Their posture (prayer) sends out prayers and intentions to those involved (including all witnesses). Their green color will also send healing to those in need. If your mantis is brown, that's good, too, as it will send grounding energy; it's easy to feel shaken up when you've seen something disturbing.

Take a moment to visualize the mantis sending its energy to all who need it. Share the image as a temporary post with no caption—sometimes the image with your intention behind it is enough. You can also use this spell for any traumatic event or experience where healing is needed but you do not want to share the details.

🖼 🎥 FOR THE BARISTAS ♥

Sometimes paying upward of five dollars for a cup of coffee (or more for fancy drinks) is hard to swallow, but you're not just paying for coffee—you're paying for craftsmanship. Favorite coffee and tea shops are hives of activity, especially behind the bar. The baristas manage and create personalized drink after personalized drink with a smile. Tip them a little extra with this spell—and boost it to fill their cups with good things.

WHAT TO DO: Do this NOW so that you're ready the next time you visit your favorite beverage shop. Set up your camera to record. Take paper money in any denomination (a new bill if you can get it) and inscribe it with this spell: *Rewards and respect rain down for all you do. / Know that I appreciate you!*

Fold the bill into a heart. (If you don't know how to do this, it's easy, and a quick online search will give you many instructional videos.) The next time you visit the coffee or tea shop, take a quick snap of it. Get your beverage, pop the heart into the tip jar, then post the picture of the shop and your video together to amplify barista love. Seal the spell with the hashtags #boostsforbaristas and #baristamagic.

# ONLINE JOB SEARCH

Whether it's your first job, you're ready to make a move, or it's time to change careers, tap into the energy that drives change to bring success to this effort.

WHAT TO DO: First, do the practical work: spruce up your resume, fill out any online applications or proposal forms, and research jobs or projects. Stones like tiger's-eye (success), malachite (money), and jade (balance) lend their energies to these tasks.

When you're ready to submit, think about what you want out of your new job. Say this mantra aloud each time before you hit the submit button: *I find work that . . .*

★ *uses and grows my talents and skills.*

★ *allows me to grow personally and professionally.*

★ *brings satisfaction and purpose.*

★ *is in harmony with my life outside work and adapts as I do.*

★ *takes place in a healthy environment.*

It's important to articulate all the things you require. Adapt the incantation to suit your personal needs and desires. Tell the Universe what you want, follow through, and when the time is right, it will be yours. Trust!

🎥 @ COFFEE CLEANSING

Just as there's tea magic (January 5), there's coffee magic, too. You can practice divination with coffee grounds; in many cultures, coffee is a ritual beverage, and as an ingredient in magical spells, coffee is, among other things, cleansing. We all have judgy little thoughts that stop us in our tracks and throw off our groove. Whether it's a worrisome news story, guilt over past indiscretions, or a failure you just can't forget, coffee can help cleanse the brain and set you free.

WHAT TO DO: You'll need a baking tray, a paintbrush or quill pen, a sturdy piece of paper, and some coffee. On the piece of paper, use your paintbrush or quill pen to print or write your intrusive thoughts with the coffee and allow it to dry. Pour some of the coffee into the baking tray so that it fills it and make a shallow bath. When your paper is dry, set up your camera and start recording: Place your paper into the coffee "bath" and watch the writing blend into the coffee and disappear. Share the video on your platform of choice with the caption: *Thoughts that haunted me, cleansed and gone!*

▶ @ DO IT SCARED

Chickens are not cowards—they totally own their space. The ancient Romans knew this; they took chickens along on battles as good-luck charms and symbols of courage. Real courage is moving forward (after common sense has been considered) even if you're scared. Allow chickens to help you find this inner strength—you've got this!

WHAT TO DO: Get a piece of paper and trace your hand to make a chicken; your thumb forms the head and your fingers, its tail feathers. Add a beak, feet, a comb, and any other details that make you happy. Don't worry about perfection, it's the shape and intention that count! Write all the things you're afraid of on the chicken. Let her absorb everything. Set up your camera and start recording on time-lapse. Put the chicken in a fireproof dish, take a deep breath, and expand your chest (like chickens do!). Light her up and say this spell: *I do it scared. / I act, as if, / I strut, I dare!* Keep recording until only ash is left. Share your video with the spell as a caption and spread courage to all who see it.

🎥 CHIME CANDLE MAGIC

Chime candles are cheap, come in a lot of colors, and can be carved, rolled, and pierced to your personal needs.

WHAT TO DO: Record the burning of each of these spells in time-lapse mode and share on your platform of choice, with or without a caption. Visualize your intention, and . . .

★ Use a green chime candle and a nail (October 23). Carefully carve the words "CASH NOW" into the candle. Slather it in olive oil and roll in gold glitter. Place it in a fireproof dish and safely light up.

★ You'll need four black chime candles, four cloves (for protection), and some salt (to create a boundary). Make a square of salt on a flat surface to represent your home. Pierce each chime candle with a clove, then set one in each corner of the square in a fireproof dish. Safely light up and let the candles do their work.

★ Use a pink chime candle, rose oil, fresh rose petals, and pink sea salt. Make a ring of rose petals and set your fireproof dish or candleholder in the center. Lightly oil the candle, then roll it in the sea salt, pressing the crystals into the wax. Set it in a fireproof dish, then light, love, and be merry.

ANNOUNCE A NEW JOB

When you start a new job, you may think—I've arrived! But really, it's the beginning of a new adventure with new challenges. To prepare yourself for the journey, and make sure that your new position lives up to everything YOU want and need it to be, try this spell to set the stage for success.

WHAT TO DO: Not everyone needs to know the thought behind your actions. When you share that you're starting a new job, do so with intention. As you create your announcement, visualize that your new position is all you want and need it to be. Picture yourself going to work and being happy and fulfilled. To help you focus your energies, hold a piece of tiger's-eye (for success). You can also burn some frankincense incense (for emotional well-being) and anoint your temples with lavender oil (new beginnings and balance). Post your announcement and carry the tiger's-eye with you or keep it in your workspace to maintain the enthusiasm of the "new" throughout your tenure.

10
02

🖼️ @ HERA'S HELPER

Sacred to Hera, the queen of the ancient Greek pantheon, peacock feathers are an emblem of queenship and the Divine Feminine (ironic, as the feathers come from the male bird). A peacock's call sounds like they're crying, "Help!" (And Hera, though she has her imperious moments, *is* a helper, if she believes in the cause.) Use a peacock feather like an antenna to find help when you need it.

WHAT TO DO: This spell is simple. Hold a peacock feather in your dominant hand, extend your arm outward, and point the feather like it's a magic wand (it is). Visualize it and yourself surrounded by indigo and violet light (the color of the third eye and crown chakras). Keeping your arm extended, slowly turn in a clockwise circle to invoke. When you've completed the circle, make an arch over your head from north to south, then east to west, touching the ground at each point. Essentially, you've surrounded yourself in an indigo-violet bubble. Say: *Send help when I need it, and help me to see it!* Snap a close-up picture of your feather on your platform of choice with the spell as the caption to expand your vision. Keep your eyes (all of them!) open.

@ 10-4: I HEAR YOU SPELL

....

Today is October 4 or 10-4, a police code for "message received" or "I hear you." Have you ever felt that your message (whatever it may be) wasn't seen or heard by anyone, least of all those who needed to hear it? Use this spell to boost your signal.

WHAT TO DO: Use the magic of the day (literally, 10/04) to get your message out. The day's potency can be spelled out numerologically: $1 + 0 + 4 = 5$. Five is a number of knowledge, justice, and understanding. "Five" days are ruled by Mercury, the planet of, among other things, communication. Put a dab of jasmine or sandalwood oil on your temples and pulse points. These scents are good for boosting communication, clarity, and getting the word out. Take a moment to ground and center before composing your message, imbibing the scent of the oil as you do so. Visualize your throat chakra glowing bright blue so that your messaging is clear. Picture your third-eye chakra as intense indigo to see and be seen. Compose your message. Before you send it, say out loud: *Hear me and respond.*

@ NO MEANS NO

We've all heard "No means no" before, along with another favorite, "No is a complete sentence." For those of us who have trouble using this spell—because it is a spell—it should be practiced often for big and little things where NO is the answer.

WHAT TO DO: You don't want to do it, whatever it is: go out with friends, agree to help, take the next step, etc. You have the right to refuse—and own the consequences. This is probably what makes saying no hard. Saying no may mean that someone gets mad at you. Saying no may mean confrontation. Saying no may mean discomfort—but so does not saying no. And the anger and resentment from not saying no can be far worse than asserting yourself.

To help you with this work, create a post with the word "No" or "Just NO" (the "NO" being larger) with blue or green letters on a black background. Black is protective, while blue conveys peace (for you) and green conveys healing (also for you—and saying no is often a part of the healing process). You can use red as well, but keep in mind that red can convey aggression and anger as well as confidence. Share the post on your platform of choice. Likes, views (which you may not see), shares, and comments will add strength to your spell.

@ SIGN OF THE WITCH

It's October, the season of the witch! Seal your posts, emails, and texts with a witch emoji; it's seasonal and carries its own magic.

WHAT TO DO: We've explored emojis as magical sigils, and the witch is no different. Look at the elements that make up this symbol, which spells out what witches do:

</:)

★ The "less than" symbol expresses that witches seek to expand their knowledge—go from less (the tiny point at the top of the hat) to more (the wide brim at the bottom).

★ The forward slash is divisive; witches often walk in two worlds, the magical and the mundane.

★ The colon is a pause, to think before acting (which should always be practiced in magic).

★ The close parenthesis denotes closure, which is what magic seeks to do.

Seal your emails, texts, and posts this month with the sign of the witch to express your magical intentions and connect to the season!

It's inevitable that people may throw negative energy your way. You have done it, too, as we all have. Sometimes this is done unconsciously, like if you're frustrated or mad at someone. But there are times when it is on purpose, and you know it. Time to send that bad energy back. All you need is your camera, a rubber band, and some good old Elmer's (or other white glue).

WHAT TO DO: Remember the old schoolyard chant, "I'm rubber, you're glue. What you say bounces off me and sticks to you"? It's a spell. Ground and center, then think of the energy coming your way, and its source. Visualize it and keep it in mind as you set up your camera to record. Set the rubber band on a flat surface and say: *I'm rubber!*

The glue is next. Squeeze a small amount next to the rubber band. (White glue is pretty benign, but make sure that it won't stain the surface of your space.) Say: *You're glue!* Then with your finger, touch the rubber band and "bounce" over to the glue puddle, saying: *Whatever you've sent bounces off me and sticks to you. Sending it back!*

Share your video with the spell as an impermanent post. The energy should start to dissipate once the post expires but repost as needed.

10
07

@ PROSPERITY PENTACLES

Look at the images in the Pentacles suit of the tarot, and the word "solid" may come to mind. In this spell, the court cards will represent you on your journey to prosperity. You'll also need three quartz crystals.

WHAT TO DO: Pull out the Pentacle court cards and lay them out in a row: Page, Knight, Queen, and King. Place a piece of clear quartz crystal between the Page and the Knight, the Knight and the Queen, and the third between the Queen and the King.

★ The Page represents the beginning of your prosperity journey—the initial ideas that start the flow.

★ The Knight takes those ideas to the next level with movement; the crystal connects them.

★ The Knight's movement inspires the Queen's nurturing nature; the Queen incubates your idea and makes it real. The crystal connects the Knight's movement to the Queen's care.

★ What the Queen nurtures, the King brings forth and spreads to the world. The crystal connects the Queen's care to the King's support.

Snap a photo of this assemblage and post with the spell: *Ideation to action, nurturing to execution, my work brings great prosperity!*

🖼 @ SHARING SPELLS

Ever come across a post that captures exactly what you're feeling or going through? In that moment, you realize that you're not alone. Someone shared that post. It might not be someone you know. And maybe a different someone created it. Both may have had or know someone who has similar experiences and were called to share a message of hope. This is magic, the post is a spell—and now you are called to propagate it.

WHAT TO DO: When you access a post that speaks to you, keep the magic going.

★ Express gratitude to the person who made the post, and the original creator if you have access to communicate this to them. Your message does not have to be long or complicated. Something like *Thank you for this* ♥ will suffice.

★ Repost or share the post, being sure to tag the person whose post you saw and the original creator if you can. Add your own comments if you feel called to do so, and the magic message: *For anyone who needs to see this . . .*

★ Boost the post with more magical intentions expressed through emojis (see April 29) and hashtags.

★ Visualize others benefiting as you did before you repost.

🖼 @ YOU GOT THIS

Two tens in succession, 10:10, say that you are complete and that, whatever your situation, you have the resources you need to handle it. Use your favorite platform to engage with and spread the magic of this day.

WHAT TO DO: Set a reminder to take a screenshot of the time at 10:10 a.m. (if you miss it, you get a second chance at 10:10 p.m.). Share the screenshot as a temporary post with the intention: *Angels say, you got this. / I'm all I need, / To succeed / 10-10 for the win!*

Refer back to when you needed strength; the Universe is sending you a reminder that *you got this*. Views, likes, and shares spread the angel magic!

10
10

📹 FRIENDSHIP SPELL

Social media is all about "friends." But more likely than not, as wonderful as most of these folks are, they are not the ones you can count on one hand that are with you for the long haul. These are the people who you feel like you've known forever regardless of how long you've actually known them. Use this spell to honor these relationships. You will need lengths of hearty, vine-like plants that also have associations of strong friendships. We'll be using honeysuckle for its sweetness (real friends sweeten our lives) and ivy (evergreen, like true friends) but feel free to substitute other vine-like plants or materials.

WHAT TO DO: Ground and center, and set your camera up to record. Bind your vines together at the top, then slowly twist them together, winding one vine around the other, being careful not to break stems or flowers (if you do, it's okay, don't stress it!). As you work, say the spell: *[Name], my true friend, our lives intertwine, / So glad I'm in your life and you in mine.*

When you reach the end of your vines, bind the other end. Share the video directly with your friend via text or email along with the spell, or on your platform of choice.

@ HEAL WITH BABY ANIMALS

Rarely do baby animal pictures fail to raise spirits. Their sweet fragility reminds us of the goodness in the world and the great potential of something new.

WHAT TO DO: All animals are messengers. Baby versions carry the spirit message of their species as well as the vibrancy of youth, unjaded vision, and trust. Responsibly source photos of these babies and share their unique magical messages:

- ★ Kitten sends you independence—you got this!
- ★ Puppy sends you unconditional love and loyalty!
- ★ Baby bunny swiftly sends you luck and abundance!
- ★ Baby hedgehog has your back!
- ★ Piglet sends you money, luck, and wisdom!
- ★ Baby goat sends love and pleasure your way!
- ★ Baby bear sends you deep, safe sleep and rest!
- ★ Baby seal sends you the agility to move and morph!
- ★ Cheeky monkey sends chaos magic for a fun day!
- ★ Baby elephant is here to clear the way for you!
- ★ Baby turtle sends you health and longevity!

◧ SELENITE FOR CLEANSING

Selenite is a shimmering white crystal formed in columns. It helps us take all the information we have coming in all the time and synthesize it into a real working order. Due to these properties, it's one of two stones that don't need cleansing, and selenite is the "self-cleaning oven" of crystals. Handle this crystal with care as it can be scratched with a fingernail or dissolved in water. Don't store your selenite or satin spar (selenite in long "logs" or "sticks") with other stones, as they'll get scratched.

WHAT TO DO: With a piece of selenite or satin spar in hand, close your eyes. If you don't have a mineral to work from, search for a clear photo on your favorite search engine. With your eyes closed, journey to your inner landscape (February 5). When you are standing in your etheric "start screen" or home base, invite the spirit of selenite into your space, or journey to theirs. Remember, if you're concerned at any time, you can ask your spirit guide to go with you. As you journey to visit the realm of selenite, think of things you might ask them like, "How can I best work with you?", "Do you have a working relationship with any other minerals that I should know about?", and "Do you enjoy working during any specific moon phase?" Record your observations and post a video diary entry about selenite's cleansing properties.

🖼 🎥 PUMPKIN MANIFEStATION

Pumpkin spice is nice, but the power lies with the pumpkin itself. Pumpkin is a harvest symbol and represents prosperity, good fortune, and multitasking. Pumpkins can be lanterns and planters, as well as soup bowls. They can be turned into pies and other delights. Their seeds are tasty, and one pumpkin has the potential to produce a hundred more.

WHAT TO DO: Start with a blank surface; snap a photo of it. One by one, add 5 small pumpkins, snapping a photo after each one. The number 5 represents the pentacle and the presence of all the elements: Earth, Air, Fire, Water, and Spirit. Overlay each photo with the words of the spell, which correspond to the position of the pumpkins and each element:

★ Blank: *Manifesting*

★ Earth, bottom right: *I plant, while . . .*

★ Air, middle left: *I think, while . . .*

★ Fire, middle right: *I inspire, while . . .*

★ Water, bottom left: *I feel, while . . .*

★ Spirit, top of the pentacle: *I make it happen!*

Stitch the pictures together to make a stop-motion video. Share the video on your platform of choice. Views, likes, shares, and comments will boost your manifestation.

@ GRAVEYARD DIRT

Graveyard dirt is one of the most powerful magical tools for communicating with the spirit world.

WHAT TO DO: To collect graveyard dirt you'll need a metal straw, a wooden skewer, some small plastic bags, and some flowers to leave as offerings. Visit the graves of those with whom you wish to connect. Say their names aloud. Ask permission to take some soil. If you have any feelings of apprehension, leave the site undisturbed; you can take the soil from another area of the cemetery, even if not from an actual grave; it's all consecrated ground. Drive the straw into the soil, cap it with your finger, and draw it out. Use the skewer to free the soil from the straw and store it in a plastic bag. Give thanks and leave your flowers.

Mix your graveyard dirt with equal parts of dried rose-buds and allspice, then get five tea lights and remove the candles. Line the bottom of each tin with the soil mixture and replace the candles. Set your candles on a fireproof dish and say the spell as you light them: *To the soil we all return, but here and now as the candles burn, / Speak to me, visit me in my sleep, and send me messages to keep.*

Share a photo or video of the candles burning and share it on your platform of choice with the spell as a caption to amplify your voice to the spirits.

◄)) 📠 SIGN ONLINE

Anything to which you affix your signature is magic and binding. Perform this ritual anytime you sign something digitally (especially if you find yourself in a Mercury retrograde period!).

WHAT TO DO: Begin by getting yourself some flowers—daffodils for truth, black-eyed Susans for justice, orange lilies for honesty, or any combination thereof. Keep them close by as you do this work, along with a piece of black tourmaline (for protection).

First and foremost, READ YOUR CONTRACT and make sure you understand everything in it. If there are words or phrases you're drawn to, LISTEN to your senses. Meditate on these words and phrases; do searches to find them throughout the document and examine them closely.

Once you've read the contract in its entirety and you (and your counsel) feel that you are ready to sign, take time to ground and center, and say this incantation before signing: *I find no fault, / We bind together, / I make this agreement, / In kind forever.*

🖼 @ GARGOYLE WARDS

Gargoyles are "garglers" of rainwater; it's the origin of their name, and what they were designed for (essentially, gutters). But we've come to see them as guardians of a sort, and they are. Gargoyles, gorgons, and grotesques can be found on many buildings and fences, old and new. Keep an eye out for them and tap into their special brand of protective power.

WHAT TO DO: The next time you're out and about, keep an eye out for gargoyles, gorgons, and grotesques: animal, human, and mythical figures on buildings. They like to perch on corners, gaze out over door lintels, and leer from unexpected places. When you find one, snap a picture and share it on your platform of choice with this spell: *Watcher of iron or steel or stone, / Guard and guide when we walk alone!*

Sharing the gargoyle's gaze expands his reach and takes him to places he has not seen. Likes, views, comments, and shares multiply his protective powers.

◤ HOUSE OF CARDS

Card houses are not stable houses. One shake, too much weight, or careless placement can cause the whole thing to crumble; this is the essence of The Tower card of the tarot. When something falls apart, it's because somewhere, unaddressed vulnerability and weaknesses exist. Use this spell to detect weak spots and fortify your inner house.

WHAT TO DO: Set up your camera to record. Use a black (protective) piece of paper as a base. Take a pack of playing cards, remove the jokers, and shuffle them. Without looking at the cards, start building a card house on the base paper. Build until the house falls. Turn over the cards to reveal where you should look for weaknesses.

- ★ Hearts: emotional involvement
- ★ Spades: ideas may need to be reviewed
- ★ Diamonds: you may need funding or other physical resources
- ★ Clubs: inspiration is needed; you may be stuck
- ★ Aces: a fresh start may be needed
- ★ Court cards: issues with people

Share your video on your platform of choice. Likes and comments will offer further guidance.

🖼 @ HUG A TREE

Part of living a magical life is living close to and respecting nature. This spell will literally put you in touch with the natural world around you. Trees have seen a lot. Many are long-lived, and they are sentient beings that can feel pain, community, and affection.

WHAT TO DO: This spell is very simple. Go to a green place in your neighborhood where there are trees, keeping in mind that the trees are also your neighbors. Safely make your way over to a tree that calls to you. (Be careful when traversing grassy areas, which can be uneven.) Place your hand on the tree's bark and visualize its energy. Feel the life running through it.

Now give it a hug. Feel the energy more strongly. Can you hear its voice? What does it say to you? Stay for as long as you feel comfortable. Share a photo of your hug (you may need a friend to help with this). If you can't get an image of you and the tree, take a close-up of its bark and a distance shot of the whole tree. Before parting say these words (or ones you compose yourself) as a magical pact to look after each other: *Magical being, neighbor and friend, / Love and protection I shall send.*

Share your image(s) on your platform of choice with the spell as a caption. Seal the spell with the hashtags #naturemagic, #magicaltrees, #hugatree, and #treemagic.

FAIRY-TALE MINI SPELLS

One way that magic and the Divine Feminine survived through the years is through fairy tales and folktales.

WHAT TO DO: Reread your favorites, and try these mini spells:

★ Baba Yaga: To reveal the truth, set up your camera to record and grind up some chilies with a mortar and pestle à la Baba Yaga. As the scent of the herb reaches your nose, say the spell: *Truth, turn your front to me!*—and reveal that which is hidden. Share your video to magnify the spell.

★ Briar Rose: Keep a rose—thorns and all—by your bed for restful sleep. Snap a photo and share to expand the love and its protective magic.

★ Hansel and Gretel: Think of something you want and write it on a piece of paper. Place a fireproof dish or bowl at one end of a flat surface; at the other, make a trail of gumdrops leading up to it. If you want something very specific, like cash, use an appropriate color (green). Make a video "following" the trail. When you reach the dish or bowl, light up the paper and let it burn to ash. Share your video to amplify the potency of this spell.

🎥 @ JUNK DRAWER ORACLE

Any collection of items can have meanings assigned to its components and be used for divination.

WHAT TO DO: Open your junk drawer and snap a photo of the contents. Next, pick up each item. What do you think each one means? Here are some suggestions:

- ★ Bandage: health and healing
- ★ Mystery key: the answers you're seeking
- ★ Random penny: luck
- ★ Twist tie: closure
- ★ Pencil: expression
- ★ Screwdriver: connections
- ★ Nails: communication, protection
- ★ Batteries: power
- ★ Pad of paper: a blank slate, beginnings

Meanings you come up with yourself based on personal experience are valid and will make this oracle all the more powerful. Create a video of yourself selecting an item from your pile. Share your video as a general reading for everyone with the meaning of the item as a caption and the hashtag #junkdrawerdivination. Do friends and followers see synchronicities?

◾️ @ IN-BETWEEN SPELL

Today, the sun moves from Libra to Scorpio, a time of in-between. It's one of the year's many "in-between" times. Perform this spell to tap into the balancing aspect of this shift. Soon, the scales will tip (from Libra to Scorpio!), and you'll be moving forward once more.

WHAT TO DO: Life is about balance. Finding, holding, losing, and recapturing your equilibrium with ease is a skill where magic can be helpful. Set up dominos end on end in a circle. Start recording and knock them over, capturing the chain reaction. Use the boomerang feature on your camera to reverse the fall. Share the video on a loop, overlaid with the spell below as text or a voice-over: *I stand, / I wobble, / I fall, / I rise again. / I always regain my balance.*

🎥 @ NAILED IT!

Think of what you "normally" use nails for, add intention, and you have magical correlation.

WHAT TO DO: When you have an intention in mind, choose a nail. Keep your intention in mind as you're working; it's the difference between hammering a nail and magically nailing it!

★ Drive IRON nails into the ground at the corners of your property (or the property where your home is situated, if allowed) to help keep out unfriendly energy, spirits, and people.

★ Hammer BRASS nails into the corners of the doorways that are entrances to your home to welcome helpers and deter unwelcome visitors.

★ Carry a STEEL nail as a talisman for strength, or an ALUMINUM nail to promote invisibility (June 10).

★ If you're making over a room in your home, hammer a NICKEL nail in an unobtrusive place to start spreading its energy to the space. Hammer a nickel nail in the room where you get ready for the day to boost transmutation (new look, same you!).

Create a video of yourself "nailing it" (suggested above). Share with relevant hashtags to seal the spell: #nailmagic #metalmagic #nailedforprotection #nailedforstrength #nailedforchange

✦ GOOD TIMING!

Just as each month, day of the week (February 18), and direction (May 28) can boost your spells, so can the time of day you perform or start your spell.

WHAT TO DO: Think of the spell you're doing and what time of day would correspond best. Don't discount times that are special and unique to you: The exact time of your birth, or of a full or new moon, or the birth or passing of a loved one—we all have our own special, powerful times!

★ Perform spells for beginnings in the morning and endings in the evening. There are many online resources that will give you the exact time of the sunrise and sunset for wherever you are in the world. Make sure to set your alarm at least fifteen to thirty minutes before to ensure you don't miss them!

★ Afternoons are great for growth spells.

★ Overnights are good for incubation spells—especially the ones where waiting is involved. The results of magical work are rarely instantaneous, and nighttime is great for the workings that you may never witness.

★ Witching hours: Noon and midnight are the full and new moons of time. Express gratitude and go for full power at noon. Plant seeds and make intentions at midnight.

🎥 🔊 @ HYGGE MAGIC

Besides the general power of words, every language has unique terms for which there is no literal translation. "Hygge" (hoo-gah) is the Scandinavian term for coziness, contentment, and comfort. Try this spell to tap into this energy.

WHAT TO DO: Set up your camera to record, making sure to capture sound as well as action. ASMR (autonomous sensory meridian response) is a reaction usually caused by a combination of sights and sounds; this is part of the magic of this spell. Using a mortar and pestle, roughly grind cinnamon and cardamom pods in equal parts. As you grind these spices together, use the scent to visualize the comfort that they conjure up and feel yourself relax. Next, put a pot of water on the stove to simmer, and when it is steaming, put the spices into it. Capture the plips and plops as the spices hit the water. Record the water as it simmers and be sure to capture its purring sound.

Share your recording with the caption: *Look and listen, bubble and steam, be content, relax and dream.* Seal the spell with the hashtags #hyggemagic and #asmrmagic. BONUS POINTS for using alt text to describe your creation for all five senses for those who may not be able to experience your ritual visually, audibly, or olfactorily.

@ A SPELL TO SEE ALL

Would life be simpler if we were able to see all perspectives? Omniscient beings see all. Try this perspective spell to give you omniscient vision and encourage others to be omniscient and emphasize.

WHAT TO DO: You'll need a crystal that facilitates empathy. Try larimar, chalcedony, aragonite, or rainbow moonstone. Go to a high place where you can safely look down (safety first ALWAYS). If this is difficult for you, go with a friend who can do this without experiencing mental or physical distress; they can capture the photo or video for you.

Take a snap or video looking down—make sure you also capture the crystal in your photo! Note how small things look and how much there is to take in. Post the video or picture with the caption: *See all, / Feel all. / Gain perspective, / Be selective / With your words, actions, and deeds.*

🎥 @ IT'S RAINING MONEY!

We can all use a little extra cash. Use this spell to give the Universe a poke about your financial needs. You'll need some Monopoly money and a few essential oils to give this spell a POP—literally: Peppermint, Orange, and Patchouli.

WHAT TO DO: This spell is all about the uplifting pop that the essential oils will give your focus and intention. For efficiency, and to avoid contact with the essential oils on the skin (especially if you have sensitivities or allergies), dilute 3 drops of each oil with water in separate spray bottles so that you have one for peppermint, one for orange, and one for patchouli. Shake each bottle gently to mix before spritzing.

Lay out your Monopoly money as single bills in rows. Set your camera to record. One at a time with each oil, lightly spritz the bills, taking in the scent. For each essential oil, say: *It's gonna rain money!*

When the bills are dry, gather them up, toss them in the air, and capture the money raining down. Share the video on your platform of choice (you may have to edit, depending on how seamless you want it to be) with this spell as the caption: *It's raining money! / If you see this, / Cash is coming / If you believe it!* Likes, shares, comments, and views pop up the power of this spell.

📹 @ FROM THE DARKNESS

It is a dark time of the year. Darkness isn't bad and should not be feared. Darkness is the tomb, but it is also the womb (both are places of germination for the next beginning). If the unknown of the darkness scares you sometimes, try this spell to help you embrace the cyclical nature of death and rebirth, darkness, and light.

WHAT TO DO: You'll need a black candle (taper or pillar), matches, and your camera. Place your candle in the middle of it. Make the room you're in as dark as possible, then set your camera to record. Begin in darkness. Whisper the words: *In shadow, all things begin.*

Strike your match and light the candle. Let the candle flicker for a second or two, then incant the rest of the spell: *In darkness, there is light, and in light, the dark. / There is no "nothing," only the dormant spark. / Awaken!*

Stop recording. Share your video on your platform of choice with the caption: *Let the darkness nurture you, and rise like the light.*

10
28

🖼️ 🎥 @ YOU'VE GOT MAIL!

People manifest their wishes and dreams through the mail: we settle debts through the mail, seal deals through the mail—the post office is a magical hub! The acceptance and recognition, and the passing from hand to hand, adds energy to an intention. Writing it makes it real—and sending emphasizes that solidity.

WHAT TO DO: Document each step of the spell as either a photo or a short video. At the conclusion of each step, say the spell: *What I send, I manifest!*

★ On a clean sheet of paper, handwrite out what you wish to manifest. Write it down in as much detail as possible.

★ Lightly spritz the paper with clary sage oil diluted in water to give it a boost.

★ Fold the letter in three and place it in an envelope.

★ Seal the envelope, write your address on it, and stamp it.

★ Take your letter to a mailbox and put it in the slot.

Share your images or videos (stitched together) with the words of the spell as a caption. When you receive your letter, share in another post, captioned with the spell to continue to boost your powers of manifestation.

▶ CANDY CORN CREATIVITY

Once upon a time, October was the only time of year where candy corn was readily available to satisfy Halloween sugar dreams. Did its inventors realize the magical associations of its colors and ingredients? The traditional white, orange, and yellow kernels are a recipe for creativity: white is great for beginnings, orange is the color of creativity, and yellow brings joy. Combine color magic with the flavor of candy corn (vanilla for success, marshmallow and honey to sweeten the pot) and you have potent energies for magic.

WHAT TO DO: Get yourself a bag of traditional candy corn. Set up your camera to record in time-lapse mode. Use the candy corn to spell out your creative dreams. Be creative! Use it also to create magical designs and sigils to add power to the spell: spirals for the creative process, equilateral crosses for balance, and eyes to draw eyes to your work. As you place each piece of candy corn, see yourself transforming through creativity. Visualize your work blossoming and giving you and others joy. Share your video on your platform of choice with the hashtags #candycorncreativity and #candycornmagic to seal the spell.

10

30

🎥 @ 🖼 ANCESTOR ALTAR

Knowing where you've come from can be instrumental in healing. Many of us are recovering from generational trauma, hurts that have been passed down—consciously and unconsciously—from one family member to another (in fact, sometimes whole groups of family members are affected). Acknowledging the past can honor a beloved ancestor, or the pain caused by things that happened in the past. By building a virtual ancestor altar—that you can add to or ultimately delete—you're taking necessary steps to peeling back the layers of your own persona, to heal and empower.

WHAT TO DO: Starting at the beginning of the month, build an altar to your ancestors—this can include personal photos, but also think about including images from the era in which they lived, objects you feel they might have liked, colors, poems, etc. Make the board public or private; invite family to post on the board as well if you feel called to do so. Arrange the images on the board as you add them; this will make the work living and organic, and something you can turn to continually. Let your eyes guide you. Take some time to be still and quiet with what you are looking at. Are your ancestors whispering in your ear about what is important or aesthetically pleasing to them?

10
—
31

🎥 @ ALL THE SAINTS

The days of spirit are upon us (Halloween, today, and tomorrow, November 2). Make a candle altar to your personal saints. You'll need some seven-day candles (pillar candles in a jar).

WHAT TO DO: Think about your needs and those who have passed into spirit that you admire; a famous person, or a friend, family member, pet, familiar, or other loved one. Use candles in colors to suit those spirits and embellish the jar with decorations and photos.

Arrange your candles in a way that has meaning to you. Before lighting the candles add some extra magical ingredients to each with an accompanying incantation:

★ Jasmine essential oil to facilitate communication: *Hear me, and may I hear you.*

★ Crushed lavender to facilitate vision: *See me, and may I see you.*

★ Rose water for love: *For the love that is between us.*

Once all the candles are lit, make a short video of them, and share with the caption: *May all the saints see you, may all the saints hear you, may all the saints bless you.* #allthesaints

 @ ALL SOULS

The days following Halloween are sacred. In many cultures, this day is celebrated as the Day of the Dead, or All Souls' Day. We all have our own ancestors with whom we commune—but there are many other souls whose names remain unspoken. Use this spell to honor them.

WHAT TO DO: Go into a local cemetery and find a random headstone you're drawn to. Read the names on the headstone aloud to honor their lives. Snap a photo of the grave and post with this spell: *These lives are a gift. / What's remembered, lives.*

Be sure to include a transcription of the headstones. BONUS POINTS for also posting or adding your images and data on crowdsourced genealogy websites such as Find a Grave so that others may know and find them.

@ HOW TO RETROGRADE

When a planet goes into retrograde motion, the areas it rules come under a microscope.

WHAT TO DO: Keep these aspects and timings in mind to be ready for when retrogrades happen:

PLANET	RULES	RETROGRADES EVERY . . .
Mercury	Communication, technology, contracts	Three times a year, lasts about 3 weeks
Venus	Love, relationships	Every 18 months, lasts about 40 days
Mars	Actions, desires, energy	Every two years for about 2½ months
Jupiter	Business, law, luck, religion, travel, wealth	Every year for about 4 months
Saturn	Structure	Once a year for about 4½ months
Uranus	Surprise, the unexpected	Every year for about 5 months
Neptune	Dreams, psychic powers, creativity	Every year for about 6 months

Share upcoming retrograde dates on your platform of choice and swap tips and tricks for dealing with them.

🖼 🎥 PRESS PAUSE

Feeling overwhelmed? Like everything is moving so fast that you can't even think? It's time to press "pause." When life is overcrowded and overbearing, use this spell to pause and collect yourself.

WHAT TO DO: You will need some lavender oil and amethyst. Both the stone and the flower (scent) are excellent for calming and restoring balance. Begin to ground and center by putting a dab of the oil on your wrists and temples; the act of having to stop and do this will start the process. The scent will activate your senses to help your body cooperate. Lavender's spiritual qualities will assist in focusing, as will the amethyst.

Place the amethyst on a flat surface and make a video. Move around the stone. Record for about one to three seconds, then pause. Snap a photo of the amethyst, and then continue recording for another one to three seconds. (Alternatively, you can record the video in slow-motion—be sure the film stops for a second in the middle; this is your "pause.") Share with the spell: *#stop for just a moment / I catch my breath. #breathe / #stop*

◢ DEFUSING THE LOVE BOMB

It's hard to escape the love bomb—from friends or lovers—especially if you are confidence challenged. Know the early signs (superfast emotional intimacy, being showered with gifts and compliments), and use this spell to defuse that bomb and stay safe.

WHAT TO DO: Because love and friendship are sensitive and private topics, if you suspect you're being love-bombed and try this spell, keep your post neutral and general to avoid reciprocity, stalking, or unwanted attacks. Love bombers don't bomb with real love; most likely, their motives come from a more selfish place. Get yourself a dozen red roses (or pink if you're dealing with a friendship, and yellow if it's a family member). Fill a large shallow bowl with water. Make a video showing just your hands; film yourself clipping the heads of the roses as if you're cutting the wires on a bomb, one by one, to defuse it. Go slowly, and carefully. As you cut each rose, say: *Love bomb defused, I am free!* Set each head in the water so that it floats freely. End with the roses floating in the water. Post the video on your platform of choice, no explanation or spell needed. Look at it when you need strength to remind you that you are free and enough.

📹 👁 MAGIC MIRROR FOR VISION

Mirror, mirror, on my phone, show me now, how I have grown . . . Mirrors are powerful magical tools for self-examination, scrying, and trance work. When you look into the mirror of the great web, what do you see? What will you say?

WHAT TO DO: The internet is an expression of our collective consciousness. Use the selfie mode on your camera as a magic mirror to see and get guidance. Do this work in a quiet place where you will not be disturbed. Set up your camera beforehand so that it captures your face. Ground and center; breathwork will help with this. When you're ready, look into the camera the way you would look into the mirror. Look straight into your own eyes (this can be startling). Breathe. If you've practiced with mirror work before, speak from your heart—or you can try this incantation: *Web, deep and wide, what do I need to know? / Where shall you guide, and your wisdom show?* Breathe. Then stop your video. Edit it so that only your spell is captured. Share as a temporary post (one rarely scries once). You may get responses (block and ignore trolls if you post publicly—and see April 14). If you're camera shy, only share with those you trust. Either way, you have "spoken" to the web—watch for signs.

▶ COMMUNICATION CANDLES

Need help finding the right words? A communication candle will help. You'll need a yellow candle that comes in a jar—the kind where you can take the candle out. (Yellow is for good outcomes, and the color associated with the planet Mercury.) You will also need some jasmine stick incense (for communication), aluminum foil, a manicure stick, clary sage oil (good for communication!), silver glitter, and chopped pine needles.

WHAT TO DO: Set up your camera so that it records the creation process: Take the candle out of the jar. Light the incense and place it in the jar. Loosely tent a piece of foil over the top to contain the smoke; this will prime the vessel. Using the manicure stick, carve the names of people you wish to communicate with and the symbol for Mercury (☿)—the planet that rules communication—all over the candle. As you work, say the spell: *I hear you, and you hear me, / Many thanks to Mercury!*

When you're done carving, dress the candle liberally with the clary sage oil, and then rub the silver glitter and pine needles all over it. Take the incense stick out of the jar, replace it with your candle, and, saying the spell aloud one last time, light it up. Post the video with the spell overlaid in text or with your voice. Likes, shares, views, and comments will help to clarify communication.

📹 CHECKMATE ROADBLOCKS

Chess is about strategy. But even with the best planning, you may hit roadblocks and walls. Turn a chessboard into a spell board for roadblock removal.

WHAT TO DO: Set up a blank chessboard. Select a piece to represent you; do not use any of the pawns, rooks, or bishops. Whatever color you use for yourself, use the opposite color for the other pieces. Place your chosen piece at the intersection of the center four squares (between the fourth and fifth horizontal and vertical rows). In the squares immediately surrounding the center four, place the rooks and bishops at opposite corners, and fill in the eight squares with pawns; this formation should create a box around the piece that represents you. Snap a photo. Say the spell (repeat as you complete each step): *Clear the path, out of the way! / That I may move ahead today.*

On one side of the box, move one of the pawns diagonally into the next square, then take a photo. Do the same with the other pawn and take a photo. One square at a time, move the piece that represents you out of the square and off the board.

Stitch the images together to make a stop-motion video and overlay it with the spell as text or a voice-over. Leave the video up until your roadblock has been removed.

@ DIGITAL CUTUPS

Cutups are nothing new, and the concept is simple: You cut text out of larger works—sometimes a handful of words, a whole line, or even paragraphs—and then rearrange and assemble them to create something unique.

WHAT TO DO: You can do this magic completely online or you can actually cut up pages (or copies of pages) from books and magazines. Think about what you are trying to manifest and keep it in mind when you're online (or reading). When you're drawn to a piece of writing, be it a poem, blog post, novel, or other work, highlight or cut out passages that speak to you—or you can choose randomly. If you're working digitally, use a tool like Snip and Sketch rather than typing out the lines to emphasize the collective nature of this spell.

When you have a collection of words and phrases, ground and center, then play with them. What are you drawn to based on your current needs? Arrange and rearrange your words until it feels right. If you've physically cut paper, snap a photo of your final spell. Save the image of your cutup spell if you've worked digitally. Post the spell as a picture on your platform of choice with your intention, along with the list of works and authors you cited (this also adds the energy of each individual author and work to your spell)!

🖼 @ WHEEL OF BLESSINGS

Never underestimate the role of chance and randomness and luck in our lives. We like to believe we have control, and we do, over our own reactions to whatever life throws at us. In the tarot, the Wheel of Fortune reminds us of the certainty of change, and that nothing is permanent, good or bad. That said, create a divinatory tool to share to help yourself and others through the process.

WHAT TO DO: Create an online spinner to send blessings. Use a free game-making generator to create a spinning game. Remember, computer-generated randomness is not random; if enough people participate, a pattern will emerge. The spinner is a tool to prompt magic that comes with views and tries and likes, and comments—which you may not see or be aware of.

Ground and center, and make a list of all the blessings you would like to encounter: kindness, respect, acceptance, love, success, contentment, peace . . . then feed them into the spin generator. Share on your platform of choice with this incantation: *Here's the deal: / Spin the Wheel. / Where it stops, / The blessings drop.*

Any blessing you bestow on others through this tool will also be bestowed on you whether you witness them or not. And you can play, too!

@ TAKE NOTE—BE GRATEFUL!

Count and share your blessings and they'll grow. Let's create a virtual blessing ledger.

WHAT TO DO: Open the notes app on your phone. You can also do this as a document on your computer, laptop, or tablet. Before you enter anything, take three deep cleansing breaths and ground. Next, consider why you're here and doing this (intention!). Be honest and be grateful.

At the top of the page, enter "Blessing x 3." Every day make at least one entry about something that makes you happy, even if it's small. If you have more than one, enter that, too—enter it all. You can also date each entry, especially if the day was an occasion you want to recall in detail or celebrate later. You don't have to share every blessing, but each week share one in some way, whether it's a text or an email to a friend or posting a temporary story or permanent post. Just putting it out there encourages growth. When others support or give it a heart, it gets bigger. It comes alive when others comment or share their appreciation inspired by you!

When you open the document or note, read it fully before making the next entry. Save your list to track happiness patterns across months and years. Swap lists with a friend to grow each other's joy. Watch more blessings roll in and begin the process again!

📷 🎥 @ AN APPLE A DAY

Apples—from which the pomander gets its name—bring their magic to this spell: love, abundance, and health. Cloves are cleansing, and rosemary is protective.

WHAT TO DO: You'll need an apple, a jar of cloves, and a sprig of rosemary. Use a nail or a needle to puncture the apple's flesh and core; this will make it easier to insert the cloves and rosemary sprig. Ground and center, and focus on intentions for being healthy, overcoming illnesses big and small, and feeling your best. Picture this radiating outward to all who will encounter the spell. Capture a video of the creation of your pomander. Cover the whole apple in cloves, but be sure to keep a small area at the top and bottom clear—this is where the rosemary will go in. As you drive in each clove say the spell: *By rosemary sprig, apple, and clove, / Good hale and health to all who behold!* Once the apple is completely full of cloves, pass the sprig of rosemary through its heart, top to bottom. You can share a video of the pomander's crafting, or a video or image of the finished spell, sealed with the words as a caption. BONUS POINTS for using alt text to describe your spell for all five senses for those who may not be able to experience your ritual visually, audibly, or olfactorily.

MINI GROUNDING SESH

Taking time out to ground and center is necessary for magical practice—and it also boosts our energies for mundane purposes.

WHAT TO DO: Use your calendar app to set reminders and send invites for regular, short group magical practices. Try to do one of these a month. The important thing about this ritual is that it is consistent and fast. Set a time for your group ritual; make it the same time each time. Keep the length of your session consistent and brief, about five minutes max. Having your background image and music (soft and peaceful!) on as people come in will limit distractions. Give people two to three minutes to join, and start and end the ritual on time. For example, set the time for noon, begin at 12:03 p.m., and end at 12:08 p.m. Whoever can make it, makes it. Understand that sometimes you might be a party of one. Be mindful of the time if you are working with people living in different time zones. Keep it simple and scripted: *We are here to ground and refresh together. We'll take three deep breaths, in through the nose, out through the mouth* (lead the breathing by count). *Now we share the frequency of om* (lead a chant for as long as you can hold the note). *We are grateful for this time together. Hail and farewell!* Say goodbye, and close your meeting app.

🖼️ @ MANIFEST WITH WANDS

In the tarot, the suit of Wands represents the element of fire, inspiration, and creativity. Use this tarot spell to jump-start your process (especially if you're stuck).

WHAT TO DO: Pull out the Ace, 2, 3, and 4 of Wands cards. One at a time, lay them out in order, layering each card slightly over the next. As you place each card, say the accompanying spell that goes with it:

★ The Ace of Wands symbolizes beginnings. *It starts with a spark, a twist of fire . . .* To this line of the spell, speak about what you're stuck on.

★ The 2 of Wands represents your plan to bring your idea to fruition: *Each step brings me close to what I aspire . . .* Speak about the steps you've taken so far.

★ The 3 of Wands is a moment of waiting: *Part of magic is waiting and noting, wishing and watching, believing and hoping . . .* Speak about where you need help, or what you are waiting for.

★ The 4 of Wands is a card of celebration and harvest: *We did it!* Add words about how you would like whatever it is you are waiting for or working on to turn out.

Snap a photo of the cards with the words of the spell. (You don't have to share your personal details.)

# @ CRYSTAL GRIDS

Crystal grids draw on the power of patterns and stones to facilitate intention. For this grid, we'll use stones that support healthy relationships:

★ Trust: rose quartz

★ Clear communication: clear quartz

★ Attraction: hematite

★ Shared interests: lapis lazuli

★ Mutual respect: sodalite

★ Selfless love: rhodochrosite

★ Passion: carnelian

WHAT TO DO: Set your camera to record. Take a moment to visualize your relationship—either with a specific person or generally, if you are looking to make new connections. When you're ready, place your stones one by one: Starting from the outside, make an outline of a heart with one type of stone. Build the heart inward—what you use may depend on your supply. Keep your relationship in your mind and intentions as you build! When you get to the center stone, use it to trace what you've built before setting it in the center. Be sure your video shows the whole grid before you stop the recording. Share the video on your platform of choice with the spell: *Day to day, stone to stone, / Build bridges of love and bring it home!*

✨ see PAST SENSATION

We're assaulted with information on a daily basis, and sometimes it's hard to tell what's real, what's not, what's been embellished, or what's been left out. Be aware of your feelings as you scroll. If you start to get overwhelmed, use this spell to help you keep your cool and not allow your emotions to be manipulated.

WHAT TO DO: When a first impression imprints itself in your memory it may trigger an emotional reaction that's hard to erase. It's difficult, even if more information comes out, to unsee that first exposure. When you encounter a story or image that pushes your buttons, STOP READING/VIEWING (unless, of course, it is an emergency that requires you to act immediately). This is not to say that you should be uninformed—go back later, from a different place with a different frame of mind. Light up some rosemary, cinnamon, or sandalwood incense—all good for clarity—and take some time to ground and center. When you feel grounded, think about the information to which you were exposed and examine your feelings. Say the spell: *Opinion? Fact? The story told, / Keep clear and calm until I see, know all.* Give yourself some space and return to the information, keeping in mind how you feel. If you need to ground again, do it! The one thing we can control is our reactions—don't give up that power!

🎥 A SPELL TO QUELL ANGER

Anger, like any human emotion, is natural and should not be repressed. Anger helps us emphasize our worth. But like anything, when taken to an extreme, anger can be damaging, especially to the person carrying it. Use this tarot spell to help navigate anger and let it go.

WHAT TO DO: Use the 7 of Swords for this ritual. In this card, a figure sneaks away from a fairground, carrying off a bundle of five swords He leaves two behind. This image can be interpreted in many ways, but for our purposes, the five swords that the figure clutches symbolize the anger you're carrying.

Take a video of yourself (or just your hands if you're camera shy) holding the card, and then dropping it. As you do, say: *I let my anger go. / I no longer need you, / But I thank you.*

Layer the spell over the video either as text or as a voice-over when you post it—or you can leave it off. The important thing is that your intention is embedded into the video. (Everyone does not need to know what you're up to!)

◤◢ SWEETEN JOB PROSPECTS

Create a honey jar to sweeten your job prospects (or current situation if there's some bitterness). You'll need honey, a small jar or bottle with a cork lid, paper, pen, a single star anise (to boost success), cinnamon powder (for inspiration), a piece of tiger's-eye that will fit into the jar, and a gold candle.

WHAT TO DO: Set your camera to time-lapse mode.

First, think of your intention. Are you looking for work or does your current job need sweetening? You can also use a honey jar to "sweeten" a deal if you're gigging (ask for more money, better terms, etc.). Keep your intention in mind, or even say it aloud as you work.

Keeping your intention in mind, place the star anise in the bottom of the bottle or jar, then fill it about halfway with honey. On the piece of paper write out what you want to sweeten in as much detail as possible. Sprinkle the paper with cinnamon, then wrap it around the tiger's-eye before placing it in the jar. Top the jar up with more honey, then cork it. Seal the jar with drips of wax from the candle, and stop the video without showing the finished jar—that's for you!

Sharing the video of the jar's creation magnifies the sweetening. Keep the finished jar in your workspace to maintain a sweet environment for your endeavors.

🎥 @ BOX FULLA secrets

When Frigg, queen of the Norse pantheon, has a secret, there's one other deity she trusts enough to keep it: Fulla, her sister-goddess and handmaiden. Fulla watches over Frigg's most prized possessions: her golden circlet (crown), her shoes (of course!), and her box of ash wood; to this day, the contents of the box are uncertain. Fulla is *that* good. Use this spell to invoke Fulla's energy to keep your secrets under lock and key and be discerning about who you trust with them. You'll need a shoebox, and some gold (to represent the goddess) and black (protective) ribbon.

WHAT TO DO: Ground and center. Take some time to write your secrets on a piece of paper, then fold it up. Set up your camera to record. Take the lid off the box, place the paper with your secrets inside, then replace the lid. Using the black and gold ribbons, tie up the box and secure it with three knots, saying: *Box Fulla secrets, safekeep what's inside, / And help me discern in whose trust I may rely.*

Take the box to a place where it is safe to burn it. Record this, too (you may need to pause your video and restart it again). Share your video with the spell as a caption to magnify the protection of your secrets.

👁 🖼 NAME YOUR PC DAY

Accept it: we have relationships with technology. We work with it, play with it, and communicate with it. We use it for planning and purchasing, socializing, and, of course, magic. Today is "Name Your PC Day." You have a magical name—do the same for your technology.

WHAT TO DO: Your tools are your allies. Arthur has Excalibur; the Blue Meanie has his glove. Swords, hands, and computers are objects associated with the air element that embody thought and intellect. What does your device do for you? How do you feel about it?

Ground and center, then meditate on this. Gloves and scabbards of old were embellished with spells, charms, and monograms; take this magical step for your device. Once you've chosen a name, create a badge or sticker with it to put on your device's cover. As you place it on your device, say: *Process quickly / Protect all data / Please serve me well, this is my will!* Snap a photo and share as a temporary post to strengthen a healthy bond between you and your device.

LOVE SLIDE MAGIC BOOST

The love slide (heart-eyed smiley on a sliding scale) is a quick and easy way for friends to drop some love on your intentions and boost them up.

WHAT TO DO: Ground and center, then post an image of your desire—it can be the actual thing or a symbol, depending on what you're comfortable with. Make the post with intention—visualize whatever it is you're trying to manifest coming to pass. Add the sliding scale heart and picture that as it slides up, your vision and desire become more clearly realized. Every time your post is loved up, someone else has lent their energy to it. BONUS POINTS for returning the love to all who engage.

🖼 @ WHERE TO? SPELL

We're in Sagittarius season! Join the travelers of the zodiac with this spell for adventure.

WHAT TO DO: You'll need a paper map and some tumbled crystals. Set your camera up to record. Think of the purpose of your trip and use the list below to choose your stones (you'll need three of whichever you choose):

★ Business, money: tiger's-eye

★ Love: rose quartz

★ Adventure: sunstone

★ Rest and relaxation: fluorite

★ Spiritual: selenite

★ Bonding time with friends: blue agate

Lay the map out on the floor in front of you. Close your eyes, say this spell, and drop or toss the stones on the map: *Where shall I go? [name of stone], tell me so!* Where they land will give guidance. If some of the stones land off the map, try again. If the stones go off multiple times, you may want to consider doing a different kind of trip or expanding or shrinking your borders. Take a photo of the map and share on your platform of choice with the caption: *Where shall I go?* to get further input and energy from friends and followers. Remember to hashtag the names of the towns, states, etc., along with your caption.

⁄˟ THE DARK QUEEN

As we've explored, we've found that astrology can tell us much about ourselves (January 6, February 12, May 8, June 15, July 12, September 16, December 22). There are placements and aspects that mostly everyone knows about, but the more obscure aspects can be just as revealing. Black Moon Lilith is one such. Named for Adam's ill-famed first wife (equal to Adam, rather than having been made from a part of him and banished from Eden for asserting her rights), Lilith is the location opposite of the moon at its farthest placement at the moment of your birth.

WHAT TO DO: Enter your birth date, sign, and place into an online natal chart generator or Black Moon Lilith Calculator. You want to retrieve the zodiac sign and house where Lilith sits. Black Moon Lilith is the *Mano Figa* of astrology (August 14). Finding her location in your birth chart and the house and zodiac sign that sits with her will reveal your primal instincts, and your deepest desires. Share your findings with trusted friends and loved ones—we are all on this journey together, and sharing will bring insights for both you and them. Note: it's worth repeating not to share your personal details—birth date, time, and place—publicly! #bewarewhatyoushare

🖼 @ DOORWAYS TO FAIRYLAND

Fairies will visit you and bless your house with sparkle and mischief, but they need a door to pass through. You'll need 2 cups of cinnamon powder (passion), 1 cup of applesauce (healing), and about ¼ cup of nontoxic craft glue (this will make your door sturdier). You'll also need a small round crystal (for the doorknob).

WHAT TO DO: Set up your camera to record the creation of your fairy door in time-lapse mode (or you can just share images of the final, magical object). Mix all the ingredients together (except for the crystal) until they're thoroughly combined. Add applesauce if the mixture is too dry, or more cinnamon if it's too wet. While you're working, chant: *Faerie doors all over town / Greetings, fae friends, come on down!* Roll the dough out so that it's about ¼ inch thick. Cut your door into any shape you desire; you can also add details like windows and texture. Carefully place the door on a baking tray and dry it out in a low oven (200° Fahrenheit) for about two hours. The door should be completely solid before you handle it. Use hot glue to attach the doorknob. Take your door outside and lean it carefully against a tree or lay it flat on the ground like a trapdoor. Snap a photo and share the image with the spell overlaid as text or a voice-over.

 @ FOODIE PICS MAGIC

Pictures and videos of food awaken the senses; there are some posts where you can literally taste what you're seeing. Watching food preparation is also strangely comforting. Images of food you see on social media may inspire you to try some recipes yourself, or to support a small business if the meal is from a restaurant (December 10). The next time you feel inspired to share a meal on socials, do so with the intention of ensuring that healing food is always on hand for you and all who see your post.

WHAT TO DO: Before you post the creation of or a finished meal on your platform of choice, think about the ingredients and the magical properties they convey.

★ The colors of the fruits and vegetables

★ The healing properties of herbs and spices

★ The elements used in preparation: water, earth (salt), fire, and air (a convection oven)

★ The love and skill that went into the meal

Visualize all these things present in the food you're about to share. Post with the caption: *Nourish the body, nourish the soul. / Fill empty bellies, but no empty calories. / May you never know hunger and always know health!* You can also post this spell when you are reposting someone else's food pics!

@ TREASURE THIS DAY

Every day is an adventure that puts opportunity in your way. Let go of expectations and open your mind and heart. Today you will find treasure—will you recognize it?

WHAT TO DO: This spell will require you to be in the moment. Do NOT capture anything on or off camera, not a picture, sound, or video. Don't even make a note about it. Whatever you come across, commit it to memory so that you can talk about it later. When you begin your day, or when you read this, ground and center. Say aloud: *I'm finding treasure today!* Dab patchouli oil on the backs of your knees, on your wrists, at your temples, and behind your ears. Patchouli grounds, helps with focus, reduces stress, and facilitates connection to the spirit world. It's also lucky. By using it, you activate your mind, body, and spirit to connect to the world and to *see*; this will help you be aware of the treasure(s) in your path. As you go through the day, make a mental note of any treasure you encounter. Repeat it to yourself along with: *I found treasure today!* At the end of the day, write a post, words only, that tells the story of the treasures you found. BONUS POINTS for using colored text. For example, if you met with someone who, whether they know it or not, healed you in some way, use green (healing) text. End with the spell: *I found treasure today!*

 PURGE!

Everyone has value—and yet, sometimes our online world can become a crowded and cluttered place that is peppered with posts and news that we do not need or want to see. Spring is not the only time for cleaning. Take time to revisit what needs refreshing in your virtual *and* physical houses. Unfollowing and muting accounts is nothing personal. Clearing and cleaning is looking after yourself.

WHAT TO DO: Take this day to look through the accounts you follow. If this is something you want to share, you may want to make a post about it—but that's entirely up to you. You may even want to write the post *without* posting it to examine your own feelings—why are you unfollowing certain accounts? What does this desire reveal about your motivations? What are you really after? Keep a beautiful piece of rose quartz close by to give you strength and resolve, and to remind you that what you are doing is an act of self-love and self-care.

When you're ready, examine each account that you follow and meditate on it. Is it time for you to set this person or account free? Visualize the account bathed in pink light and unfollow with love. This subtle magic initiates the release in a positive way. If you cannot bring yourself to unfollow at this time, mute the account and revisit it in the spring.

NEED A HAND?

Everyone needs a hand sometimes. Whatever the lift, try this spell to assist in getting the helpful hands you seek.

WHAT TO DO: Take a moment to ground and center and meditate on the kind of help you need. Keep this in mind as a mantra throughout the day: *SOS! Lend a hand!* Communicate your intention and need through imagery. Hands can be just as expressive as the face; capture images of people's hands doing the kind of work for which you need help (writing, heavy lifting, holding, etc.). Videos will work as well; use whatever medium you are most comfortable with and works best for you. Post the images and videos as a series with the caption: *SOS! Lend a hand! / I need help with [name your intention].* Likes, views, shares, and comments will boost your intention and the magic.

 **@ SOUND UP!**

Sharing the magic of place and space makes magical locations and the energy they lend more accessible, particularly places where sounds are healing.

WHAT TO DO: Where are you right now? A bustling city street? Feel the energy and passion of the people around you. By the sea? Let the soothing sound and sight of the water wash over you.

Walking a forest path? Listen to the call of birds and the whisper of the wind as it passes through leaves and branches all around you . . . magical, right? Stop (where it is safe to do so). Pull out your camera and take three deep breaths. Make a thirty-to sixty-second video of your surroundings, being sure to also capture the sound. Post your video with this caption: *At this moment, be with me. / Stop. Breathe. Listen. See!* BONUS POINTS for using alt text to describe your place for all five senses for those who may not be able to experience your ritual visually, audibly, or olfactorily.

Icons—religious paintings—were created to be windows into the spirit world. Their eyes watch over and protect those under their gaze. They also serve as prayer portals. Who lives in spirit now who would be your icon? Use this spell to honor their memory and connect with them for comfort and guidance when you need it.

WHAT TO DO: Find an image of a person that you admire, and that has passed into spirit. Head and neck shots work best, with the person gazing straight into the camera or out of the canvas. You can post the creation of your icon or just the finished spell. If you're capturing the creation, start recording. Mount the image on a piece of cardboard and paint out the background in gold or silver (many icons incorporate metal). Surround the head of the person with a halo of lapis lazuli (to connect to the spirit world), celestite (angel crystal), and quartz crystal (to amplify the powers of the other stones and your intention). As you place the stones and glue them in place, say the spell aloud: *Dear [name], / Bringer of comfort, a light in the dark, / Watch, protect, and open your heart.*

Post your video or the image of your icon on your favorite platform(s) and caption with the spell. Repost as needed when you or anyone else need your icon's wisdom.

@ **RABBIT! RABBIT!**

It's the first of the month, and so many people are posting "Rabbit! Rabbit!" for luck for the next thirty or so days. How? And . . . why? The "rabbit" part is obvious. Rabbits have long been seen as symbols of luck in many cultures (March 30). The trend to begin the first of the month with a rabbit fest started over a hundred years ago with a magazine featuring the phrase, and it stuck. But just because something is having a moment doesn't mean it's not magical.

WHAT TO DO: Incorporate and spread *Rabbit! Rabbit!* magic starting today.

★ Set your calendar and reminders to send you or wake you up with the spell. *Rabbit! Rabbit!* will be the first thing you hear when you wake up or check your texts or email.

★ Share a *Rabbit! Rabbit!* post on your platform of choice. BONUS POINTS for snapping a picture of a rabbit and overlaying it with the text of the spell.

★ Say the *Rabbit! Rabbit!* spell for luck on the first of every month (doesn't hurt to try!).

★ Before you go to sleep, say *Hare! Hare!* to seal the luck. You can also share a photo of a hare (different from a rabbit—longer ears and back legs) and overlay it with the spell. *Hare! Hare!* sounds like *Here! Here!*, which denotes agreement.

🎥 BEAT THE WINTER BLUES

As the days get shorter, it's easy to slip, without even realizing it, into the winter blues. Try this spell to nip those feelings in the bud and lighten things up.

WHAT TO DO: Record a video of this mood-boosting ritual. This is also another way to create sacred space as all the elements are present. Fill a clean spray bottle with water and add three fingerfuls of salt to it (that's water and earth accounted for!). Next, add at least 9 to 12 drops of bergamot oil; not only is this citrusy scented oil uplifting, but it also facilitates connection to spirit. That leaves us with two more elements to add. To represent fire, add a piece of amber (vitality) or sunstone (blessings—and it embodies the sun!). For air, add blue apatite or blue lace agate; both are great for clarity. Take note that it's not just about the individual elements, but how they work together; the blue and gold stones, constantly cleansed in salt water and heightened by the bergamot oil, uplift visually and through scent.

Swirl the bottle clockwise to mix and invoke the powers of the elements. Create a video showing your creation in action. Say the spell and give a spritz in the direction of the camera as if you are sharing it with all your friends and followers: *Lighten up! Feel joy! Feel safe! Feel inspired!*

@ POWERFUL POMANDER

Share the creation of a magical pomander. You'll need your camera, some oranges, lots of cloves, ribbon in colors that mirror your intentions, a marker, and a tapestry needle.

WHAT TO DO: Set up your camera to record in time-lapse mode. "Write" your intention in cloves on the orange (keep it short!) or create a symbol for it. Use the marker to draw out your pattern in dots on the orange's skin; every dot marks where you'll place a clove. Use the needle to drive a hole into each dot before pushing the cloves into the orange to save your fingers. Thread the ribbon through the tapestry needle and pass it carefully in through the bottom and out through the top of the orange. Pull the ribbon through, then pass the needle back through the top and out at the bottom so that you have a loop at the top of the orange and two loose ends at the bottom. Knot off the loop (make sure it's large enough so that you can hang the pomander), then slide the orange up the ribbons so that it lies tight against the knot. Tie a tightly knotted bow at the bottom to secure the orange in place. Share your video and caption it with: *Sending joy and protection to whoever sees this!* Whatever your personal intentions are will be magnified, and the general powers of the pomander will be shared with everyone.

🖼️ @ HEAL ANCESTRAL TRAUMA

For this spell, we'll use AI to create a tool for magic that can help you start to heal deep-seated hurts.

WHAT TO DO: Generational trauma suggests that we carry the burden of our ancestors—if not in our DNA, then in our habits. The way we were raised is based on the actions of previous generations, which may result in deep scars. Actually seeing ourselves in the past can be a catalyst for healing.

Use photo creation apps to blend actual pictures of you into historical portraits (many will do a first session for free). If you are aware of family issues that occurred during a specific time period, choose that era. If you have no information, look at the historical periods offered. Is there a particular time period that you're drawn to for any reason? As you make your choices, speak this incantation aloud: *Place my face in the glass of the past, / That I may see the pain that lasts.* When you have a collection of images, look through them. Some will be way off and not look or feel like you at all—but which ones do? Post the image or images of your choice with the incantation overlaid or as a caption. Likes and comments will boost this magic. Keep an eye out for signs of ancestral communication (found objects, music, scents that seem to appear out of nowhere and in dreams).

@ 🎥 DAMAGE CONTROL SPELL

Cleaning up messes (especially other people's messes) is not fun. When you have to do damage control, try this spell to assist your work and ease the cleanup. BONUS POINTS for having a specially designated broom for this purpose.

WHAT TO DO: Ground and center and think of your situation. Set your camera to record a video and take it with you around your home. Say aloud, "Where is the damage?" (because you can't always see where the damage is). Look for accumulated dust and dirt (because when you do damage control, the effects of that damage are starting to build).

When you find dust and dirt, stop, pause, and take a breath. Visualize the damage from your situation in the accumulated dust and dirt that you've found. Next, slowly and gently sweep the dust together (try not to just stir it around). As you do so, say the spell: *The damage is done, but I am not. / Cleanse the slate so that all may move on.* Pick up the accumulated dust with a damp cloth and discard it. (The water will further work to rectify your situation; as you throw the cloth away, picture the damage caused in your situation also being tossed.) Share your video with the spell as a caption (you may want to speed up parts of it). Keep the post up until your situation is resolved.

🖼 @ MAGIC COOKIE EXCHANGE

While you can't swap actual cookies online, you can share recipes (just about every ingredient in a cookie recipe has magical properties).

WHAT TO DO: Collect photos of magical cookie ingredients and overlay the magical properties of the ingredients with the photo (adapt this list; these are just suggestions):

GINGER: luck, longevity • CINNAMON: passion, money • CHOCOLATE: love, balance • CLOVE: focus, mental ability • LAVENDER: cleansing, calming • CARDAMOM: stress reduction • COCONUT: purification • RUM: dispel negativity • ORANGE: happiness

Stitch the images together in a sped-up video (or use a generator for this) and share on your profile with this caption:

Baking's first ingredient is love; screenshot another from the post above / To share the season's warmth and spirit and energize all those who see this! This is a magical cookie exchange! Screenshot this post—that is your ingredient, and what you are called to share.

Before the winter solstice, bake some cookies and post your recipe with the spell and the hashtag #magiccookieexchange. All who see will share in this magic.

@ GNOME HOME MAGIC

Whether they're kitted out in biker duds or in their traditional pointy red hats, everyone loves a gnome. Our favorite garden decorations are cousins of Scandinavian *nisse*, ancestor spirits who also symbolize abundance, fertility, and prosperity.

WHAT TO DO: Because they embody the earth element, gnomes are excellent magical partners for finding, creating, and manifesting "home," whatever that may mean to you. Keep your camera handy and your eyes open for gnomes in the wild. You may see them in front yards, community gardens, or while shopping. When you see one and it calls to you (this is important, and you'll know when it's calling—you will want to stop and look!), ask permission (of the gnome) and snap its photo. Share the image with the incantation: *My home needs help, dear magical neighbor. Please, help me with this labor!* Then state what your home needs to be more of a haven for you. If all is well, simply ask for a blessing: *Guardian spirit, earthly gnome, send your blessings to my home!*

@ ASSEMBLAGE ALTAR

Found objects are Divine messages. Coins on the street, playing cards, feathers, a single earring . . . What does your collection of found items spell out for you?

WHAT TO DO: This spell is a ritual that will start today (or whenever you decide to begin) and will build over time. This will be the spot for your altar. Some people like to use a cloth, slab of crystal, or smoothed wood (like a natural-shaped charcuterie board) as a base; use what feels right for you. Snap a picture of the empty altar and save it.

Go about your day and keep your eyes open—what does the Universe throw in your path? An interesting stone? A coin? What you find does not need to be something dropped on the street. Perhaps you're in a store and something catches your eye—something you were not looking for—that counts, too. Every time you add something to the altar, take a picture. When it feels complete to you, take a final picture. Stitch the individual images together to make a stop-motion video of the altar growing, and share it with the spell: *Into my path, and into my hands / The Universe put these— / What should I understand?* Feel free to add your own interpretations; likes and comments will grow your understanding.

WRITTEN IN STONE

Crystals convey messages, and when put together (so long as they're not frenemies; April 16), they form spells. How do you say that in "crystal"?

WHAT TO DO: Arrange your crystals and snap a photo. Cast some quickie crystal spells by sharing images of crystal combos infused with intention. Remember, arrangement and background add further energies to the spell. Think of what your intention is, and your spell will work accordingly. Use the above combos as a guide; be inspired and create your own, based on your needs.

★ Be gone!: rutilated quartz, black tourmaline

★ Live, laugh, love: amber, rhodochrosite, aquamarine

★ Leave me alone!: selenite, moonstone

★ She persisted: blue lace agate, black onyx

Caption the photo with the names of the crystals and the hashtags #writteninstone, #sayitwithcrystals, and #crystalspell. Ask friends and followers for the vibe they get from your photo. You can reveal the spell if you wish in the captions and comments.

12
—
09

🖼 @ SMALL BUSINESS SPELL

When you support a small business with your attention and dollars, you support years of practice, skill honing, emotional ups and downs, and sweat. It's a worthy investment—throw some magic at that, too!

WHAT TO DO: Whether it's a restaurant, artist, or delivery service—whatever service or product they provide, give your fave small business a shout-out to raise their visibility, then add magic and intention to amplify. Share an image or video of the small business you want to support. Take an image of the business's product, logo, or service and surround it with these crystals (chips or tumbles work just as well as points!).

★ Malachite transforms; it helps spin straw into gold, and it's also suitable for surviving change.

★ Tiger's-eye protects and facilitates strength and prosperity.

★ Amethyst opens intuition and empathy.

★ Quartz crystal amplifies the power of the other stones, plus it draws useful people.

Snap a photo and caption it with the business's name (tag them if they are also on your platform), and this spell: *[name of business]: Try them! See them! Support them! #supportsmallbusiness*

@ 🎥 TIES THAT BIND

You can cut cords to end a binding (July 16)—but you can also knot cords to seal a commitment. Be sure not to tie the knots too tightly; even in long-term relationships, no one wants to be bound and trapped.

WHAT TO DO: You'll need some cords in the color that defines your relationship. (You can use multiple cords if your relationship is multifaceted; yellow and orange cords can represent a friendship that is also a creative partnership; green and red cords can represent a business relationship that is passionate about what it produces; red and pink cords can represent a romantic partnership that is also passionate. Use the colors that resonate with you, your traditions, and your culture.) Set up your camera to record. Have each person in the relationship pass them through their hands, then clasp hands and wrap the cords comfortably over your hands, visualizing the relationship as it is today. Wrap the cords a second time, visualizing your future path together. Then wrap a final time, tie a loose knot, and say the spell together: *By the law of three times three, bound in love for posterity. / Bound, not burdened, called, not compelled, / May these cords support and serve us well.* Share your video, or a picture of your bound hands with the spell as the caption.

@ COMFORT AND JOY

Here at the year's end is the last day to tap into natural and recurring successions of numbers through month, date, and time. Multiple twelves indicate completion, comfort, and joy. Added up and funneled down to a single digit, we get the number 6, which indicates renewal (end of one year, beginning of another). Take the time into consideration—12 + 12 + 12 + 12 and you will work down to 3, the perfect number (see February 14).

WHAT TO DO: Set a reminder to take a screenshot of the time at 12:12 p.m. (sorry, only one shot at this one!). Share the screenshot as a temporary post with the intention: *To all who see this, / Receive comfort and joy! / Share to spread the love* ♥ Views, likes, and shares amplify; and by sending comfort and joy out, the Universe, like a mirror, will send it back to you.

12
12

🎥 POTATOES FOR PROBLEMS

Potatoes are practically perfect in every way. Besides being delicious, they're great for grounding spells and rituals because of the way they grow. And being in the nightshade family and because they're 80 percent water, they are connected to the moon. Use this spell when you need to shrink something, be it a situation, an attitude, a seemingly impossible project—potato is there for you!

WHAT TO DO: Ground and center. Set up your camera to record. Wash the potato in salt and water, then carefully pass it through the flame of a candle and incense to bless it with the elements. Hold the potato in your hand. It's solid but *feel* its water (it may actually feel wobbly!). Now peel it, and as you do so, say this spell, visualizing that which you want to shrink get smaller and smaller: *What no longer serves, I slice away, piece by piece, day by day.* Keep peeling until the potato is completely gone, or until it feels right to you (progress, not perfection!). You can also use this spell to remove unwanted energies—use a potato that has some dark spots or overgrown eyes. Peel those parts away, using the same spell and visualizing any negativity falling away with every slice you make. Compost the peelings and share your video with the spell as the caption to magnify its power.

🎥 @ NUTMEG MONEY JAR

Use this spell to conjure up some cash (or equivalents; read on!). You'll need a mason jar, whole nutmegs (money drawing and practicality), and pennies—lots of these! Even if they are no longer true copper, pennies are excellent conductors of energy.

WHAT TO DO: Start recording. In the center of your space, place a mason jar. Set it down so that you can hear the glass meeting the surface of the space (but not hard enough to crack or break it)—sound is important in this video! Next, say the words of the spell: *Pockets are empty, account is drained, / Money, fall down on me like rain!* And drop a single nutmeg into the jar. Make sure you capture the *plunk!* as it hits the glass. Keep repeating the spell while more quickly dropping more nutmegs into the jar. As you start to run out of nutmegs, start dropping the pennies in, too. Keep adding pennies—fistfuls if you can, until they dash out over the sides. End with the spell. Share your video on your platform of choice with the caption: *Money, fall down on us like rain!* Shares, likes, and comments will amplify! Note: financial resources may come in the form of cash, a gift, more time, or a cancellation.

 # @ TIME MUNCHERS

Time munchers turn a five-minute conversation into an hours-long engagement—and not because you're an active participant. Use this spell to reclaim your time.

WHAT TO DO: As always, take practical steps to protect yourself. This may include letting that call go to voicemail, scheduling strict periods for engagement, or having a preplanned exit strategy. Go into your favorite board game and select a red piece to represent your time muncher, and a black piece to represent you (checkers work well for this spell!). Draw or print out an image of an hourglass. Decide how much time you can or want to give to this person. Write the number in black right directly over the throat of the glass (where the upper and lower globes meet, and where the sand passes through). Anoint the red piece with sandalwood oil (to promote peace and quiet) and place it in the upper globe of the hourglass. Anoint the black piece with peppermint oil (for strength—you may need it to make a hard stop) and place it in the lower globe. As you place the pieces, say the spell: *[X] minutes is all you get, our convo is over, don't be upset.*

Snap a photo of your hourglass spell and share with the caption: *Time is valuable.* No need to name names to share the whole story. The spell image is enough.

@ WINTER TRAVEL SPELL

Holiday season is travel season! In addition to practicing practical travel safety, post a safe travel spell so you and your friends and followers stay safe while you revel.

WHAT TO DO: Open your favorite online map tool to create a map of your trip. Travel safety isn't just about getting from point A to point B; it's about being safe in your destination environment, too, so include any stops you think you'll be making. Print the map out on the largest piece of paper you have available (you can also do all this digitally if you wish). Use a black (protective) marker to trace your route. As you do this, visualize yourself arriving at and enjoying every destination safely. Next, outline your route with a blue highlighter to give your trip a protective aura in case of detours or a change of plans. Write a protective spell around the border of the map; this covers more area and gives voice to your intention: *Wherever I go, I am aware. / Wherever I go, I am safe. / Wherever I go, I am prepared. / Wherever I go, I am protected.* Blur the map before sharing it, then post on your platform of choice. By not sharing your coordinates publicly, it will protect your travel plans (as well as yourself and your home).

🎥 @ VANILLA STAR AMULET

Like a human baby, vanilla pods take about nine months to ripen. That may not seem like a long time, but when compared to other "beans" that take only weeks to mature, it really is! This built-in quality makes vanilla good for work that requires time and endurance. Vanilla also brings warmth to ignite passion (for love or projects) and keep you going. You'll need five vanilla pods.

WHAT TO DO: Set your camera to record the center of your space. One at a time place each vanilla pod to form a star. Speak the accompanying spell as you place each pod:

★ Top to bottom right: *Spirit to Fire, burn, inspire.*

★ Bottom right to center, left: *Fire to Air, time and to spare.*

★ Straight across from left to right: *Air to Water, thought and emotion.*

★ Middle right, and down to the left: *Water to Earth, time is worth.*

★ Lower left to the top: *Earth to Spirit, live it, feel it.*

Share the video on your platform of choice with the caption: *For now and tomorrow, as long as it takes. I am empowered by elementals' embrace.*

🎥 @ MINT COCOA SPELL

You can share a cup or bowl of your favorite cocoa—and all of its magic—even in cyberspace.

WHAT TO DO: Before you perform this spell, think about the power of the ingredients:

★ Milk: cleansing, purifying, and nourishing newness (plant-based milks will carry the magical properties of those plants)

★ Chocolate: love of all kinds

★ Marshmallows: a concoction of corn syrup (corn, abundance), honey (healing, cleansing), gelatin (healing), sugar (attraction), water (cleansing, water element), salt (protective, earth element), and vanilla (long-term magic, December 17)

★ Peppermint: healing, money magic, banishing negativity

Make your cocoa. Use a peppermint stick and stir clockwise to invoke the energies of the elements used to make the brew. Drop in some marshmallows. Before you sip, set up your camera to record a video. Then, raise your mug and say: *Farewell, Autumn, Winter is upon us, / I raise a toast to love and abundance. / Protection for all in the coming year, / Minimal stress, and nothing to fear!* Share your post with the toast as a caption.

 @ FLAT LAYS FOR SUCCESS!

Flat lay shots are magic spells "spelled" out in clothes!

WHAT TO DO: Think about your needs, then start pulling out clothes, shoes, and accessories. Visualize success. See and feel yourself moving easily through whatever it is you have planned—and pivoting if those plans are disrupted in any way. ALWAYS go with your personal style and wear what makes you feel your best:

★ Expecting confrontation? Pair black fitted garments with a dash of red for confidence, gold jewelry for success, or silver if you want to hold anything back (silver = mystery).

★ Consider comfy green and blue garments for doctor's appointments. Green is healing, blue will maintain peace and calm.

★ Date night? Try reds and pinks for passion, lavenders and purples for cosmic connections. Blind date? Incorporate some black for protection.

Also think about stance: place sleeves akimbo for confidence. Legs can dance for happiness. Share your flat lays with the hashtags #magicalflatlay and #dressforsuccess. Any engagement will magnify your energy. If you have to choose between outfits, get the vibe from your community.

🎥 CRACKERS FOR WISHES

Whatever holiday traditions you follow, consider adding crackers (the paper pull-apart kind rather than the crunchy kind) to your celebrations. If you've ever pulled a wishbone, you're ready for crackers. (Birds' breastbones are lucky charms; each person takes hold of one side of the breastbone and pulls. The bone cracks—and the person holding the larger end gets their wish.) Crackers work the same way: the person holding the larger end wins the prizes inside—a paper crown, a toy, and a piece of paper with a joke or motto on it—magical gifts. Turn holiday cracker pulling into a ritual.

WHAT TO DO: Create a sacred space with a salt circle (August 20). Have your cracker pullers stand inside. Set your video to record. Have each person take hold of one end of the cracker. Instruct them to take three deep breaths, then say this spell before they pull: *A crown for the God at the end of the year, / Words that the wise are ready to hear. / A toy for fun, for mirth, for cheer, / And blessing for the one who luck holds dear!* Read the joke, wear the crown, and show off the toy; all who see share in the moment. Share the video, if you can, and make the actual cracker pull in slow-motion.

🖼 @ ACORN TO PINECONE

Sometimes it's hard to remember that we spend the better part of December in the fall. As we say farewell to autumn and hello to winter, do a virtual ritual to ease this transition. Part of magical practice is building an awareness of the seasons and their changes, which are often subtle.

WHAT TO DO: Safely go to a green place where you can collect acorns and pinecones. You're not looking for the "perfect" specimen, but one of each that speaks to you. If you wish you can record and share your foraging; that is up to you. What you'll be sharing are the representatives of the season in a sacred space together. Place the acorn in your sacred space and say: *In this acorn, oh so small, is the essence of the fall. / Help me balance, help me heal, at this turning of the wheel.* Now place the pinecone next to the acorn and say: *In this perfect spiral of seeds, rests the endless evergreen. / Winter comes as it always will, in the new year hopes and dreams are fulfilled.* Snap a photo of the acorn and pinecone together with the spell overlaid as text or a voice-over to help others balance as the year turns.

✳ YOUR SATURN RETURN

It's Capricorn season, and Capricorn is ruled by the planet Saturn—but Saturn influences everyone's lives. When Saturn comes to town, get ready to work.

WHAT TO DO: Saturn pays all of us special visits two to three times during our lives. These happen every twenty-eight to thirty years or so: the "Saturn Return." This aspect often ushers in broad changes and brings challenges that help you evolve (or not, you have to embrace it). In your first Saturn Return, you may get your first "real" taste of adulthood. In your second, you may find yourself faced with career and priority shifts, empty nests, and changes that come with midlife. What will you do with these changes to level up? Knowing when your Saturn Returns will occur will help you prepare and make you aware of upcoming challenges and opportunities to be your personal best. Plug your birth date and time into a Saturn Return Calculator—there are several free ones online. Your Saturn Return in your birth chart shows the exact place Saturn was on the day you were born. Every time he comes back to that spot, you experience a Saturn Return. Get ready to face down bad habits and personality aspects that no longer serve you. Share your Saturn Return dates with trusted friends and loved ones to see who will share this transit with you, and to be prepared to support each other.

🎥 HOLLY AND IVY

In December the world is awash in red for blood and life, and green, from the evergreen trees and plants that hold the promise of life and hope. Life always finds a way, and energy is perpetual. Spread this truth with a little ritual.

WHAT TO DO: Holly and ivy are two seasonal evergreens memorialized in song and imagery, with various cultures and religions attaching different significance to them. From a magical perspective, holly and ivy represent duality: fire and water, male and female, the sun and the moon. Holly imparts protection and resilience. Ivy heals and brings love and abundance. Pair these powerhouses together and they become a vehicle by which you can share all these things. Set up your camera to record. Ground and center and bind a sprig of holly and an ivy vine with white ribbon or string (white for new beginnings; we're at the threshold of a new year). Put three fingers full of salt into a vessel with water and stir clockwise to invoke. Dip the branches into the water and "bless" your camera—actually, you are blessing the folks who live on the other side of it: your viewers, friends, and followers. Say the spell: *Bounce back from ills, / Love to fulfill, / By ivy and holly, water and fire / May the coming year bring all you desire!* Share this blessing on your platform of choice.

🖼 🎥 @ ORNAMENT ORACLE

Holiday ornaments and decorations hold unique special meanings for all of us—and you can use them for divination!

WHAT TO DO: This year, give the gift of a unique, year-end reading that you'll create with your personal symbolism: Select ten to twenty of your favorite holiday decorations. The more, the merrier! Assign a meaning or a blessing for each one. For example, candles of all sorts (which transcend many cultures) can mean illumination, the "light at the end of the tunnel," passion, creativity, or anything associated with fire. Round ornaments can mean completeness; completeness of *what* will depend on the color. Evergreens can symbolize longevity, cleansing, and good health. Use your personal traditions and imagination to create meanings for these objects. (Keep in mind that the viewer will also bring their own connotations and meanings to them, too.) Take a picture of each and stitch them into a video and set it to play at high speed. (Alternatively, there are apps into which you can feed the photos to create this high-speed slideshow.) Post the video and caption it with the list of meanings. Have viewers screenshot the slideshow—whichever ornament they get is their fortune or blessing for the coming year. When recipients post their "gift" in the comments, that gift also comes to you!

🎥 @ 🔊)) SHARE THE YULE LOG

Burning a Yule log is an ancient and sacred tradition that marks the return of the light as the days grow shorter—and you can share on your platform of choice!

WHAT TO DO: You'll need a log (composite or natural), a few magical items, and your camera. To emphasize your log's "specialness," try these magical additions:

★ Write intentions on your log. If you're having a gathering, have every person in attendance write out at least one intention for the coming year.

★ Bless your Yule log with essential oil. Pine, juniper, and cedar are scents of the season, but you can also include cinnamon, clove, and orange oil for some solar power.

★ Bind herbs to the log; try rosemary, to remember all the good times of the past year; lavender, to usher in a calming, peaceful new year; and sage, to banish any lingering negativity and ensure a fresh start. Use cords in the colors of the season to add their powers.

Share the magic of your Yule log by making a video of it burning. Back it with music or sound effects that mean renewal and fresh starts and post with this spell as the caption: *To all who see the log alight / Know health and wealth and peace from this night!* Views, likes, and shares will amplify the blessings of the season and send them back to you.

12
—
25

📹 UNBOXING DAY

Who doesn't love a good unboxing video? There is SO much energy that is released in an unboxing—the revelation of a mystery, honoring a gift that was given, sharing excitement. Unboxing is also unpacking what we've been carrying to face, enjoy, or bring closure to anything. Whatever it is, you have to take it out of the box first.

WHAT TO DO: What you unbox is going to depend on what you are willing to share. Maybe you'll unpack your real feelings about the holiday season. Or maybe you'll unpack questions, or an intention, or a project you want to bring to light. Think about what you would like or need to unpack. Write it on a black piece of paper with chalk, a white marker, or crayon. Write large enough so it can be read when it is unboxed. The black paper is protective; the white text, renewal—once you've unboxed, time resets so that you can move onto a new phase. Anoint the corners and center of the paper with a dot of rosemary oil (courage and clarity), then put it in a box and seal it. Later in the day, or whenever you're ready, set your video to record and "unbox" with intention: *Unboxing my [intention]. What comes next?*

🖼 @ POINSETTIA SPELL

WARNING: POINSETTIAS HAVE TOXIC PROPERTIES—BE EXTRA CAREFUL AROUND PETS AND SMALL CHILDREN! As flowers go, poinsettias are a staple in the month of December. While they've only been a global holiday tradition for about two hundred years, they've had magical properties since they've existed. Their pointed, star-shaped petals cut negativity and their bright red color brings luck and joy. Periods of darkness encourage them to bloom, which makes them great for "behind the scenes" magical work.

WHAT TO DO: Place poinsettia plants around your home so that they are in view of entrances and exits. (Note: use this plant with caution if you have pets or small children as these plants are toxic.) Visualize the flowers cutting any negative vibes before they can come into your space. See them bathing anyone who comes and goes from your home with joy and blessings.

Snap photos of the plants and stitch them together to make a slideshow. Share it on your platform of choice with the caption: *Star-shaped flower, share your power!* #poinsettiajoy #poinsettialuck. All who see, like, comment, and share multiply the flower power!

12
27

🎥 @ JUST SAY IT

Never underestimate the power of the simple, direct approach.

WHAT TO DO: Meditate on your intention, whatever it may be, and for whatever purpose. Then, just say it. Literally. How you choose to share your intention is up to you. (You know your privacy and security needs.) You can create a video of yourself stating it. You can create a text with the words or send it to trusted friends and loved ones via text. But that's all you need to do: say it. And keep saying it aloud or to yourself (and keep your post up) until you see movement, or your desire comes to pass.

VOICE ALTAR

When people of note pass into spirit, being able to see and hear them through videos and recordings is comforting, though it is a shadow of who they were when they were here. This can be doubly powerful when we have treasured recordings of people to whom we were close. Voice altars use the power of sound to increase love energy and keep memories and spirits alive.

WHAT TO DO: To create a personal voice altar, save messages on your phone and on other devices as backups, especially if it's a message just for you. You can attach an image of the person who is speaking or an image of something that symbolizes them. Keep these virtual icons in a safe place and back them up. Take this one step further and create a living voice altar by exchanging personal, recorded affirmations with friends. Select three friends and make a recording for each of them. Record one to two sentences for each that state their name and how you feel about them. Keep it simple and specific. Ask each friend to do the same. (This magic works best if you're all in agreement to do it; this is NOT a voice altar chain voicemail game!)

🖼 SCREEN OF PEACE

Sometimes inaction is the best action. Turning off for a day renews strength. Try this spell at least once a quarter to restore balance and inner peace.

WHAT TO DO: We all dread the "blue screen of death" as it's usually the signal that a laptop, tablet, or phone is about to die out and we'll lose everything we've just worked on. But blue, when we choose it, is the color of peace and clarity.

Today, post blue across all your platforms. Choose a shade that says "peace" to you. Step it up a notch by filling your screen with an image of blue stones.

★ Blue lace agate is calm and stabilizing; it lowers stress and boosts immunity.

★ Kyanite repels all negativity and aligns the chakras.

★ Aquamarine is crystal seawater and is linked to Atlantis; it also brings good luck, happiness, and protection.

Set the post with the intention of being balanced and at peace and sending balance and peace to others. The magic will multiply with every view.

@  WHeeL OF THe YeAR

The year is ending and a new one is beginning shortly. It's a good time for some divination. Try this tarot spread for yourself, friends, and followers to envision the coming new year.

WHAT TO DO: Shuffle your deck, then lay out the cards.

★ Turn over your first card—this is your card for the year.

★ Starting directly above your year card, turn over your second card, which represents January.

★ Continue to turn over cards, forming a circle around your year card. Lay out one card for each month. The entire spread is a central card surrounded by twelve more cards, for thirteen cards total.

Rather than hard, fast predictions, think of this reading as a weather forecast for the year with your overall vibe or message depicted in the central card. Use your favorite resource to interpret the cards, or simply read the story you see unfolding in the images (February 16).

Snap a photo of the spread and post it on your platform of choice. Ask friends and followers for insights. Don't be surprised if someone asks you to do a personal reading for them!

SPELLS BY CATEGORY

ALL-PURPOSE

1/2 Charging for Magic • 1/4 Your Online Magical Name • 1/16 Alert! Time for Magic! • 1/21 Aquarian Candles • 1/22 Crystal Collection • 2/10 Magical Playlists • 2/18 Daily Magic • 2/26 Magical Memes • 3/5 Your Book of Shadows • 3/7 Make Your Own Rules • 3/25 Crystal Ethics • 4/16 Crystal Frenemies • 5/14 Caption This! • 5/28 Witch Way? • 5/30 Background Magic • 6/16 Step It Up! • 7/27 Lemonade Lightning • 8/12 Words to Live By • 8/27 Crystal Shapes • 10/1 Chime Candle Magic • 10/6 Sign of the Witch • 10/9 Sharing Spells • 10/24 Good Timing! • 11/3 How to Retrograde • 11/9 Digital Cutups • 11/21 Love Slide Magic Boost • 12/3 Powerful Pomander • 12/6 Magic Cookie Exchange • 12/8 Assemblage Altar • 12/9 Written in Stone

ASTROLOGY

1/6 Discover Your Astrology •2/9 Discover Your Moon Sign • 2/12 Finding Your Venus • 5/8 The Nodes Know • 6/15 Find Your Vertex • 7/12 The Part of Fortune • 9/16 Wounded Healer Magic • 11/23 The Dark Queen • 12/22 Your Saturn Return

BALANCE

1/20 Liftoff! • 2/1 Peaceful Parting • 3/23 Benzoin Oil for Calm • 4/15 Quiet Quest • 4/23 Isua for Strength • 5/4 May the 4th Be with You • 5/5 Stability Under Stress • 5/17 Kambaba Jasper • 7/23 Peanut Magic • 8/18 Uranus for Change • 9/15 A Spell for Lateness • 10/22 In-Between Spell • 10/28 From the Darkness • 11/16 See Past Sensation • 12/5 Damage Control Spell • 12/21 Acorn to Pinecone • 12/30 Screen of Peace

BANISHING

2/25 Bye, Drama Llama! • 3/21 Banishing the Ick • 3/27 Protective Clove Magic • 3/31 Banish with Dragons • 5/7 Death Becomes Her • 5/26 Banish Energy Vampires • 5/27 Labyrinthine Layers • 5/29

Release with Bay Laurel • 6/27 Drama Be Gone! • 7/15 Black Pepper Spell • 7/25 Harmony Helper • 8/29 Pumpkin Spice Banishing

BINDING
2/8 Stitch It Shut! • 4/14 Binding Trolls

BLESSING
4/6 Serendipity Sharing • 4/24 Affirmation Stones • 6/30 Hook 'Em and Hold 'Em • 9/12 Share, Scry, and Seal • 11/10 Wheel of Blessings • 12/23 Holly and Ivy

BUSINESS AND CAREER
1/25 Business Relationships • 3/3 Building Your Niche • 4/27 E-Empowerment • 5/23 See Your Success • 6/8 New Job Collage • 8/10 Look at Me! • 9/17 Team Tarot! • 9/28 Online Job Search • 10/2 Announce a New Job • 11/18 Sweeten Job Prospects • 12/10 Small Business Spell

CELEBRATION
1/27 Joyful January • 2/2 A Circle of Light • 4/30 Walpurgisnacht • 5/1 It's Beltane! • 6/21 Litha Lessons • 8/13 Blessed Nemoralia! • 8/15 Hekate's Harvest • 12/25 Share the Yule Log

CLEANSING
1/12 Sleep Magic • 1/23 Saturn Cleansing • 2/15 Spiritual Bath Spell • 3/1 A Spell for Post Remorse • 3/10 Drop That Hot Rock! • 3/11 Cleansing with Smoke • 4/1 Cleansing with Sound • 5/9 Misfortune Averted! • 5/18 Share a Little Smoke • 7/1 Release with Sunflower • 9/7 In the Garbage • 9/29 Coffee Cleansing • 10/13 Selenite for Cleansing • 11/27 Purge!

COMMUNICATION
5/11 House Magic Flow • 6/18 Gone Fishing • 8/1 Lavender Does Not Lie • 9/9 Amazonite Knows • 10/4 10-4: I Hear You Spell • 10/16 Sign Online • 11/7 Communication Candles

CONFIDENCE
2/19 Crystals for Confidence • 6/9 Strut Your Stuff • 7/6 Reclaim Independence • 7/13 Pyrite for Leadership • 7/28 Hold Your Own

Hand • 8/4 Queen of Everything! • 8/5 Tiger's-Eye Independence • 8/6 Mane Magic • 8/7 Count on Pearls • 8/14 Reclaim Power with Figa • 9/19 Be Your Own Advocate • 9/25 Body Temples • 9/30 Do It Scared • 10/5 No Means No • 10/10 You Got This

DIVINATION

2/16 How to Tarot, by Pixie • 3/16 The Oldest Spell • 3/17 Get the Big Picture • 3/19 Intuition Check-In • 3/28 The Lovely Lenormand • 3/29 See Clear with Coriander • 4/11 Tarot for Clarity • 5/16 Playing Card Oracle • 6/1 Rose Divination • 6/12 Aura Captcha! • 6/13 Yes . . . Or No? • 7/26 Anything Altar • 7/31 Divination with Runes • 9/4 A Little Bibliomancy • 9/14 Magic Word of the Day • 9/24 Found Feathers • 10/18 House of Cards • 10/21 Junk Drawer Oracle • 10/26 A Spell to See All • 11/6 Magic Mirror for Vision • 11/22 Where To? Spell • 12/24 Ornament Oracle • 12/31 Wheel of the Year

FERTILITY

6/2 Strawberry Success • 6/19 Corn Magic, Air Magic • 9/2 Fertility Crayons • 9/5 Rays for Days

GODDESS

3/6 Be Like Persephone • 4/17 The Divine Spark • 6/28 Syn Slams the Door • 7/29 Nemesis for Justice • 8/24 The Feminine Fire • 8/28 Cats for Courage! • 10/3 Hera's Helper • 11/19 Box Fulla Secrets

GRATITUDE

1/19 Found Family Photos • 3/26 Nesting Gratitude Face • 4/25 Body Acceptance • 5/13 Thanks, Knight of Cups! • 9/22 Word Cloud Magic • 9/27 For the Baristas ♥ • 10/19 Hug a Tree • 11/11 Take Note—Be Grateful! • 11/26 Treasure This Day • 12/10 Small Business Spell • 12/12 Comfort and Joy

GROUNDING

1/9 Touch of the Season • 4/5 Sounds of the Season • 4/7 Diffusing Anxiety • 5/12 Perspective Power • 7/8 Energy Bubbles • 8/20 Salt Circles • 8/21 Peace Be with You • 8/30 Altar in a Bottle • 9/1 Acacia in the Kitchen • 9/26 Accidents and Aftermaths • 11/4 Press Pause • 11/13 Mini Grounding Sesh

GROWTH
2/5 Your Inner Landscape • 4/2 Stop-Motion Seed Spell • 7/2 Virtual Scarecrow

HAPPINESS
1/10 Send a :) • 1/31 Happiness Holder • 3/15 Orange Blossom Spell • 4/21 Cheerful Expression • 5/10 Melt a Hard Heart • 9/21 Sweets for the Sweet • 10/25 Hygge Magic • 12/7 Gnome Home Magic • 12/18 Mint Cocoa Spell • 12/27 Poinsettia Spell

HEALTH AND HEALING
1/15 Healthy Heart • 1/30 Healing for Others • 2/27 Wild Wellness • 3/30 Choco-Bunny Magic! • 4/9 Thyme of Healing • 4/22 Rainbow-Healing • 4/26 Music Makes the Magic! • 5/21 Open Your Heart • 6/22 Smash Beauty Standards • 7/24 Cicada Song • 8/16 Healing Onions • 9/10 Pause for Mental Health • 9/11 Healing for Tragedy • 10/12 Heal with Baby Animals • 11/12 An Apple a Day • 11/17 A Spell to Quell Anger • 11/25 Foodie Pics Magic • 11/29 Sound Up! • 12/4 Heal Ancestral Trauma • 12/13 Potatoes for Problems • 12/26 Unboxing Day

JUSTICE
2/23 Social Media Justice • 3/9 Just Desserts • 6/23 Crystals to Win in Court • 7/30 Monogram Magic • 10/20 Fairy-Tale Mini Spells

LOVE
1/29 Love, Sweet Love • 2/14 Sealed with <3 • 3/18 Ouroboros Amorous • 4/8 Virtual Carnations • 4/10 For Ishtar, for Love • 7/14 Firefly Magic • 9/3 Honey Love Spell • 9/13 Chai Tea Love Spell • 11/15 Crystal Grids

LUCK
5/19 Matchstick Magic • 6/4 Lucky Ladybugs • 8/11 Bananas for Luck! • 12/1 Rabbit! Rabbit!

MANIFESTATION
2/6 A Bit of Celtic Magic • 2/22 Thrice Two • 2/28 Cabinet of Curiosities • 2/29 Happy Leap Day! • 3/13 Manifest with Oakmoss • 3/22

Secret Gardens • 5/2 Balloon-a-Moon • 5/20 Get-It-Done Spell • 5/24 Spring Pansy Ring • 6/5 Manifest with Myrrh • 6/26 Slow or Speed Up Time • 7/4 Written in Fire! • 8/2 Burning Man • 8/26 Regarding Reply • 9/8 A Lost Pet Spell • 9/23 Magic Sunflower Seeds • 10/14 Pumpkin Manifestation • 10/23 Nailed It! • 10/29 You've Got Mail! • 10/30 Candy Corn Creativity • 11/14 Manifest with Wands • 11/28 Need a Hand? • 12/17 Vanilla Star Amulet • 12/28 Just Say It

MEDITATION

7/22 Labyrinthing • 8/31 Water Meditation

NATURE

2/7 Marvelous Moon Phases • 2/17 Herbs of Power • 2/20 Find a Familiar • 5/15 The Witches' Garden • 7/7 Almond Appreciation • 7/19 Time of the Season • 7/20 Wax and Wane • 7/21 Squirrel Power! • 8/8 Feral Cat Protection • 9/18 Step into Fairyland • 11/24 Doorways to Fairyland

NEW BEGINNINGS

1/1 Rise and Shine! • 1/14 Rewind and Shine • 3/20 Aries, Rebooted! • 6/6 Number of the Beast

MONEY AND PROSPERITY

1/5 Prosperi-Tea • 2/21 Prosperity Candles • 4/20 Mint Money Mandala • 6/3 Basil Debt Banishing • 8/9 Money Maven Oil • 8/17 Fierce Fiery Fumes • 8/25 Blackberry Spell • 10/8 Prosperity Pentacles • 10/27 It's Raining Money! • 12/14 Nutmeg Money Jar

PROTECTION

1/7 Protective Sepia Filters • 1/8 Online Sacred Spaces • 1/17 Creativity Castle • 1/18 Foolish Technology • 1/24 Manipulation Shield • 1/28 Houseplant Magic • 2/3 Protection Philter • 2/11 Mini Me, Mighty Me • 2/13 Good Boundaries • 3/4 Mind Your Business • 3/8 Street-Smart Protection • 3/12 Password Protect • 3/14 Help! I've Been Hexed! • 3/24 Protective Ringtones • 4/3 Protective Thorns • 4/18 MRx Backup! • 4/19 The Spirit of Olive • 4/28 DIY Hero(ine) • 4/29 Emojis for Protection • 5/3 Warding for the Home • 5/31 Angelic(a) Protection • 6/14 Protect Pride! • 6/24 Summer Travel

Charm • 6/25 Filtered Potential • 6/29 Return to Sender • 7/5 Security in Rosemary • 7/11 Psychic Protection • 8/3 Orange Ovation • 8/23 Crystal Boundaries • 10/7 Rubber and Glue • 10/17 Gargoyle Wards • 11/5 Defusing the Love Bomb • 12/15 Time Munchers • 11/20 Name Your PC Day • 12/16 Winter Travel Spell

RELATIONSHIPS

2/24 Help Wanted • 4/13 Pine Pitch Sitch • 7/9 The Earl of Asking • 7/10 Immortality Spell • 7/16 A Spell for Breakups • 8/19 Family Love Spell • 10/11 Friendship Spell • 12/11 Ties That Bind • 12/29 Voice Altar

ROAD OPENING

3/2 Tapping the Web • 4/12 Lifting the Shadow Ban • 5/25 Clear the Way! • 11/8 Checkmate Roadblocks

SELF-CARE

1/3 Dig in, Introspection • 2/4 The Beauty Inside • 4/4 4 x 4 x 4 x 4 • 4/17 The Divine Spark • 6/11 Hypersthene Spell • 7/17 FOMO: Oh No! • 7/18 Ransom Note • 9/25 Body Temples • 12/2 Beat the Winter Blues

SPIRITS AND ANCESTORS

9/6 Dream Candles • 9/18 Step into Fairyland • 10/15 Graveyard Dirt • 10/31 Ancestor Altar • 11/1 All the Saints • 11/2 All Souls • 11/30 Modern Icons

SUCCESS

1/11 Magical Herb Inventory • 1/26 Stay Golden • 6/10 Crushing It! • 7/3 Ginger Beer Success • 8/22 Take Control • 12/19 Flat Lays for Success!

TRANSFORMATION

1/13 Snow Magic • 6/7 Before and After • 9/20 Butterfly-Moth

WISHES

5/6 The Wishing Cup • 5/22 Word-Find Wishes • 6/17 Sandalwood Wishes • 6/20 Dandelion Wishing Spell • 12/20 Crackers for Wishes

ABOUT THE AUTHORS

Arts and history advocate by day and magical writer by night, NATALIE ZAMAN has been exploring mystical practices for decades. An avid tarot reader and storyteller, she is the author of the award-winning books *Color and Conjure* and *Magical Destinations of the Northeast* and the coauthor of several young adult fiction books. She is also a regular contributor to publications from Llewellyn Worldwide and BBI Media. Curiously, she shares a birthday with her home state of New Jersey, though she is a bit younger. See what Natalie is up to at NatalieZaman.com.

AMY BLACKTHORN is the award-winning author of the bestselling Blackthorn's Botanicals series. She has been described as an "arcane horticulturalist" for her lifelong work with magical plants and teaching. She incorporates her experiences in British Traditional Witchcraft with her horticulture studies. She is certified in aromatherapy and has been ordained through the Order of the Golden Gryphon. Amy's company, Blackthorn's Botanicals, creates tea based on magical associations. She has appeared on HuffPost Live, Netflix's *Top 10 Secrets and Mysteries* in an episode about supernatural abilities, and the Associated Press. Amy lives in Delaware. You can keep up with Amy's new releases with her newsletter at AmyBlackthorn.com and view her tea shop at BlackthornsBotanicals.com.